# WOODY HAYES
## and the 100-Yard War

# WOODY HAYES
# and the 100-Yard War

## by JERRY BRONDFIELD

Random House  New York

*Library of Congress Cataloging in Publication Data*

*Brondfield, Jerry, 1913–*
    *Woody Hayes and the 100-yard war.*

    *1. Hayes, Wayne Woodrow. 2. Football coaching.*
*3. Ohio. State University, Columbus—Football.*
*I. Title.*
*GV939.H35B76      796.33′2′092 [B]      74–9070*
*ISBN 0–394–49091–6*

Grateful acknowledgment is made to Wells Twombly and to The Sporting News for permission to reprint material from Mr. Twombly's article which appeared in the January 19, 1974, issue of *The Sporting News.*

Photograph credits for photo insert: Columbus *Dispatch,* page 6 (both); Detroit *News,* 5; Mary Hayes North, 1 top left and right; Ohio State Alumni Office, 1 bottom left, 2 (both), 3; United Press International, 4, 7 (both), 8.

Manufactured in the United States of America
9  8  7  6  5  4  3  2
First Edition

For my son Eric—quite obviously the most unusual
Buckeye fan and Woody-Watcher of all

# Acknowledgments

In approaching a book about Woody Hayes, a writer soon discovers that just about anyone within a short punt of big-time football either has a story to tell about him or has an opinion about him —and is eager to get on the record as a licensed Woody-Watcher.

I wish I could personally salute everyone I talked to, but in this case, where my research operations provided such a deep source of riches, it is obviously impossible.

But to certain people and certain sources I owe an unmistakable debt, and I acknowledge it, now, with gratitude and appreciation. Thanks, then, to Woody Hayes himself, and his wife Anne; to Woody's inspirational book, *You Win with People;* to his sister, Mary Hayes North; to Woody's assistant coaches who were so generous with their time and total recall: George Chaump, Chuck Clausen, George Hill, Rudy Hubbard, John Mummey, Esco Sarkkinen, Ralph Staub, and Dick Walker.

Thanks, too, to many of Woody's former assistant coaches, most notably Larry Catuzzi, Ed Ferkany, Lou Holtz, and Lou McCullough; to Joe Falls, sports columnist for the Detroit *Free Press;* to Paul Hornung and Kaye Kessler, sportswriters for the Columbus *Dispatch* and Columbus *Citizen-Journal;* to Lou Berliner of the Columbus *Dispatch;* to Frank Tate, managing editor of the Ohio State University Alumni Monthly, and to so many former Ohio State players whose memories I mined for some of the richest ore of all.

—JB
Roslyn Hts., Long Island, N.Y.
March 1, 1974

# Contents

# WOODY HAYES
and the 100-Yard War

# 1
# "Up North"

"In addition to working my ass off the way no assistant coach ever dreamed of working, they said I'd have the privilege of experiencing Woody's minitons, megatons, and hundred megatons . . . His staff measures his rages that way."

—Ed Ferkany,
former line coach,
Ohio State University

\* \* \*

The crisp February night was moonless and starless, with a predicted threat of snow. The temperature was in the twenties and traffic was at a minimum on the Michigan highway leading south from Flint toward Toledo, Ohio.

Ed Ferkany, an Ohio State offensive line coach, took one hand off the steering wheel to glance at his watch. With luck they should be in Columbus in three hours.

Next to him, head coach Woody Hayes sat with hands folded across his ample middle, half dozing. Rarely does he do any of the driving when on a recruiting trip with an assistant coach.

If Woody felt like talking there would be talk. Otherwise

there wouldn't be. This much Ed Ferkany knew, although it was his first year on the staff. (In fact, his first month.) This much he had been warned. And more . . .

Ferkany glanced out at the forbidding dark sky. A few scattered snowflakes flickered and danced at the windshield.

Some inner voice of the experienced traveler pulled Ferkany's attention to the dashboard—to the gas gauge. The tank was considerably less than quarter full.

He hesitated. Then: "Woody, I think maybe we'd better stop for gas at the next station."

First a brief silence, followed by a grunt. Followed by: "Naagh, keep going."

A mile ahead was a gas station. Ferkany passed it by.

Five minutes later Ferkany glanced anxiously at the needle of the gas gauge, inexorably headed for the big E on the left. It was no night to be stranded on a highway, out of gas. And if it happened, Ferkany knew who'd do the hitchhiking to the nearest station.

Up ahead loomed the lights of another filling station. Ferkany stole a glance at the semisomnolent Woody Hayes.

"Uh, Woody," he began tentatively. "There's a gas station up ahead and I really think we'd better pull in and fill up."

Woody Hayes turned his head slowly toward his driver. "No, goddammit!" he growled, "We do *not* pull in and fill up. And I'll tell you exactly *why* we don't. It's because I don't buy one goddam drop of gas in the state of Michigan!" He paused an instant. "We'll coast and *push* this goddam car to the Ohio line before I give this state a nickel of my money!"

Ferkany knew immediately that it was not a gag. Hayes

was not putting him on. Woody Hayes' complete dislike of anything relevant to the state of Michigan is almost legendary in Ohio. He will not even mention the Michigan team by name. It is only "that team up north."

Obediently Ferkany fled past the gas station and offered up a silent prayer that they'd make it to the Ohio line. They made it by about the length of a first down, sputtering their way into the first filling station in Ohio territory.

Ed Ferkany should not have been jolted by what just happened. He had been warned. In fact, he confided later to his wife Jeanine that the incident brought back into focus his job interview with Woody Hayes just a few weeks earlier.

Hearing about a vacancy on the Ohio State coaching staff, Ferkany, then an assistant at Navy, decided to take a shot at it. It's the kind of shot taken by a couple dozen young coaches around the country every time there's an opening at Ohio State. The opportunity to work and learn under Woody Hayes is an attraction tantamount to Michelangelo hanging a sign outside his studio saying: APPRENTICE STONECUTTER WANTED.

But what the young assistant coach walks into if he gets the job at Ohio State is a situation that defies belief. Ed Ferkany's job interview should have been a tip-off that things would be nothing short of riotously unpredictable.

"First thing I did," Ferkany recalls, "was to phone a couple of friends of mine in Columbus, as well as a former assistant under Woody, who had left for a head coaching job elsewhere. What they told me, if I read them right, was that a guy had to be out of his mind if he took a job with Woody Hayes but he'd also be out of his mind *not* to take it. Which leaves a guy just where he *ought* to be—making up his mind. Although it didn't help me much when they tossed a bit of mystery at me."

Mystery . . . ?

"In addition to working my ass off the way no assistant ever dreamed of working, they said I'd have the privilege of experiencing Woody's minitons, megatons and hundred-megatons."

His what?

"His rages. The staff measures them that way. I asked for examples but they just snickered and wouldn't cooperate. They said I'd have to learn the same way they did.

"Anyway," says Ferkany, "I wrote to Woody and told him I was very much interested, and after getting permission from the Navy athletic director, he invited me to come on over and talk. I showed up the very next Saturday and went to his office. I'd carefully rehearsed all my X's and O's and was ready to put on a helluva display at the blackboard."

Ferkany's face registered a bewildered recall. "I didn't scrawl a single X or O. Hayes started asking me about my family and my impressions of the Naval Academy and lots of other things. An hour went by and I realized he hadn't said anything about football. Then he suggested we go to lunch.

"That's where it'll happen, I figured. Now we'll be getting around to football. Some private corner of some nice restaurant and he'll talk football until it comes out of our ears.

"We got in his car and drove about a quarter of a mile. I look up and we're in front of something called 'Big Bear Supermarket.' We got out of the car and Woody started telling me that the Big Bear was the first supermarket in central Ohio history, and how farmers and other people for miles around still came here because it had such a small-town farmers' market sort of atmosphere. I looked around. "There they were, all right. The farmers, the small shop-keepers, the housewives in bulky sweaters, galoshes and scarves on their heads. And no restaurant in sight. But what there was, against one wall, was a lunch counter, and Woody headed right for it. Guys slapped his back and said: 'Howzit goin', Woody?' Or, 'Hey, Woody, where you been?' Stuff like that. And Woody waves and gives the stuff right back to them, as though he were on Main Street or in a country store.

"Next thing I know, Woody's ordering a couple of hero sandwiches and some coffee in big mugs, and we're standing there having lunch. I picture Bear Bryant or Ara Parseghian hosting a coaching candidate at the fanciest place in town, or perhaps the faculty club. And here's ol' Woody springing for huge country sandwiches at something called the 'Big Bear Supermarket.'

"Not that it meant anything to me." Ferkany grinned. "I'm no snob and I like a homey atmosphere as well as anybody. But suddenly I knew I was being introduced to the real Woody Hayes, one of the world's most unpretentious great men."

So unpretentious, in fact, that after lunch Woody suggested that they go over to his house in Upper Arlington, a suburb of Columbus, hard by the Olentangy River which borders the university. But first, if Ferkany didn't mind, Woody wanted to pick up his laundry.

So they stopped to pick up Woody's laundry, with Woody muttering something about the shoddy quality of services these days, and then they went on to Woody's house.

Here it comes, thought Ferkany. Now we'll talk football in the comfort of his living room.

"Hey, there's a Big Ten basketball game on TV," said Woody, flinging his laundry onto a chair. "Let's watch it."

His wife came in, and Woody introduced her to Ferkany. Anne Hayes chatted with Ferkany while Woody snapped on the TV set and dialed the proper channel. They all sat down. Michigan was playing Purdue. Anne kept chatting, asking Ferkany about his family and other homey stuff. Woody was absorbed in the basketball game. Ferkany tried to follow the game with sidelong glances while talking to Anne. What the hell, Ferkany thought. Am I supposed to show him I'm interested in basketball, too?

Five minutes later Ferkany did a double take. Woody Hayes was fast asleep.

Anne excused herself to do some household chores. In came a substitute, Steve Hayes, their sixteen-year-old son. Ferkany chatted with Steve. Woody slept on.

"I felt as though I was being interviewed by the whole family," Ferkany recalls. "Except that I was harboring some doubts that I was being interviewed at all.

"Suddenly I looked over at Woody. He sort of stretched and opened his eyes. Didn't bother him in the slightest that he'd fallen asleep. He looked at his watch and said, 'Let's go back to my office . . .'

"Finally! So he drove us back to his office, and all the while he's talking politics, the Vietnam war, the problems of youth and every damn thing except football.

"Suddenly he frowned slightly and popped a question at me. 'You've been an offensive backfield coach at Navy. I need an offensive line coach. What makes you think you can coach centers and guards?'

"Well, I wasn't going to be defensive about it, and if he was looking for me to be intimidated I wasn't going to show it. So I just told him that I was a football coach, period. And a football coach had better be able to coach any phase of the game or get out of the business. Or words to that effect. Well, he just sort of stared at me an instant and then he asked me what were my favorite plays at Navy, and which ones worked best and why. I spent a few minutes telling him, and that was the end of my interview with Woody Hayes. He said he had a couple of other people to interview and he'd let me know in a few days. He didn't ask me to stay for dinner, or anything, and I just got out of there as soon as I could. I caught a 6:30 plane back to Annapolis and told my wife to forget it—that we wouldn't be going to Columbus.

"Nine days later Woody phoned and asked me to join his staff. It was my first indication that Woody Hayes does not make judgments and evaluations like ordinary people do. Subsequently I was to find out that Woody Hayes makes a lot of judgments on instinct and that he is rarely if ever wrong."

# 2
# Mountain
# of Contradictions

"He is so effective . . . so capable of mesmerizing an
audience, that if you don't want to like Woody Hayes,
don't ever listen to him speak!"
                                        —Kaye Kessler,
                                        Columbus *Citizen-Journal*

*   *   *

Ed Ferkany's early exposure to Ohio State's Wayne Woodrow Hayes was one view of the man who has been called the
most colorful, most charismatic, most nonconformist, most
controversial coach in football. Pro, college or rinky-dink.
Wherever they pump up the ball. No matter. He may some
day be approximated but never duplicated.

Hayes is capable of exquisite kindness and consideration;
of quaint honesty in a world that no longer seems to appreciate honesty; and of a high degree of old-fashioned
morality and ethics. All quickly followed by a flag on the
play which proclaims he is also tyrannical, cantankerous,
abusive, mule-skinner-mean, and callously manipulative.

If some key quality or trait has been omitted here, there are countless fans, players, alumni, reporters, officials and other observers who are ready to supply a few more from Column A and a few from Column B, none of them repetitive, and all apparently true.

In personal, people-to-people relationships he can if he chooses be a certified softie with the instincts of a Mr. Chips or an Albert Schweitzer. In politics and philosophy he ranges somewhere to the right of Calvin Coolidge, Pat Boone, Richard Nixon and Friedrich Nietzsche. He carries on an admitted love affair with history and the military. His hero of heroes is General George Patton. And with accuracy and aplomb he can quote by the yard from Herodotus, Lee, Karl von Clausewitz, Confucius, Chief Justice John Marshall, Otto von Bismarck, Teddy Roosevelt, and yes, by God, Ignace Paderewski, both as a pianist and Polish premier. Having majored in college in history and English, he eventually developed such protean tastes in reading that he can be described as a Renaissance man in his versatility and breadth of knowledge.

His reading habits reflect the organization he has brought to life. He scans newspapers and magazines and clips items of wide variety. Their subject matter ranges from science to politics to ecology to medicine to philosophy to religion to exploration to God knows what, and a secretary carefully pastes them in huge notebooks. Woody keeps at least a dozen such notebooks, each as thick as a Gutenberg Bible and almost as heavy. They're at his office, at his training headquarters where he has a hideaway and a cot, and at home. When he has time to read he simply grabs a notebook and wades in.

His ability as a speaker (always off the cuff; never with a

single note) gets him invited to such disparate events as serious college lecture series; corporate sales conventions; Ohio State alumni meetings; and coaching clinics. And the only time he usually talks football is at the clinics. He is so effective, so able to mesmerize an audience that Kaye Kessler, sportswriter for the Columbus *Citizen-Journal,* once observed, "If you don't want to like Woody Hayes, don't ever listen to him speak."

Four times he answered the Pentagon's request to go to Vietnam and speak to servicemen during the war. He took football film with him, but he talked about everything and anything that came to mind. He became a fast friend of Major General Lew Walt of the U.S. Marines, and Walt eventually became a regular visitor to Ohio State home games as Woody's guest.

In the words of one veteran Woody-Watcher, he packages as "a fascinating curmudgeon," and by another as "a classic study of contrasts and a mountain of contradiction."

Woody Hayes has passed his sixty-first birthday. He stands an even six feet tall and before his heart attack last spring was a paunchy 220-pounds plus. The straight, combed-back hair, parted on one side, is full and snowy. Three sportswriters who once watched him striding across a hotel lobby compared their best descriptions.

"Looks like a bailiff in a county courthouse," one offered.

"No, I make him the sheriff in Sunday clothes," said the second.

"I say a bailiff on vacation in Atlantic City," suggested the third.

But such images disappear in a puff once Woody Hayes opens his mouth. He launches any subject at a brisk, purposeful pace, working slowly to a full, vocal orchestration which keeps anyone from getting a single word in until he has had his say.

His voice sometimes seems to carry the barest hint of a lisp, and when he gets into an animated mood or is chiding someone, it reminds some people of Jonathan Winters' character, Maude Frickett, with her flat Ohio diction. On the telephone, if he is originating the call, there is no "Hello, Jim, how are you?" The person on the other end barely says hello when Woody is launching into "Jim, I think we ought to do such and such about this such and such . . ." Bang. Right into it.

He is easily the most quoted football coach around, either for a solicited opinion or when he's winging it— much of it due to his rich gift for original thought and inspired phrase-making. Woody is never at a loss for a germane thought nor the pithy way to express it. When defending his team's Rose Bowl invitation in 1973, for instance, after Michigan tied the Buckeyes in the huge, thunder-filled Wolverine stadium, he declared, "It was an even game played on an uneven field."

His broken-field impetuosity is not only legendary but alien to even his closest associates. His compulsive and resourceful cursing is legendary, yet he savors the niceties of the English language and would feel personally offended if he had to listen to someone tell an off-color story in the presence of ladies.

He has been accused of whacking his own players—and his accusers have also been aware of the punishment he used to inflict upon himself with his own fists before his illness.

His offense has been called "Three Yards and a Cloud of Dust," an erroneous label because (a) the mathematics wouldn't produce a first down in three cracks, and (b) because of the brilliant long-gainers of star running backs such as "Hopalong" Cassady, John Brockington and Archie Griffin. Yet it is true that he is one of football's most conservative coaches, putting his faith in a running game that is mostly straight ahead and to hell with lots of ball-handling tricky reverses and delayed stuff. The pass? Everyone knows he considers a football in the air as horrendously out of its element.

Chuck Knox, coach of the Los Angeles Rams, noted for his wide-open, freewheeling offense, has a favorite aphorism: "Conservative coaches have one thing in common: they are unemployed." This doesn't exactly square with Woody Hayes' twenty-three-year record of spectacular success at Ohio State.

Woody leads a very limited social life and has few intimate friends; according to the gossips, the last time he took his wife to a movie it was the Ohio State-Michigan game film.

He is incredibly un–money-conscious, and it doesn't bother him a bit that he is the lowest-paid head coach in the Big Ten. In fact, says one athletic administrator, in a list of the top fifty big-time football schools, Woody Hayes' salary of about $27,000 would place him somewhere around 45th. Even with outside earnings, such as his reported $12,000 for a seasonal TV show, he has never approached the income class of a Bear Bryant or a Darrell Royal.

He has never asked for a raise at Ohio State. When they tried to give him one a couple of years ago, he rejected it, saying he didn't need it; there was too much inflation abroad in the land already; but if they wanted to increase his assistants' salary, that would be okay with him.

If there is one facet of Woody Hayes' life and times more universally known and discussed than any other, it's his combative, ferocious behavior on the football field—and slightly off it, with the press. For this he has drawn more adverse comment from fans and the news media than anyone who has ever hung a whistle around his neck. Yet many people have never learned of his impassioned efforts to help quell student riots and demonstrations such as followed the Kent State massacre, or the kindnesses he still performs for players he coached three decades ago, now down on their luck.

He is the most peripatetic, busiest, most intense and most-traveled recruiter college football has ever spawned.

When the wolves have been after opposing coaches for losing seasons, Woody Hayes has come to their defense— usually on the day before he has played them, breaking a prime rule of psychological warfare.

As the son of a former superintendent of schools, Woody Hayes is so sold on the subject of education that people, not knowing his background, regard some of his attitudes (since he is a football coach) as phony posturing. Nothing could be further from the truth.

Like him or not, in his twenty-three years at Ohio State, Woody Hayes has become a legend in his own time, and there is no doubt that any future history of football will find him ranked with such coaches as Amos Alonzo Stagg, Pop Warner, Fielding Yost, Knute Rockne and Jock Sutherland. Perhaps not for his inventiveness, but for his total impact on the game. (And for his consummate artistry in designing a play to be forever known as FULLBACK 26—RIGHT OR LEFT.)

For support, the record to date will show that he has won

nine Big Ten titles and three national championships; has twice been named Coach of the Year (a distinction he shares with Southern Cal's John McKay); has appeared in six Rose Bowl games and was denied a record seventh appearance by a recalcitrant faculty that, in a burst of highly charged academic emotion, decided that some sort of brakes be applied to football fervor at Ohio State and refused to allow the football team to accept the invitation.

Ten times Woody's teams have made the wire services' top ten polls. He ranks second among all active coaches (behind Bear Bryant) in number of victories, with stats of 192 wins, 60 defeats and eight ties for a .762 percentage excluding ties. Only twice in his twenty-three years at Ohio State has he had losing seasons: 3–5–1 in 1959 and 4–5 in 1966.

The record also shows that Woody Hayes has developed more All-America players (twenty-eight) and has had more players drafted by the pros than any other coach in history. Another fact, all shiny and impressive, is that no other coach has had as many of his assistants or former players tapped for head coaching jobs elsewhere—at least twenty-four. If not a form of flattery, this record is at least tacit recognition that something of the master's winning ways must have rubbed off on the pupil. Not one has ever been a loser. Hardly a season goes by when somebody on Woody's staff isn't approached for a head job by another school. Over the years the list of those who accepted includes Ara Parseghian, at Notre Dame; Bo Schembechler, at Michigan; Carm Cozza, at Yale; Lou Holtz, at North Carolina State; Bill Mallory, at Colorado; Earle Bruce, at Iowa State (as well as Lou McCullogh, Iowa State athletic director); Paul Dietzel, at South Carolina; John Pont at

Northwestern; Bill Hess at Ohio University; and Rudy Hubbard at Florida A & M. A number of Woody's disciples also
became coaches in the pro ranks, including Bill Arn-
sparger, the new head coach of the New York Giants, and
Larry Catuzzi, offensive coordinator of the Houston club in
the new World Football League.

For a statistic that warms the hearts of those entrusted
with making bank deposits in the name of Ohio State University, Woody Hayes has also seen his team lead the nation
in home attendance in twenty-one of his twenty-three years
with the Buckeyes, with a current average of around 87,000
per home game. Nobody at Ohio State talks about no-
shows. It is an alien figure which brings naught but bewil-
derment to anyone you mention it to out there.

When people damn him and indict him, he doesn't even
bother to shrug it off. None of it ever penetrates his tough
hide. He makes the best newspaper copy of any man in the
game. There are only two coaches in football whose nick-
names conjure up instant, almost universal recognition:
Woody and Bear.

Around the man has grown a cult of Woody-Watchers.
Their solemn observation has made him the subject of
more varied and colorful anecdotal material than any other
coach past or present, including fabled Knute Rockne.
These stories, showing the coach in varied guises and attitudes, make the man and all his contradictions come to life.

# 3
# The Woody Stories

"I'm gonna kill myself," Woody was screaming. "I'm gonna jump off a goddam Alp!"

Slowly the soft chant went up in the football office back in Columbus: "Jump! Jump!"

"I will, I will!" Woody bellowed back.

\*　\*　\*

After graduating from Ohio State with a sparkling academic record, one of Woody Hayes' best ends went off to Harvard Medical School. Woody was inordinately proud of the boy, both as a football player and a student, and was stunned—and hurt—when he got a letter from him during the winter of the boy's first year of med school.

The letter divulged the distressing word that the boy was planning to drop out of medical school. The pressure was intense, the work load was staggering, and he was feeling depressed and defeated. But he wanted to tell Woody he was leaving Harvard before Woody heard it second hand.

It was in the midst of a tough recruiting season and Woody's time, as usual, was splintered and tight on all sides. But a moment after he'd read the letter, Woody checked some flight schedules, grabbed his hat and coat, and hustled out to the airport. A half-hour later he was aboard a plane for Boston.

Marching unannounced into the boy's room, Woody sat him down and for thirty minutes nonstop laced into the boy unmercifully. He accused him of breaking faith with his family, with himself and—yes, by God—with his former football coach, and Woody would hold himself to blame if the young man dropped out. Woody Hayes didn't produce quitters on the football field, dammit, or anywhere else, for that matter.

Woody and the boy's family expected him to become a doctor and Woody was there to make sure they wouldn't be let down, understand? He laid on a lot of other stuff, too, as only Woody can.

Woody allowed just one dramatic moment of silence after he'd finished, then got up and left the room to catch his plane back to Columbus.

The boy stayed in Harvard Medical School and graduated with honors. Today he is chief of neurosurgery at a prestigious Midwestern medical school. He frequently speaks at seminars and sports banquets and often wanders onto the story of how Woody Hayes kept him in school.

*  *  *

It was early June, and Lou McCullough, who was Woody's defensive coordinator at the time, picked up the ringing telephone. It was an overseas operator asking if he would accept a collect call from a Mr. Woody Hayes in Bellino, Italy.

Certainly, said Lou. Woody was mountain-climbing in the Alps, but if there was something on his mind it had to be football, and he'd head for the nearest phone.

Unfortunately, McCullough sensed what it was. Football players' grades for the spring quarter had just come in, and Woody knew it. No matter where he was during that week each year, Woody Hayes would grab a phone to find out how his kids did and—God forbid—whether anyone had become an academic casualty.

McCullough knew that Woody's primary interest at the moment was the best freshman halfback anyone had seen in years, but a boy who was considerably less impressive in the classroom. (Call him Smith.)

The instant Woody got on, McCullough started babbling some light-hearted delaying palaver about Woody's vacation, and how was the Italian weather and the mountain-climbing and the pasta and ravioli.

At least those were McCullough's intentions as he tried to put off the inevitable until Woody returned to Columbus. No chance. Woody cut right through the subterfuge. "How did Smith do?" he barked across the Atlantic and the Alps.

"Coach, I'm sorry, but not good."

"Goddammit, McCullough, how'd he do?"

McCullough took a deep breath and said, "I'm sorry, Coach, but he flunked out of school."

From 4,500 miles away came a terrible sound as Woody Hayes screamed into the telephone. First there was a blistering string of four-letter obscenities, some of them new and manufactured on the spot as he raked McCullough. Then Woody demanded to know which coach was responsible for Smith's appearance at daily study table and who was responsible for liaison with Smith's professors.

Without caring for answers he then demanded to talk to every assistant coach in the football department and flayed each one, regardless of responsibility. "Have I missed anyone?" he screamed into the phone at McCullough. "I want a crack at every sonovabitch on the staff, you understand?"

Then he was off on a new tack. "I can't trust anybody back there! I go away for two weeks and you kill me! I might as well kill myself right here!" he raged.

All nine assistant coaches gathered in the room were new, some of them mentally asking themselves where there might be an opening on some other staff because Woody obviously was going to fire them all. They could hear his voice blasting through the wire.

"I'm gonna kill myself!" he was screaming. "I'm gonna jump off a goddam Alp!"

Slowly the soft chant went up in the football office back in Columbus, with McCullough desperately trying to cover the phone. "Jump! Jump!" several of the coaches were calling out.

"I will, I will!" Woody bellowed back. "I heard those sonsabitches! Tell 'em I will, I will!"

Even as muffled laughter rose around McCullough, there was a clacking sound and then silence, and everyone knew that somewhere in Italy, in some small Alpine hamlet, a horrified innkeeper for the first time in his life had seen a telephone ripped out of the wall and flung across a room.

*  *  *

Tom Perdue, a tough, hard-nosed defensive end and co-captain stood in the doorway to Woody Hayes' office. "Coach," he began, "I'm getting married next month and I'd like very much for you to be my best man."

As Woody mentioned to someone later in a reflective moment: "This is one of the things coaching is all about."

When Perdue's son was born he named him Hayes Perdue.

* * *

No one ever suggests to Woody Hayes that enough is enough. For four hours the offensive coaches had been going over the films until their eyes were glazed and their senses sagging. It was midnight. After the eighty-third rerun they still hadn't found the key to what they were looking for. As if by mutual consent, everyone sat back, semiexhausted, not a worthwhile comment extant in the room. Finally one of the veteran assistant coaches, obviously without thinking, mumbled, "Woody, we haven't come up with it yet, so why don't we break it up and come back to it in the morning?"

Slowly and ominously Woody Hayes got to his feet, his eyes beginning to widen, his chubby cheeks beginning to redden. Then, visibly, his whole body began to quiver as he gathered himself, Thor-like and considerably more menacing.

He raised his arms slowly, his hands beginning to clench into fists.

"Don't anybody—*ever*—tell me we've had enough!" he blazed, his voice breaking into a squeal. "Never, never, never!" Then, in the culmination of his rage and frustration he did something not at all unusual for him but which might be viewed as unthinkably irrational by anyone else. Larry Catuzzi, later to be head coach at Williams, but then in his first season at Ohio State, could not believe what followed.

"Woody took those two clenched fists," Catuzzi recalls in awe, "and smashed himself high alongside both cheeks, obviously as hard as he could swing his hands. Anybody else would have kayoed himself. I was witnessing, for the first time, one of Woody's hundred-megatons. When he's beside himself with rage and has no other way to express himself, he'll punch himself silly."

They ran the film again for another hour.

The next day when the defensive coaches had a rare joint meeting with Woody and the offensive coaches, they stared at a Woody Hayes sporting two gorgeous black eyes, but quite calmly holding forth over a play diagram.

The defensive coaches stared unblinkingly, not daring to raise the obvious question. Only when the meeting broke up did one of the offensive coaches slip his mute colleagues the word.

"Nothing serious. Woody got mad at us last night."

Oh.

It was all perfectly understandable.

* * *

It was 1:30 A.M. when the telephone rang in the dormitory room of John Mummey, the Ohio State quarterback. (Mummey is now an assistant coach.) Sleepily, Mummey pawed for the phone.

"John," the voice at the other end said, "this is Coach Hayes. What're you doing?"

"Coach," Mummey mumbled, glancing at the clock, "I'm sleeping. Or, I mean, I was—"

"Well, I tell you, John," Woody went on, oblivious to all, "I've been thinking that maybe I ought to let you pass a bit more next Saturday. I've got some ideas about it, so why don't you come on over to my office."

Mummey looked at the clock again to make sure his sleep-fogged eyes hadn't deceived him, although knowing

Woody Hayes, he could hardly doubt either the moment or the incipient madness.

"Sure, Coach. I'll be right over."

Mummey climbed into his clothes and trudged three-quarters of a mile through the chill November night to Woody's office in St. John Arena.

It was now 2:00 A.M. "Hi, John," Woody said. "Sit down."

Mummey sat down, waiting for the new and exciting word that Woody was—wonder of wonders—going to let him fill the air with footballs on Saturday, and had something very special to diagram for him right now.

Woody picked up a slim volume on his desk. "John," he began, "are you familiar with a poem called "The Frost Is on the Pumpkin?""

John Mummey stared.

"Let me read it to you," Woody said. And did. And then began reading several other things from the volume by James Whitcomb Riley. And then began asking the kind of penetrating questions an English professor would ask a class in covering the same material.

It went on for almost an hour. Never once did Woody Hayes discuss ambitious plans for a Mummey passing attack on Saturday. Or discuss football for a moment. "It was the strangest hour of my four years at Ohio State," Mummey recalls. "Woody suddenly looked at his watch and said something about it being late and I'd better be getting back to my dorm."

It was almost 3:00 A.M. John Mummey walked back to his room trying to figure out what the hell had happened. He finally dropped off to sleep, never knowing.

"On Saturday we creamed somebody 42–zip," he says. "We threw four passes, completing two."

* * *

Anyone who tries to put Woody down simply has to come away from his efforts with a verbal bloody nose. Witnesses who tuned in on the following exchange at the Ohio State faculty club heard one of the great squelches of history.

The faculty is pretty well split in their opinion of Woody Hayes, believing he's either a prized and shiny ornament or a bramble thicket in the grove of academe. On the one hand he is regarded as a proven leader, a positive thinker and a man who has really brought honor and prestige to the university with his football successes—and as a man who, as a gifted and versatile scholar, can more than hold his own in just about any intellectual discussion.

There are other faculty people, however, who are harshly critical of big-time football, Ohio State style, many of whom are genuinely jealous of his success and his honors. Collaterally, they think he's an outright curmudgeon and a disgrace to the university community because of the controversy surrounding his volatile behavior on the football field.

One day a professor who was a camp leader in the anti-Hayes faction decided to unlimber his anti-Woody vibes and tore into him right there in the faculty club lounge. He began putting Woody down on several counts, a number of which he invented on the spot.

Woody calmly took the abuse—remarkably restrained for one so explosive. He didn't say a word until the professor ran out of breath and invective. In a dead heat, incidentally.

Then Woody raised a forefinger and aimed it emphatically at the prof's chest.

"Okay, now you listen to me," he began. "What you say about me and about football may or may not be true. But

I can tell you one thing that is very certainly true . . ."
Woody paused and cranked up for his clincher. "Just
remember one thing. I can do *your* job, but you can't do
*mine!*"

\* \* \*

Whenever an Ohio State player suffers an injury that
hospitalizes him, Woody, of course, visits the boy immediately. But upon leaving the player's room he'll walk down
the hospital corridor and, absolutely unannounced,
abruptly enter another room or ward, stop at the bedside
of an old man or a small boy, and say, "Hi, how're you
getting along? I'm Woody Hayes and I was just passing by
and thought I'd say hello." He'll spend a minute or two
chatting, then shove off with a "Hang in there, Mac," or
some such.

"It's simply amazing," says a hospital official. "That
casual little gesture of Woody's will often do as much or
more than a pill or a visit from the doctor."

\* \* \*

No one ever disputes Woody's decisions in terms of time,
place or appropriateness. Once Woody was holding a staff
meeting on a Sunday afternoon during spring training,
preparing for a scrimmage on the stadium field the next
day. The weather had been threatening but the field would
be well protected against rain by the huge tarpaulins. Five
minutes into the meeting it started to sprinkle. And at
the same moment a student manager burst in with the
announcement that the stadium crew had neglected to cover the field with the tarps on Saturday before leaving
work.

"Everybody out!" Woody shouted to his assistants.
"We'll do it ourselves!" And he led a mad dash from the

football offices toward the stadium. Since it was Sunday, most of the coaches were dressed in good clothes. One of the assistants was Bill Mallory (now head coach at Colorado), whom Woody had just hired from Yale.

They all piled onto the huge tarps and struggled to un-roll them in a now drenching downpour, urged on by Woody, who was not only probably pushing and hauling with more vigor than the others but was pacing them with some urgent cussing.

Mallory, the former Yalie, his expensive sports jacket now a mass of sodden wool, looked over at his new boss incredulously. Another assistant coach, Hugh Hindman, now assistant athletic director, caught Mallory's expression and cracked with a straight face, "Welcome to the big-time of Woody Hayes."

\* \* \*

Woody Hayes is, as everyone knows, an authentic his-torian, and often carries his love of history to strange lengths. Often during a staff meeting he'll pause after a discussion on a new blocking angle or some such and out of nowhere snap, "Okay, who can tell me what happened at Gallipoli in the Dardanelles?" Or: "Who was the Iron Chancellor?"

Then he'll glare out at his young assistants waiting for an answer. If he gets none he'll snort disgustedly. If a lucky assistant coach reaches back successfully for some class-room recall and comes up with the right answer Woody will flip him a quarter, along with a wry "Congratulations."

\* \* \*

It was about 10:00 P.M. one winter night and Woody Hayes, at the Philadelphia Airport, had just learned that his flight to Columbus had been canceled. There wouldn't be another flight to Columbus that night. Woody mentioned something appropriate for the occasion to the ticket agent and then asked where the car-rental counters were.

A young serviceman behind Woody hesitantly asked him if Woody intended to drive to Columbus, 425 miles away. Woody said he was going to do exactly that. Uh, would Woody mind if the young serviceman hitched a ride with him? He was on his way home to Utah after two years overseas and he had an 8:00 A.M. connection out of Wright Field in Dayton for a flight to Utah. If he missed it he'd really be out of luck.

Woody said he'd be glad to take him along, and then made a phone call to John Mummey, one of his assistant coaches. He wanted Mummey to stand by to drive the young man from Columbus to Dayton when they got to Columbus early in the morning.

The young man said he was Air Force Staff Sergeant Dave Buller of Ogden, Utah. His benefactor merely said his name was Hayes.

About seven hours later Woody pulled into the outskirts of Columbus and phoned ahead to Mummey. "I'll drop him off at your place in about fifteen minutes," said Woody. "You be ready to take him on to Dayton."

"I'll be ready," said Mummey.

And then, as Mummey described it, "Woody continued on home for a couple hours sleep before holding a staff meeting and I set out for Dayton with the Air Force man. He started telling me what a nice guy Mister Hayes was, and how engrossed he'd become in Mister Hayes' nonstop conversation.

" 'Golly, the guy is an expert on so many things, and especially history,' the kid said. 'Actually, he sounded like a history professor,' he went on.

"I looked at him curiously," said Mummey. " 'Do you mean to say you don't know who that was you were driving with all night?' I asked him.

"He shook his head negatively. The man had simply said his name was Hayes."

"Yeah, his name was Hayes, all right," Mummey said he told the boy, "But that was Coach *Woody* Hayes of Ohio State."

The boy stared open-mouthed at Mummey. "Holy mackerel! He never even mentioned it . . ."

Mummey nodded. "Yeah—and if I know Woody he was too busy talking history to mention football . . ."

A couple days later a reporter for the Salt Lake *Tribune* heard about it and broke the story nationally.

\* \* \*

A year or so ago, Woody Hayes looked out his living-room window and saw the three cars sitting in the driveway: his own, his wife Anne's, and their son Steve's. "My God!" Woody cried. "Look what this one family is doing to the atmosphere!"

He bolted from the house, drove his car down to a used-car dealer and sold it on the spot.

At Biggs Athletic Facility, the team training quarters, he puts his own energy-crisis program into effect. He prowls the building turning out lights, and much to the anguish of his assistant coaches and other staff, periodically turns off the air conditioning during August and September and then sulks and glowers when somebody surreptitiously turns it back on.

\* \* \*

At the first staff meeting of the year a couple of years ago, Woody strode into the conference room with a small red book in his hand. Without a word of explanation he began reading and lecturing from Chairman Mao's famed *Little Red Book*. He went on for more than an hour, discoursing on Mao's philosophy.

When he was finished he silently passed out sheets of paper to his coaches. "Number your papers from one to ten with a couple inches of space between each number," he instructed.

Then he demanded answers to ten questions based on the reading and his lecture. When they were finished, the coaches were told to trade papers and grade them, with Woody supplying the answers. Then he went over the results while they sat there silently and uneasily. Finally Woody looked up, gave a small grunt of satisfaction and said, "By now you should have realized you've just had a test on the subject of discipline." That ended the first staff meeting of the season. The subject of football never came up.

*    *    *

Woody had just finished writing a football instruction book which was almost ready for the printer. His various assistant coaches had served as editor on certain chapters. Now it was early summer and they were trying to get away on vacation before Woody could find other chores for them.

Apparently getting away from Woody for a vacation isn't easy. ("Avoiding Woody in the halls," says one, "is one of the great games we play. We have to. You see, anytime Woody can find two or more coaches he'll hold an impromptu staff meeting.")

One of Woody's assistants had slipped away to Georgia without Woody knowing. Woody was teed off because he wanted that particular assistant to check a certain chapter in the book. Woody finally pried loose from another coach the information on where the other guy had gone in Georgia. Woody got the absentee coach on the phone and was told sorry, but there just wasn't another plane out of there that day. "You just stay put where you are," Woody snapped. "Don't you budge. I want you *today*, not tomorrow."

Woody dispatched one of the university planes to Georgia and hauled the luckless assistant back to Columbus. A few hours later Woody had him flown back to Georgia.

\* \* \*

Behavior patterns for Woody are not easily charted. No one knows where the peaks and valleys might form. During the week of the 1973 Rose Bowl proceedings, NBC television asked Woody to supply fourteen Buckeyes for a filmed introductory bit to be used prior to kickoff against Southern Cal.

Woody picked the fourteen Bucks and hustled them over to where the TV crew had set up its camera station on the practice field, the whole scene involving guys running around with headsets on, plugged in to miles of cable and gear, and orders being issued by all kinds of electronic wizards. Woody eyed them narrowly.

The director got the fourteen Buckeyes together and began briefing them in a way essentially reminiscent of Cecil B. De Mille if not more so. Woody stared for about five seconds. Then he rushed forward.

"Hold it! Hold it!" he piped in that rising inflection of his which can verge on the ominous. "How long will this take?"

De Mille figured on something like twenty-five minutes.

"Bull!" said Woody. "In five minutes we're gonna be practicing!"

Various NBC chins sagged as Woody began shuffling his players into a fast formation in which they moved up to the camera, gave their names, position and class rank, and moved swiftly off-camera.

Director, soundmen, cameramen and other supernumeraries, caught off-guard, never worked so fast and so ad-lib. The poor director had never been so *déclassé* in all his career, but then he'd never been upstaged by an expert like Wayne Woodrow Hayes. The entire production went off without a hitch with only one take—in less than five minutes, including a brief, friendly windup speech Woody made on-camera.

A sideline observer was heard to remark, cheerfully: "Hell, given those twenty-five minutes the director wanted, Woody could have made *War and Peace*. With retakes."

\*    \*    \*

When it suits him Woody will interrupt practice in a flash. Woody is quick to admire excellence in sports wherever he sees it, and before another Rose Bowl game a couple of years ago—where he is notoriously selfish about imposition upon his team's practice time—he was quick to grant a few moments to one of his favorites, Maury Wills. Wills had come over with Curt Gowdy of NBC, and the minute Hayes spied Wills he grabbed him and hustled him over to his team. "Gentlemen," he said to his players, "I ask for your total concentration just once a week at game time. Now I'd like you to meet a man who had to do it every day for 154 games a season. I believe he accomplished the greatest individual sports feat of the century when he stole 104 bases in 1962."

* * *

No one throws more things and with more abandon than Woody Hayes. The most famous prop in the Ohio State team conference room is the water pitcher on Woody's desk. Woody seldom pours from it. It is nearly always empty or nearly so. It is easier to throw. John Bozick, the equipment manager, always has a half-dozen in stock.

In between pitchers Woody has his own free substitution rule. (He once heaved a film projector at Bill Mallory, now coach at Colorado.) Recently, when something had gone badly during a staff meeting, he flung his full cup of coffee. When nothing else was handy to follow it he jerked his wallet out of his pocket and sailed it after the coffee. Papers flew from every part of the wallet. One of them skittered down smack into a puddle of coffee.

An assistant coach stared at the mess right at his feet. He could very plainly see that the rectangle of thin cardboard was Woody's Navy discharge card. Very somberly the young coach pointed and said straight-faced, "Hey, Coach, your Navy card is sinking."

There was a tiny gasp from his colleagues. Woody rushed over, rescued the card and started drying it off.

"Goddam coffee will stain, I'll bet," he said calmly and went back to his desk, the tension relieved.

* * *

On Saturday nights during the season Woody looks at films of his next week's opponent. Usually they've arrived a day or so earlier. But on this particular Saturday night a few years ago there was still no trace of them and Woody was beginning to steam. Assistant coach Ralph Staub phoned the other school's officials and was told they'd been shipped that morning via TWA and should have been there by now.

Eight o'clock and no film. Nine, and no film. Woody was building up to at least a fifty-megaton. He had Staub phoning TWA every ten minutes. Finally Woody blew the lid.

"Get me the national freight manager of TWA on the phone!" he yelled at Staub. "I don't care where he is in the whole damn country, get him!" Then he skidded to a halt.

"Hold it!" he screamed at Staub. "Get me Howard Hughes on the phone!"

Staub stared in utter disbelief. "Woody . . . Howard Hughes?"

"That's right," Woody barked. "He owns the goddam airline, get him on the phone!"

There was no way an assistant coach was going to tell Woody Hayes that Howard Hughes was never, ever, available to *anybody* on the phone.

"I'll give you ten minutes," Woody added, and stormed into his office.

The assistant went through the motions of calling TWA's national headquarters and a public-relations man or two, knowing there was no chance. Finally he put down the phone and started toward Woody's office to tell him there just was no way. At that instant a TWA deliveryman hove into sight with the film.

Staub dropped the cans on Woody's desk. "They just got here," he said, almost trembling in relief.

"Lucky damned Hughes," Woody snapped. "I'd've sure chewed *his* butt off . . ."

* * *

Woody has a very limited guest list for practice sessions and it's said that even the college president can't get in without prior arrangements. One day Red Grange was in town and Hayes invited him to practice, but an aide forgot to notify the man on the gate. Finding out that the immortal Galloping Ghost had been turned away Woody let go with a fifty-megaton.

His assistants finally got him calmed down as they prepared to board the two team buses to take them to dinner.

The rigid rule was that the first offensive and first defensive units plus Woody and the defensive coordinator, rode in the number one bus. The assistant coaches and the rest of the players (nicknamed AYO, for "all you others") would ride the second bus.

The first bus would never dare move without Woody, but somehow it did that day when Woody was already steamed over the Grange incident.

Woody got to the parking lot, saw that only the number two bus was there and loosed a hundred-megaton. He hurled his attaché case into the parking lot; it burst open, scattering his game plan and everything else to the winds. "It was a lulu," recalls Lou McCullough. "I'll never forget that two-mile ride with him to the student union where the team was having dinner. It was the first time in history that a vehicle of any kind—let alone a bus—ever careened through the campus at 75 m.p.h., with Woody bellowing every foot of the way.

"Woody just won't be upstaged and the driver knew his life wasn't safe if he didn't overtake that first bus."

* * *

Former Detroit Lion All-Pro defensive back Dick LeBeau, reaffirms that Woody Hayes in a locker room be-

tween halves is something else. Especially when he's behind in the ball game.

"We'd sit there in three rows in front of him," LeBeau
recalls, "and we'd all keep our helmets on because Woody
would walk up and down and emphasize his points by banging guys on top of the head.

"Well, this one time we'd played a real bad first half. I'd
snuck into a corner of the dressing room and was trying to
eat an orange and drink a coke. Suddenly Woody spied me.
I hadn't had time to put my helmet back on.

"Woody was in the middle of a fiery speech and grabbed
me by the neck while bellowing out his message. Everything was pretty emotional in there, but I was having trouble just breathing and staying alive. I finally was able to
smack his arms and hands off my neck, and with my first
breath—like I was all caught up in the emotion—I yelled,
'Yeah, yeah, we gotta go out and get 'em!'

"So we all ran out on the field—five minutes early."

\* \* \*

Although Woody is not noted as a humorist he enjoys
dropping little shorties that don't get too involved—especially if he can weave a bit of homespun philosophy into it.
Such as:

"Some people change, and some people change too late,
and then you have a problem. Like the one we had back
home in Newcomerstown when they had to give up driver's
ed in the high school because the horse died."

\* \* \*

On a recruiting foray into New England, Woody went
with a prospect to meet the boy's father, a lawyer, in

the father's office in Boston. Woody noticed a picture on the wall and identified it immediately. He turned to the boy.

"Chief Justice John Marshall," he said. "Fourth Chief Justice of the Supreme Court of the United States—one of the great legal minds in our history."

Then, according to an assistant coach accompanying him, Woody went on to quote from several of Marshall's decisions, including famed *Marbury* v. *Madison*, explaining how they affected the early growth of the nation.

"A great mind, an imaginative leader, a real inspiration to all Americans," Woody said, admiringly, coming within a hair's breadth of implying he'd have made a great football coach. The boy was obviously impressed. The lawyer-father stared agape at Woody, even more impressed.

*   *   *

Woody Hayes' assistant coaches discovered the lengths to which his determination can take him very early on. Two of them were looking out the window after lunch one day when they saw Woody driving into the parking lot below. There was exactly one empty space left—a very, very narrow one—and Woody headed for it.

Slowly, carefully, he just managed to squeeze into it. But after a few seconds he didn't get out of the car. Suddenly his assistants realized why. There could not have been more than four inches of space on each side of the car. There was no way he could open a door.

Finally, they watched Woody back his car out slowly. Then he got out and went to the rear of the car. Carefully, he placed his hands on the rear end of the trunk, carefully judged his down-and-distance, made an allowance for windage, and putting all his considerable muscle into it, cautiously began pushing the car. Inch by inch, foot by foot he shoved it neatly back into the narrow space. He stood there a moment, staring triumphantly at the concept of his victory, dusted off his hands and headed for his office.

"My God!" said one of the assistants. "Either the man is superbrilliant or superstubborn."

"Probably both," the other agreed, "but can you imagine what he thinks of the word 'defeat?' "

Twenty years and thirty-some assistants later, the answer —known to all—is the man's bench mark.

# 4
# Hello, Columbus!

Columbus is a city, for God's sake! where down at City Hall
the portrait which hangs in most revered civic glory is that
of Howard "Hopalong" Cassady, Ohio State's mercurial
Heisman Trophy winner . . . It is also a city where a TV
commercial tells you that if you buy a piano at so-and-so's
they'll throw in a free shotgun.

*   *   *

Wayne Woodrow Hayes, the practicing autocrat who owns
and operates the nation's most colorful and tempestuous
football stand, could not have happened to anybody else.
Not Notre Dame, not Michigan, not Colorado, not UCLA,
not anybody. Of this there is no doubt.

Woody Hayes could only have happened to Ohio State
and Columbus, Ohio, and all three deserve each other in
a coexistence that almost defies description. But why not
try, right?

Claims are variously made by football powers and communities around the country that they are The Football

Capital of the World, or have the nuttiest fandom extant, things like that. All claims are palpably invalid except those put forth in Buckeyeland. Sorry, Nebraska. Sorry, Alabama. Sorry, Texas. Sorry, all.

Ohio is a state, first of all, which if it has raised any kind of False God before the Lord, looks upon football with idolatrous eyes. It is a state which has about 650 high school football teams, providing more than 1,500 players currently on college teams throughout the nation. It is a state which produced a phenomenon in the town of Massillon, whose team has, in turn, produced more state champions, more high school All-Americas, and more college players than any other high school in the United States, and where time was, for year upon year, the Chamber of Commerce presented every baby boy with a football before he left the hospital.

It is a state which has high school teams which draw more spectators than 85 percent of all college teams in the nation, and where an appearance at the Friday night high school game is probably more obligatory than at church on Sunday morning.

It is a state where the high school teams are ranked each week not by sportswriters and sportscasters, as is done elsewhere. In Ohio it is done by sophisticated computer programming to take the partisan politics and personalities out of the system.

It is a state, too, where a veteran sports editor from Akron named Jim Schlemmer can take a puff on his pipe in the Ohio State pressbox, glance at his watch and remark, "They're just about coming down the aisle."

When a colleague next to him asks for clarification Schlemmer draws himself up grimly and explains. "Son's getting married back home right about now."

"And you're not there?" the colleague asks, incredulous.

"If the damfool hasn't got the good sense not to get married on the day Ohio State opens its football season," Schlemmer growls, "how in hell can he expect me to be there?"

Which brings us to Columbus, Ohio, (pronounced by natives as "C'lumbus") where a few decades ago a humorously fey sports columnist for the United Press was sent to cover Ohio State's football opener. It wasn't a super-spectacular, although the opponent was Texas Christian, which was led by one of the most exciting players of his day —little Davey O'Brien. But UP thought that their star columnist, Henry McLemore, should be on hand.

McLemore, as was his fashion, came a couple days ahead of time and filed a perceptive and immortal opening game lead for Friday papers: "Columbus, O. (UP)—Tomorrow, promptly at 2:00 P.M., the city of Columbus will throw a fit."

It is a city, for God's sake! where down at City Hall the portrait which hangs in most revered civic glory is that of Howard "Hopalong" Cassady, Ohio State's mercurial Heisman Trophy winner.

It is also a city—you'd better prepare yourself for this— where a television commercial tells you that if you buy a piano at so-and-so's establishment they'll also give you a free shotgun. When a dumbfounded visitor hears this for the first time, the merchandising concept escapes him.

It is a city about which an advanced middle-aged sports writer, now living in the East, recalls a weird moment while growing up in Columbus. "We had just moved there from a small town," he recalls. "On my first morning in the fifth grade, the class stands and pledges allegiance to the flag,

then sings 'The Star-Spangled Banner.' Then—Good
Lord, I'll never forget it—this crusty old biddy of a teacher,
pushing sixty-five or more, stands poised with arms aloft
like John Philip Sousa, a sacklike brown dress down to her
ankles, just barely exposing a pair of clumpy, no-nonsense,
English-countryside shoes. 'And now,' she says, 'we will
sing the "Buckeye Battle Cry." '

"With that she sweeps her arms down, her face breaking
into some sort of pagan exhilaration, and leads this class of
ten-year-olds into the first stanza of Ohio State's rousing
football fight song. She sings right along with them, swing-
ing those arms of hers like she has a halberd or mace in
each hand. The kids aren't much behind her in their zeal,
either."

The middle-aged sportswriter shook his head as he described it to a friend. "I tell you it was something. I was only
ten years old myself and I didn't know what the hell was
coming off. 'The Star-Spangled Banner,' sure, and maybe
a chorus of 'America the Beautiful,' but this was my first day
in this school and they hit me with this 'Buckeye Battle Cry.'
I got the idea I'd better learn the goddam words before
next week because they sang it once a week, right on
schedule, every Friday."

The ardent and noble attachments for Ohio State football in Columbus manifest themselves in strange and won-
drous ways. Sophistication has more recently come to the
city and environs, but it wasn't too long ago that on the rare
occasion when the Buckeyes were upset, Saturday-evening
parties were known to be canceled because people were
just not in a partying mood.

Literate Columbusons who have read James Thurber
continue to bask in some of Thurber's witty views of his

days as an Ohio State student. Especially the one about the huge tackle, Bolencevicz.

Thurber tells of the difficulty Bolencevicz has in a geography class when he is asked to name three forms of transportation. The big tackle gets by with horse and automobile, and then he's stuck. The prof, full of sympathy and a desire to keep Bolencevicz academically eligible for football, gives him all sorts of strong hints.

He makes *chuf-chuf-chuffing* noises and emits a fairly good imitation of a steam whistle, but the big tackle doesn't get it. In frustration the prof asks, "How did you come here to school, Bolencevicz?"

"M'father sent me," says Bolencevicz desperately.

"But *how?*" the prof pleads.

Finally, when the prof once more makes a noise like a locomotive whistle, Bolencevicz sees the light. "On a train," he says happily, receiving his passing grade.

As Thurber described him, "Bolencevicz may not have been dumber than an ox, but he was certainly no smarter."

It still makes C'lumbus fans chuckle with understanding.

And natives still approve of the stand taken by a politician running for office in Ohio. What, he was asked, were his ideas on a suitable foreign program? That was an easy one. "Beat Michigan," he uttered promptly, and it was printed exactly that way.

Not that politics aren't taken seriously around here. After all, the state legislature sits in the capitol downtown, and its pressure is felt not only in the city but by Ohio State University, much of whose financial aid it controls.

On balance, Columbus may be considered a lovely city, a clean city and—truthfully—as many have said who have left the place for other climes, other opportunities: "It's a great place to grow up in."

It has a population of 600,000, four of whom are not Ohio State football fans, and it is largely Anglo, Northern European, with no sizable ethnic groups. It has proportionately few Slavs, Poles or Latins.

It's only 15 percent black, which gives it one of the smaller (again proportionately) black communities among major American cities; in fact, it doesn't have much of a ghetto problem. Blacks, indeed, do quite well in Columbus, with an obvious segment of successful black professionals and businessmen. There is only a small Puerto Rican population, with nothing like a New York, Philadelphia or Washington *barrio* to be found. The Jewish population is also quite small (fewer than 10,000) and mostly to be found in the contiguous suburb of Bexley.

An ear trained to detect shades of diction and dialect would pick up essentially an amalgam dominated by clean, unadulterated, unaccented Midwest speech, although there is still a 1920-ish residue of *Warshinton* for the nation's capital or president; *Pairiss* for the French city; *merried* for the state of matrimony; *kewpons* for the things rich widows clip, and *goff* for the game played by most of the city's doctors on any Wednesday afternoon.

Columbus is a city that for years has been remarkably free of political scandal; one of its recent mayors was a typesetter at a local newspaper. He had never gone to college and was fond of strolling downtown High Street at night, bracing an obvious out-of-towner and saying, "Howdy, I'm the mayor. How d'you like our city?" Columbusons never thought it very unusual, however, because this is a city whose inhabitants seem remarkably friendly and casual.

It is a city where in the 1920s and 1930s, when they still had trolley cars, newsboys were given badges which allowed them to board the trolleys anyplace along the line and peddle their papers up and down the aisle. A city, too, that initiated a charming custom called "Charity Newsies": on Charity Newsie Day, rich and influential citizens donned newsboy clothes, staked out downtown corners and sold papers for charity, seldom bothering to make change if you handed them anything more than the two cents for the paper.

It is a city where the state penitentiary is only a half-dozen blocks from the state capitol, and nobody makes invidious comparisons or comments. In the last two decades it has been a city where with some justification, despite an overlay of Midwestern corn and kitsch, civic leaders can point with pride to its cultural and civic instincts. Its famed Rose Garden is the world's largest, and Children's Hospital leads the nation in admission of patients. Columbus also has a modest reputation as a pretty fair stop on the lecture and concert circuit. Not burgeoning, mind you, but you can't call it an intellectual wasteland by any means.

Until recently a single skyscraper of forty-eight stories stuck out over the vast downtown business plains like some lonely and embarrassed Stonehenge freak. When it was erected in the mid-twenties, a perplexed spire of tannish sandstone, not quite sure of its architectural origins, it was called The American Insurance Union Tower and acquired a couple of other corporate names after that. It never reached 85 percent occupancy in its palmiest days. Today there are a half-dozen twenty-five -story-or-more beauts that give Columbus one of the Midwest's nicest skylines, including an absolutely round high-rise motel that is still a visual come-on for the over-nighters from Piqua, Wapakoneta, Chillicothe and Mingo Junction.

But despite the state capitol and its attendant bureaucracy, the biggest deal in town is Ohio State University, three miles up North High Street.

Here, where Woody Hayes is the dominant Natural Resource and a continuing cause célèbre rolled into one, is a fair prototype of the Populist dream of higher education—the diverse, sprawling land-grant college which Congress blessed with free acreage in the 1860s and which America built by the dozens in the nineteenth century—as its state universities.

It is well worth a look . . .

* * *

A foreign dignitary, visiting Ohio State University a few years ago, had just approached a part of the campus known as the Oval. It is the main vista of the university and funnels in from High Street and 15th Avenue, flanked by two memorial gateways. The wide entrance road quickly merges into two embracing driveways which form The Oval. It is a lovely, vast grassy area accented with stately trees, and crisscrossed by numerous walks splaying out in every possible direction. Surrounding The Oval, on two sides, are many of the university buildings.

Just as the visitor and his escort reached the area, the sharp, clear notes of a lone bugle spilled out from somewhere onto the frosty autumn air.

Along the various walkways hundreds upon hundreds of students were on their way to or from class. With the first notes of the bugle they all came to a stop. "Frozen motionless" might be a better way of putting it.

In any direction as far as the eye could see, they were

caught in their transfixed postures. The visitor quickly recognized what the bugler was playing. It was taps. The visitor looked questioningly at his escort.

"It is Wednesday, eleven A.M.," his escort said. "Ever since World War One, taps is blown at this moment and everyone hearing it on campus comes to a halt out of respect for all the Ohio State men who died in the war."

The visitor said it was one of the most impressive and touching sights he'd ever seen in his travels from around the world.

"You should see it from the top of the library tower," his guide said quietly. "It gives you goose pimples."

On this same Oval there is something called the Long Walk, a wide path splitting the Oval straight up to the library for about 250 yards. There was a time when any male freshman found walking on it could be dragooned by upperclassmen and thrown into nearby Mirror Lake. That custom ended in the mid-twenties, to nobody's regret. Up until then, too, every male freshman had to purchase, his very first day on campus, a scarlet and gray freshman beanie and could also be dunked in Mirror Lake if caught without it.

It was about this time, too, that they held an election for homecoming queen, and the embryonic politicos at the Law School decided to put up a candidate named Maudine Ormsby. They flung up posters all over the place without a picture: VOTE FOR MAUDINE ORMSBY—LOVELIEST GAL ON CAMPUS. The law schoolers did such a great job that their gal won in a landslide. Then they produced Maudine Ormsby. She was a prize cow at the Ag School cattle barns.

At one time there probably was no more typical huge land-grant state university in America than Ohio State. She was a late starter but a fast bloomer, founded by the legislature in 1870 as the Ohio Agriculture and Mechanical College, stuck out on some rustic acres in the bucolic north end of the city of Columbus, with the idea in mind that it would turn out expert agrarians and engineers and ultimately some schoolteachers. It was hoped that all of them, of course, would remain in Ohio and put their newly learned skills to work on behalf of the state which had educated them. The first class had twenty-four students.

And so the sons—and soon the daughters—of Ohio's farmers, merchants and businessmen from small towns and cities alike, began flocking to the growing campus where tuition, until as late as 1940, was less than a hundred dollars a year, and the only thing you needed as an entrance requirement was a diploma from a high school in the state of Ohio. This opened the door for a lot of dummies who wanted in on four years of rah-rah, but the faculty learned how to get even. The law said they had to be admitted, but there was no law saying Ohio State had to keep them, and the flunk-out rate at the end of the autumn quarter became fearsome.

Today Ohio State's big, beautiful campus, its architecture a blend of traditional and modern, is home to 36,000 undergraduate students, and its academic standing commands a lot of respect, with acknowledged eminence in liberal arts, medicine, law, dentistry, engineering and dozens of other disciplines.

There is now a sizable interlacing of students from all the other states in the union and from about fifty foreign nations, and except for the unknowing from Nigeria, Pakistan or Greece, the student body is aware that Football (and it deserves its capital F) is the most provocative and visible facet of campus life. And if Football is King, then Wayne Woodrow Hayes is its Grand Vizier, in whom great power rests. And few have any doubts about who Woody is. In a recent trip to the campus, a visitor asked three questions of twenty random students, sought out in modern, high-rise dorms, the $300,000 fraternity and sorority houses, and in campus eateries and hangouts.

1. Who is president of Ohio State University?
2. Who is chairman of the department in your major?
3. Who is Woody Hayes?

Granted, that the result of this less than earth-shattering poll is immediately tipped off by your psyche, the breakdown is still another thing. Ten of twenty knew that Dr. Harold Enarson was prexy. (Of course this was only his second year on the job, but what the heck . . . ) Five of twenty knew who their department head was.

Nineteen of twenty knew who the football coach was. The twentieth was a little freshman girl from a small farm community. Unexpectedly, she knew who Harold Enarson was. She wasn't sure of the chairman of her department. Then she frowned and repeated Number 3. "Okay," she said, "so who's Woody Hayes?"

The inquisitor smiled and told her he was the Ohio State football coach.

As if on some strange, guilt-ridden reaction the little freshman broke into tears and turned her head away. Embarrassed or ashamed—take your pick.

It's difficult to deny Woody Hayes' stature and place in the community. Traditionally each fall the fraternity and sorority houses and all the dormitories stage an ambitious competition for best decorations for the homecoming game. Invariably, the focus of a half-dozen of these will be a colorful 20-to-25-foot papier-mâché colossus of Woody Hayes, complete with short-sleeve shirt, red pants, black baseball cap, glasses and a football. Sometimes animated. Little kids come from all over to gawk. Just as they gawked in 1973 at the state fair, where the Ohio Dairyman's Association fronted their promotional display with a life-sized refrigerated statue of Woody Hayes—carved in butter.

But the head football coach at a place like Ohio State cannot be examined in a vacuum by himself. It helps to understand a man like Woody Hayes by understanding, first of all, the enormity of the entire athletic setup. To begin with, there is an Athletic Department budget in excess of $4,000,000 annually. At first blush, a staggering amount of money to be spent on fun and games. But no one really looks at it that way. Neither by the university administration nor by the state legislature, which must allot its general funds.

The Athletic Department not only operates at least fifteen varsity sports but provides intramural activities for thousands of nonvarsity athletes—men and women—in a dozen different sports. It is football, of course, that provides the funds for minor varsity sports and this tremendous intramural program. Football itself spends $350,000, exclusive of salaries for Woody Hayes and nine assistants. Also excluded, are scholarships for approximately 110 players which are reported to total $250,000 per year.

The physical plant is spectacular. The Roman emperors were pikers. The plant at Ohio State includes the stadium, seating 87,000; St. John Arena, a gorgeous basketball hall, which seats close to 14,000; French Field House, used for track; a hockey rink for varsity games, physical education and free-time student skating; two golf courses; about fifty tennis courts; a natatorium for varsity swimming meets, seating 3000; three other nonvarsity pools; three varsity baseball fields; a men's gym which has five basketball courts; wrestling and weight rooms; handball courts and fencing rooms.

There are acres upon acres of intramural fields, and across the Olentangy River, just a mile from the stadium, is Biggs Training Facility, which services varsity football. Here are coaches' conference rooms; squad conference rooms; trainers' quarters; therapeutic devices for injuries; equipment repair rooms; and last but not least, a lush, red-carpeted varsity locker room that is sprayed daily with a long-lasting scent that could easily be lilac or apple blossom.

If football is a religion here, Ohio Stadium is its mecca, and a football Saturday in Ohio Stadium is a spectacle which once observed is forever retained. From a vantage point high in the uppermost of its three decks you can see hordes of people streaming across the parking fields and intramural sports fields, coming from every possible direction.

Kickoff is 1:30 P.M., but by 12:30 the huge stadium is already three-quarters filled with fans who want to see the teams work out. By 1:00 it is full. In the East it is common for people to wander in fifteen minutes after the kickoff, waving diffidently to friends already seated. This kind of indifference in Ohio Stadium can easily get you killed for thoughtlessly blocking somebody's view. There are only four certifiable reasons for being late for a kickoff in Ohio Stadium:

1. Your car lost its transmission sixty miles west, on U.S. 70.

2. You left your tickets back at your motel, you idiot.
3. The doctor was all thumbs in putting a fresh cast on your broken leg.
4. You died that morning.

At 1:15 there is a blare from unseen clarion trumpets at the north end of the stadium. The Faithful know what it heralds, and everyone strains for the first glimpse of an old ritual. From a ramp at the far end of the stadium comes the Buckeyes' famed blue-uniformed, white-spatted, all-brass marching band, originator in the early 1920s of the quick-stepping formations later adopted by almost every band in the nation.

Suddenly, up through their ranks bursts this booted, high-shakoed drum major. By the time he gets up front he is in full flight into an improbable high-stepping, backward-leaning routine that would land any normal person in an orthopedist's office. He flings up his baton, the band breaks into "The Buckeye Battle Cry" and the place goes ape.

Delirium! Ecstasy! The 87,000 lose their gourds. Kill! Kill! Kill! Bring out the lions! Where the hell are the Christians? Go, Woody! Go, Bucks!

You don't even have to go to Ohio State to feel your scalp prickle, say jaded sportswriters in the pressbox.

Five hundred uniformed Boy Scouts (they're the ushers, an honor gained on recommendation by scoutmasters throughout the city) and several tons of burly state troopers come to salute. Two dozen lovely khaki-uniformed R.O.T.C. coeds (called Angel Flight) march smartly to the flagpole with the color guard to raise the flag for the national anthem.

A helluva sight. A helluva show. Who'd want to miss it, hey?

Nobody, if they can help it.

There is a famous picture of Ohio Stadium filled with umbrellas. Umbrellas of every color and size. No people are visible. Just umbrellas, looking for all the world like a colossal, spreading mass of dripping wet mushrooms. On drenching days like this, the civilized notion would be to opt for a cozy sofa at home, near a radio. The caption with this famous picture merely proclaims: 87,000 RAIN OR SHINE.

Ohio State once played Michigan in the season finale, with the Big Ten title at stake. The last day of the season came up with a record-setting 29-inch snowfall and temperatures hovering around a nice, even four degrees. All roads, highways, bus and rail lines, and airports were shut down throughout the state. Somehow, close to 60,000 fans fought their way through the drifts and howling winds and made it to Ohio Stadium.

There they saw astounding sights as the frozen tarpaulin protecting the field had to be hacked apart with axes. Only half of it came up. There were no yard-line markers visible. Within minutes after half of the tarp was removed the field was again covered with almost a foot of snow. In the concrete stadium aisles, people built bonfires to stay alive.

The blizzard winds made a mockery of recognition on the field, not to mention progress. Not a first down was registered all afternoon. There were thirty-five punts. No back had a gain of more than four yards. The game was decided when somebody from Michigan dug a blocked Buckeye punt out of a deep snowpile in the Ohio end zone.

At game's end a horrible rumor swept the stadium: in attempting to roll up the frozen tarps one of the Boy Scout ushers assisting with the chore was inadvertently rolled up inside of it. The question was, which of the rolled-up pieces of tarp now held the Boy Scout? Now undoubtedly frozen solid, but if dead, then certainly dead in a good cause. Of course, it turned out to be just a rumor, but a helluva football story to add to the insanity that is C'lumbus on game day.

It was not too many years ago that a football game in Columbus was preceded by a Friday night that had a flavor all its own. A flavor compounded of equal parts Roman holiday, old-time American Legion convention and some leftovers from the French Revolution. And have you ever been to a barn-burning?

A few thousand students would open the proceedings with what was euphemistically called a "nightshirt parade." More realistically, it was a license to put on some old clothes and take High Street apart, from the university district southward to the state capitol three miles downtown. Snake-dancing in a four-block long phalanx, the students (fortified by hundreds of young "townies") would rip trolley-car wires from the overhead power lines; bring automobile traffic to a snarled standstill by opening hoods and disconnecting battery wires; soap store windows; and romp up and down the aisles of every movie theater along the way while the bedeviled theater managers had no choice but to turn on the house lights and stop the projection machine until the hordes had found their way back onto the street.

Al Jolson once said his most harrowing evening in show business came in the mid-twenties when he was playing the Hartman Theater in Columbus and his performance was rudely interrupted by "what looked like thousands of ruffians advancing menacingly down the aisle toward me. I knew my reviews in the local papers had not been that bad."

Hotel managers quickly learned to remove all furniture and rugs from their lobbies the night before a game but were never completely able to prevent campus pranksters from getting to upper floors from which they bombed pedestrians below with bags of water.

But if Ohio State was notorious for the participating fervor of its earlier fans, it was even more so for its much-publicized label as the "Graveyard of Coaches." It wore this label for years, and the years did not treat Ohio State kindly . . .

# 5
# Graveyard of Coaches

The Columbus *Citizen* ran a reader poll for a new coach
. . . Paul Brown got 2,331 of 2,811 votes. The Ohio State
freshman coach was second . . . There were scattered
votes for the sports editor of the rival paper; Lassie; a
bosomy TV star named Dagmar; Harry S. Truman; actress
Lana Turner; comedian Ed Wynn; Senator Robert A. Taft;
and a lifer in the state pen. Only Brown was considered a
serious candidate.

\* \* \*

Woody Hayes, the architect of the modern Ohio State football image, might never have had the chance if it hadn't
been for Charles W. Harley, of Columbus East High
School. The Buckeyes were the last team to be admitted to
the Big Ten in 1912 and not only was it the baby brother
in the lodge, but it had previously taken more than its share
of horrendous shellackings from such gridiron giants as
Oberlin, Western Reserve, Case, Wittenberg, Kenyon and
even Ohio Medical College. A bad scene.

This was bad enough, but what led the locals to the
depths of despair was that fact that the struggling Buckeyes

had never—repeat, never—beaten Michigan. In one stretch of eleven straight games the Wolverines had outscored them 311 points to 12, and had also handed Ohio State an 86–0 clobbering, its worst in history.

Three things turned Buckeye shame into towering pride. Admission to the Big Ten and the arrival in 1913 of Dr. John W. Wilce, a young physician from Wisconsin and a former Badger footballer who said, yes, he'd try to turn things around but he'd have to have permission to practice medicine on the side. No fool, he. If there was to be any priority it was on the order of making a living.

Two years later young Chic Harley reported as a freshman. In 1916, Harley's first year on the varsity, Dr. Wilce had himself a prescription for success.

Harley was clearly an encore of Halley's Comet, which just a few years earlier had streaked across the heavens to turn people agape with awe. Harley is Halley returned, said the joyous natives, wrong by only seventy more years to come, but otherwise right on target.

What Harley did was run, pass and kick the Buckeyes to undefeated seasons and the Big Ten title in his sophomore and junior seasons. Walter Camp, the patron saint of All-America teams, picked Harley for the honor in 1916–17, showering him with accolades which left Buckeye fans ecstatic.

After time out in 1918 for military service Harley repeated his All-America heroics in 1919. Hero-starved Ohio State was finally well-gorged. Michigan had had its famed point-a-minute teams, its Willie Heston and its fabled coach, "Hurry-Up" Yost. Amos Alonzo Stagg had made Chicago a national power. Bob Zuppke had already come to Illinois. Minnesota's Dr. Harry Williams had turned out many a Gopher All-America. Ohio State, last on the scene, had been led into the big-time by Wilce and Chic Harley.

There is no taste like that of instant success. There would have to be more of it. And for what fans and the university had in mind there must be a showcase. No more rickety wooden grandstands seating a mere 20,000. They would raise a true temple to this glorious new insanity, and alumni and local citizens climbed over each other to subscribe its $2,000,000 price tag.

The triple-decked gray concrete structure, built in about a year and a half, was dedicated in 1922. It held 65,000, which clearly wasn't big enough, and later would have to be enlarged. It was the first of the nation's huge, modern stadiums, the first built since Harvard's and Yale's, which were pre-World War One. It launched the 1920s boom in college ball parks that had all the biggies following the Buckeye lead.

What it also led to at Ohio State was something that would be called the "Graveyard of Coaches." Dr. John Wilce, producer of the Buckeyes' first champion, first All-America and first conqueror of Mighty Michigan, continued to be a winner but couldn't whip Michigan as often as the locals would like. Beating Michigan was the eleventh commandment, losing to Michigan the cardinal sin. By the late 1920s it was obvious Wilce had lost his desire to continue with pressure football and wanted to spend more time in medicine. He resigned after the 1928 season.

L. W. St. John, the Ohio State athletic director, immediately got a tip from Major John L. Griffith, the Big Ten commissioner. He knew a candidate for the job who was really interested. "Like who?" asked St. John.

"Knute Rockne."

St. John, a calm and deliberate man, calmly told Griffith he was out of his cotton-pickin' mind, or whatever was the 1928 equivalent, but Griffith knew what he was talking about.

Notre Dame's famed coach somehow thought he'd climbed all the available mountains with the Irish and was looking for a new peak. Rockne and St. John went into a long huddle. After about four hours he agreed to take the job—but only if no word was mentioned until he had a chance to get back to South Bend and ask Notre Dame officials to let him out of his contract. It was all set.

No one knew how it happened, but there was a leak. Notre Dame officials heard of it, and when Rock got home he knew there was no way they'd let him out of his contract. Those were the days when coaches felt impelled to honor those things. Notre Dame talked Rockne into staying on and Ohio State lost a chance to lay forever the Coaches' Graveyard ghost that would soon take residence in the huge, cavernous stadium alongside the Olentangy River.

Instead of Rockne, the Buckeyes got one of Wilce's assistants, a solid and capable man named Sam Willaman. Unfortunately, a nickname came with him: "Sad Sam" Willaman. He had that kind of face and manner. He also was one fine football coach and never had a losing season. But in five years he couldn't wrap up a Big Ten title. There were years when he lost only one game. The one game always seemed to be to Michigan. Alumni discontent, student discontent and a generally sour overview by the statewide press convinced Sad Sam Willaman. He packed it in.

Okay, fans said, let's get somebody with imagination, with zest and zeal and anything else beginning with Z. So, St. John got it for them. He got the zaniest, maddest, most imaginative football coach ever to hit the Big Ten, and the record still holds. He got the Buckeyes Francis Schmidt from Texas Christian, and it was Schmidt who launched Ohio State's modern era of football eminence. Schmidt was a World War One bayonet drill instructor with a loud, raucous and colorful approach to the English language, the likes of which had never been heard on this serene and conservative campus.

He also had a genius for offensive football. In his first year at Ohio State he stunned the opposition by displaying —in the same game—the single wing, double wing, short punt and, for the first time ever seen, the I-formation. He used reverses, double reverses and spinners, and his Buckeyes of the mid-thirties were the most lateral-pass conscious team anyone had ever witnessed. He threw laterals, and then laterals off of laterals downfield, and it was not unusual for three men to handle the ball behind the line of scrimmage.

In his first two years he got touchdowns in such bunches that Ohio State immediately was dubbed The Scarlet Scourge, and Francis the First was known as "Close-the-Gates-of-Mercy" Schmidt.

He was a bow-tied, tobacco-chewing, hawk-faced, white-haired, profane practitioner of the football arts—modern football's first roaring madman on the practice field and the sidelines, and so completely zonked out on football that legend ties him to the greatest football story of the twentieth Century.

So caught up was he in his diagrams and charts that there was hardly a waking moment when he wasn't furiously scratching away at them. He took his car into a filling station for an oil change but stayed right in the car while the mechanics hoisted it high above the subterranean oil pit to do their work.

Francis Schmidt, immersed in his X's and O's, simply forgot where he was. For some reason he decided to get out of the car, still concentrating on his diagram. He opened the door on the driver's side and stepped out into the void, which ended eight feet south of him in the pit. He refused to explain the limp which he carried with him to practice that day.

It had really taken Schmidt only one year to enrapture Ohio State fans for what was predicted to be forever. At his first football banquet after a sensational first season capped by a glorious 34–0 shellacking of Michigan, Schmidt, in bayonet drill tones, bawled forth two classic and historic comments. "Let's not always be called Buckeyes," he brayed. "After all, that's just some kind of a nut, and we ain't nuts here. [A debatable claim.] It would be nice if you guys in the press out there would call us 'Bucks' once in a while. That's a helluva fine animal, you know."

Ringing applause. Bucks and Buckeyes, interchangeably from now on . . .

And then: "And as for Michigan . . . Well, shucks, I guess you've all discovered they put their pants on one leg at a time just like everyone else."

Bedlam. It was apparently the first time the homely Texas line had ever been uttered in public and it swept the nation. It also launched a "Pants Club" at Ohio State: thenceforward each player and key booster who was part of a winning year over Michigan was awarded a tiny little golden replica of a pair of football pants.

There were four straight, heady, lopsided victories over Michigan, 1934, 1935, 1936 and 1937. And in 1935, with one of the most talented teams of the decade, Ohio State played the epic game with Notre Dame, often called the greatest college game of all time. The Bucks succumbed to a fourth-quarter miracle finish by the Irish, 18–13, but by then Francis Schmidt was the most talked about coach in the nation.

In 1935, too, a 200-pound lineman at Denison University, just fifty miles from Columbus, was finishing a successful but undistinguished three-year career as a small-college tackle. The big-time world of football fifty miles away was an alien concept to him. If he had any plans at all for the future they were involved with law school. His name was Wayne Woodrow Hayes . . .

But Francis Schmidt, despite his individual brilliance, coached football in a perpetual ambience of frenzied chaos. His staff was in a limbo of misdirection and uncertainty. Nobody knew from one day to another what the hell the mad genius was going to do. He heaped scorn and ridicule on his players and they hated him. There was open dissension. And after a couple of years the opposition began to catch on to his pyrotechnic style.

Then, like other coaches before him, Francis Schmidt fell victim to the Michigan bugaboo. After four straight Buckeye victories, Michigan came up with a back named Tom Harmon, and in 1938, 1939 and 1940, Ohio State dropped three in a row. The 1940 game was particularly galling as Harmon ran for three touchdowns, raising his career total to 33 and breaking Red Grange's record. He also passed for two. The 40–0 pasting was the worst suffered by Ohio State since it had entered football's big-time.

Once again in Columbus, mutinous fans were setting out a plank for a Buckeye football coach . . .

Francis Schmidt knew the Athletic Board was debating his future. He was the kind of man who'd rather die than be fired, so he quit before the board could act—as it certainly would have done. The board also accepted resignations of Schmidt's five assistants, two of whom would later make names for themselves elsewhere: Sid Gillman at Cincinnati and later in the pros; and Gomer Jones, who would become the architect of Bud Wilkinson's great lines at Oklahoma and himself head coach there.

When news photographers came around for a going-away photo, Schmidt, blatantly sarcastic to the end, told them, "You guys have dozens of my pictures in your files. Just dig out one of them and use it. And while you're at it, underneath it just say: 'Rest in peace.' " Three years later, at Idaho, he died of a heart attack. Some say a broken heart.

It had been years since there was any real or stable "peace" on the Ohio State football front. What the Bucks needed was someone who could provide it—and on a long-term basis.

The Buckeyes could have gotten their new direction from any of dozens of attractive candidates around the nation who lusted for the job, despite the perils that went with it. But for a major power they went to the most unlikely source of all. They astounded the nation by going to a high school. They astounded no one in the state of Ohio.

In the years between 1935 and 1940, Massillon High School had won six straight Ohio championships and had gone 56 games without defeat, with 51 consecutive wins in the streak, the longest in so-called Triple A competition in national prep history. In that period the Massillon Tigers averaged 40 points a game, against 2.8 for the enemy. College recruiters could literally hold a convention in this town of 25,000 on any given day. The Tigers played in a 21,000-seat stadium. Their average home crowd was around 21,400. In 1940, in eight home games they drew 171,000 fans.

The coach of this prep school colossus was youthful Paul E. Brown.

By 1940, when Francis Schmidt packed his bags in Columbus, high school coaches around the state had gotten weary of the constant clobberings Paul Brown had been giving everyone. They were tired of the 99-year lease he held on the state championship. They simply decided to get rid of him.

They peddled him to the Ohio State Athletic Board, saying, "Here's your new coach, fellas, and you'll never find a better one anywhere, even though he is just a high school guy . . . And besides, if you take him on, we promise we'll send all our best kids to Ohio State."

It was the nicest and politest brand of intimidation anyone ever dreamed up, but with nothing but salutary effects possible for all concerned. How could Ohio State resist?

A month later, on January 14, Brown was attending a luncheon meeting in Columbus when a newsman bent down and whispered in his ear: "Did you know the appointment has been made?"

Brown looked up, startled. "Who'd they pick?"

The newsman grinned. "You."

The meeting was adjourning but the chairman shouted for attention. "The man who just addressed this group a few minutes ago," he shouted, "is the new football coach at Ohio State!"

The place erupted in a roar. Ohio State's new football coach was just thirty-two years old.

In New Philadelphia, Ohio, a twenty-six-year-old high school coach, Wayne Woodrow Hayes, thought it was just fine that one of his peers had been tapped. Even though Brown's starting salary at Ohio State was just $7,000 . . .

So Paul Brown came to Columbus, along with most of his Massillon High School staff, and in his first year, 1941, he lost only in an upset to a Northwestern team led by Otto Graham. He tied Michigan and was on his way. The next year he installed the T-formation, the first Big Ten coach to do so, and won the national championship with a team of all juniors and sophomores. Critics said his 1943 club would have been the greatest ever seen on a football field, but by 1943 they had dispersed to places like North Africa, Guadalcanal and the skies above Britain. Most of them never did return to Ohio State, but even if they had, they would not have been returning to Paul Brown.

Brown had a poor season in 1943, using a strange amalgam of wartime material. Playing with seventeen-year-old freshmen and upperclassmen declared physically unfit for military service, Brown found out for the first time in his life what it meant to lose more often than he won. The following year, volunteering for military duty, he wound up coaching a strong Great Lakes Naval Training Station team in Chicago.

Brown's replacement in 1944 was Carroll Widdoes, one of the assistants he'd brought down from Massillon High School. Widdoes pulled off a miracle. Using the same sort of subpar material he'd inherited from Brown, plus a re-tread dental student who was granted another year of varsity play under wartime rules, Widdoes clobbered nine straight foes, all supposedly stronger than the Buckeyes. One of his victims was a star-studded Great Lakes naval team coached by—surprise, surprise—his former boss. The Bucks wound up number two in the nation, just behind Army.

Widdoes was named Coach of the Year and the dental student, a 168-pounder named Leslie Horvath, grabbed off the Heisman Trophy, the only time in history that the two awards went to the same school.

In 1945 Widdoes slipped a bit. He was upset by Purdue, picked up steam again to whip Minnesota and end Bernie Bierman's 21-game winning streak, and went into the Michigan finale with a chance to win the Big Ten title again. Michigan nipped the Buckeyes, 7–3, and Caroll Widdoes abruptly resigned. His very frank reasons were that he'd had two years of the big-time pressure cooker and knew with great certainty that he wanted out.

But the amazing thing was that Widdoes said he wanted to simply step down to his old job as backfield coach and let somebody else run the store. In fact, said Widdoes, the right guy would be assistant Paul Bixler, still another of Brown's helpers from Massillon. The Athletic Board promptly hired Bixler. Ohio State University was handing a whistle to its fourth football coach in seven years . . .

Bixler lost only two of his first eight games and was thought to be having a respectable first year. In his finale —at Columbus; repeat, at Columbus—his Bucks got murdered by Michigan, 58–6. Nobody at Ohio State loses to Michigan 58–6. At least nobody does and maintains any claim of respectability. Bixler quit a few weeks later to go to Colgate. Buckeye officials would now be offering the whistle to a fifth coach in eight years . . .

Once again the coaching merry-go-round was whirling in Columbus, this time to a discordant tune. Things were complicated. Everyone had accepted Widdoes as a fine caretaker in Paul Brown's absence, but Paul Brown wasn't coming back. While still in the Navy in February 1945, Brown had startled everyone by signing a contract to coach Cleveland in the new All-America Football Conference.

Nobody in the administration or in the athletic director's office shed a single tear. Nor did a lot of newspapermen throughout the state. They were shocked and disgusted that Brown should have deserted them, just when he had the makings of a dynasty ahead of him, to enter a pro game still a long way from the stature it would later enjoy.

But Brown's supporters were muttering quite loudly that Lynn W. St. John, the Buckeye athletic director, was resentful of Brown's popularity, didn't like his ruthless desire to win, and thought Brown ultimately wanted his job—St. John was about to retire.

Downtown in the Statehouse, a member of the legislature offered a resolution (passed, 66–21) to rehire Paul Brown. But St. John had tapped Dick Larkins to succeed him, and Larkins had his own reasons to oppose Brown— Brown had signed Buckeye stars who still had postwar eligibility at Ohio State to pro contracts—soon-to-be famous stars like Dante Lavelli, Lynn Houston, Lou Groza and others.

Larkins quickly let it be known he wouldn't be inviting Brown back to Columbus. Instead he hired an old buddy and All-America teammate in their playing days at Ohio State: Wes Fesler, then at Pitt. Fesler had been the most versatile and popular athlete in Ohio State history, and his selection delighted everyone.

Fesler immediately did what no other Ohio State coach had ever done. In 1947 he finished dead last in the Big Ten.

But such was his charisma that nobody let out a peep. He moved up a few notches in 1948, and in 1949 when the Buckeye kicker got a second chance at a point after touchdown because Michigan was offside, the Bucks got a tie with the Wolverines and went to the Rose Bowl, where they whipped California. It was just the beginning, crowed Buckeye fans.

The following year the Buckeyes were described at midseason as "Vic Janowicz and a supporting cast of forty other All-Americas." They were deep, talented and sure national champions. Then something happened at Illinois—nobody ever really knew what—and the Buckeyes were upset 14–7. There was still a chance for redemption in the usual finale with Michigan.

Then something even worse happened. Ohio State and Michigan played the bizzare Blizzard Bowl under the worst conditions ever seen for a football game—the infamous game of thirty-five punts and not a single first down, played in five-degree weather with hardly anybody being able to tell friend from foe. The Wolverines won when they found a blocked Buckeye punt in a snowbank in the end zone with seconds left in the first half.

It was the most vitriolic aftermath to any Ohio State game ever. Athletic director Larkins was pilloried for allowing the game to go on; and Wes Fesler was flayed for calling a punt with seconds to go in the half, instead of trying to run out the clock.

Two weeks later Vic Janowicz received the Heisman Trophy, but three days after that there was a stunner of even more dramatic impact. Wes Fesler said he was quitting to go into the real estate business with multimillionaire industrialist John Galbreath, who also owned the Pittsburgh Pirates and the very successful Dapper Dan stables, which later provided him with two Kentucky Derby winners. It had to be a Big Ten mark for sudden disenchantment. What the record didn't show was the depths of Fesler's psychic despair and disillusionment with pressure football —Columbus and Ohio State style.

For a year or more he had been privately brooding over big-time football: its pandering to teen-age high school stars and their parents; the whole recruiting rat race; the hypocrisy and the rampant hanky-panky. He was on record as advocating a complete Big Ten round-robin schedule, and to hell with the outside world. Let's control our own methods and destinies, he urged.

But there was no way to turn back the decades of Midwest chauvinism, the bred-in-the-bone fervor of Ohio State fans. And suddenly it hit him.

If he weren't sure of it during his three-year tenure as coach, he got the message straight enough within a week after the Blizzard Bowl of 1950. He couldn't believe the vicious phone calls or the hateful mail which athletic director Larkins and he got for weeks afterwards.

Fesler later confided to friends that he was almost nauseated when his wife was subjected to abuse, and he knew that any love he had for football, Buckeye brand, had come unglued. He'd been having severe headaches and couldn't sleep. So Wes Fesler quit. He just up and quit. One more ghost in the graveyard of Ohio State coaches.

So Columbus and Ohio State began playing "Here we go again" as the search began for Fesler's successor—the sixth coach in twelve years. Twenty-four hours after Fesler resigned, Glenn "Tiger" Ellison of Middletown, president of the Ohio High School Coaches Association, reported that its members were strongly urging that Ohio State bring back Paul Brown from Cleveland.

The Associated Press got into the act and polled its state sports editors on the preference. Sixteen of the twenty-nine voting picked Brown. Second, with six votes, was Chuck Mather, the highly successful coach at Massillon High School, Brown's old launching pad. There were others, such as Bud Wilkinson of Oklahoma; Wally Butts of Georgia; Bear Bryant of Kentucky; Don Faurot of Missouri.

Then the Columbus *Citizen* weighed in, as long as everyone else was. It ran a reader poll in which Paul Brown got 2,331 of 2,811 votes. Harry Strobel, Ohio State freshman coach, was second. Russ Needham, the sports editor of the *Citizen*'s arch-rival paper, the *Dispatch,* was third. Then there were scattered votes for Lassie; a bosomy TV star named Dagmar; Harry S. Truman; actress Lana Turner; comedian Ed Wynn; Senator Robert A. Taft, and a lifer in the state pen. Only Brown was considered a serious candidate.

Needham of the *Dispatch,* a leader in the drive, blared: "Ohio State is no more a coach's graveyard than Minneapolis or Madison . . . But it is a graveyard for mediocrity in football coaching."

Ahead for Ohio State lay the longest search for a football coach in big-time college coaching history. It would be known as "the seventy days."

On day forty-seven, Wes Fesler said he'd had enough of the real estate business and was getting back into football. He replaced Bernie Bierman as coach at Minnesota. In Columbus, heads reeled. If Fesler really did like football, was it Ohio State he was allergic to? Who the hell would be willing to come in here and coach on a lunatic fringe?

The answer was at least half a hundred candidates who said they had whistle, playbook, tough hides and would travel. One of them, with the toughest hide of all, was Wayne Woodrow Hayes. The trouble was, few people had heard of him and nobody wanted him.

# 6
# The Seventy Days

The time was right, and for someone with Woody Hayes'
ambition and drive, he was going to have to reach for it
now. He was thirty-eight years old. In a couple of years the
big opportunities might not have been interested in his
knock.

\*  \*  \*

"I didn't come here for the security. I came here for the
opportunity."

Thus barked Woody Hayes with a belligerent glint in his
eye in one of his early public pronouncements after being
appointed Ohio State football coach in February 1951.

With this damn-the-torpedoes-full-speed-ahead pun-
gency, Woody, the wartime Navy commander, laid it right
on.

Nobody could have put it more succinctly or in better
perspective. And nobody had sweated out a big-time football appointment the way he did—or for as long as he did.

The seventy days of search, conjecture and breathless expectancy brought forth from one wag the view that "they're conducting this thing with the solemnity and posturing of selecting a Pope. All we need now is the puff of white smoke."

It was well into the search, when a senior tackle at Miami University was playing handball with his coach. The senior tackle was a pudgy but tough kid named Bo Schembechler. The coach was a pudgy but tough thirty-eight-year-old, Woody Hayes. They swatted the ball for a couple of minutes without a word passing between them.

Suddenly the coach stopped short, the ball gripped in his hand. He stared hard at his player. "Bo, who do you think should get that job at Ohio State?"

Schembechler stared back. "I think you ought to get that job, Woody," he said.

Hayes massaged the handball roughly. "You sure of that?"

Schembechler nodded "Sure  . Yeah, I'm sure of it."

"Why?" Hayes demanded stubbornly.

"Because I think you're the best man for the job."

Hayes grunted and swatted the ball. "Really think so, hey?"

"Yeah, sure. I really think so," snapped Schembechler.

As the present Michigan coach recalls it, not another word was said, but he felt as though Woody knew all along that he was the best man for it and would probably get it but was longing for one of his most respected players to come out with an outright endorsement.

Woody Hayes had been one of the first to apply. He got into a long line that formed not only in fact but in the fantasies of every sportswriter or influential alumnus in the state. All of whom felt they were enfranchised authorities on what was best for Ohio State's football future. And were quick to let their choices be known.

Strangely enough, there weren't many actual applications from the well-known coaches of the period. Many frankly felt they wanted no part of the zany, pressure-packed situation on the banks of the Olentangy River. No Buckeye coach had ever ended it all by leaping in, but eventually somebody had to be the first, and who wanted that?

There was, of course, a search committee: the Athletic Board of twelve members. It laid down the specs for the man they wanted but not once did they formally approach anyone. They sat back and waited. The board was made up of six faculty members: two from the School of Engineering; one each from the Law School, Chemistry, Dentistry and Business Administration. There were two alumni, one a former attorney general of Ohio, the other an insurance man who'd once been head baseball coach and assistant football coach at Ohio State. An ex-officio member was the university vice-president, and another was a member of the university Board of Trustees. Then there were two student members, one a graduate student who was formerly a varsity basketball manager, and the other a junior in journalism. Some mix!

They all wanted the same thing. A guy who could win. Everybody said something about winning with honor, but nobody ever came up with a working ratio on that score.

But over everybody's thinking, over all the conjecture, superseding all the names that were being bandied about, there was the haunting shadow of one man.

His name was Paul Brown.

Yes, *that* Paul Brown.

Suddenly, a whole passel of folks—including some vociferous newspapers—got behind an incipient "Bring back Paul Brown" movement. Nobody among university officialdom was very fond of that idea. Truth is, they found it rather repugnant. They hadn't liked the way Paul Brown had cut himself loose from the school which launched him into the big-time, by announcing he was going to coach a pro team in Cleveland. But he'd been one helluva college football coach and had added to his luster with the Cleveland Browns. Who possibly would be a better man to restore the Buckeyes to gridiron supremacy than the one who'd dominated the old All-America Football Conference and had won the NFL crown in 1950 after the two leagues merged?

Of course, everyone said he'd have to be an idiot to give up his $40,000 and more as a pro coach to return to Ohio State for a third of that. But many of the same people thought that vanity and his strong love for the college game would induce him to take another crack at it.

Paul Brown wound up among eight finalists chosen by the Athletic Board to come to Columbus for interviews. Woody Hayes was another. The remaining six were Don Faurot, the highly successful head coach at Missouri; Warren Gaer, head coach at Drake; young Sid Gillman, head coach at Cincinnati; Harry Strobel, then freshman coach at Ohio State; and two high school coaches in Ohio—Chuck Mather of Massillon and Jim McDonald at Springfield.

There was only one of the eight who never formally applied for the job. Paul Brown. But because of the growing ground swell to bring him back, he just let it be known, in a friendly sort of way, that he'd be glad to come down and talk to the people if they felt there was any useful purpose involved. Just to please a lot of his friends, seemed to be the prevailing attitude among all concerned.

So all eight candidates came to Columbus for interviews with the screening committee of the Athletic Board. The committee delved into certain specifics. What were the candidates' views on, for instance, coaching and scouting methods; strategy; discipline standards; handling of players; recruiting, and general all-around sportsmanship?

Nobody ever came out and asked if the candidate thought he could win many more than he lost, and beat Michigan. Any candidate who didn't think the committee had those little items in the back of their minds would be nuts.

The alumni association formally adopted a hands-off policy, content to let the proper authorities do the selecting. But alumni leaders in Cleveland, Cincinnati, Toledo, Dayton and elsewhere sent appeals to the chairman of the Board of Trustees at the university to make sure the Athletic Board resisted pressure groups peddling their own man. In essence, the alumni leaders were anti-Paul Brown because they felt he was a win-at-any-cost sort of coach. Meanwhile, petitions in favor of Brown had been circulated on campus and came up with more than 2,000 names.

In recalling the situation, Woody Hayes says he didn't even consider himself a leading candidate—not even in the top ten or twelve—when he decided to reach out for the big time. "I wasn't even certain I was ready for it," he says.

Hayes had just finished his second year at Miami of Ohio after two undefeated seasons in 1947–48 at little Denison University in Granville, Ohio. In his second season at Miami, the Redskins had a very respectable year, winning eight of nine, losing only to Xavier in an early-season 7–0 upset. After scoring 322 points to 79, Miami received an invitation to play Arizona State in something called the Salad Bowl in Phoenix, Arizona, which enjoyed a tinge of respectability at the time but which subsequently died a largely unmourned death as a postseason attraction. Beating Arizona State 34–21 was a major upset for Woody Hayes, but it was not exactly the most impressive calling card for someone hankering to take out after the Big Boys with Ohio State.

But the time was right and for someone with Woody Hayes' ambition and drive, he was going to have to reach for it now. He was thirty-eight years old. In a couple of years the big opportunities might not have been interested in his knock.

Woody Hayes is a man who makes his own way and makes his own breaks, but he'd be the first to admit that fate took a hand in that winter of 1951. When Woody was working for his master's degree in educational administration at Ohio State summer school sessions in 1947–48, his advisor was Dr. Daniel Eikenberry of the Graduate School staff. Because Woody was a football coach, Eikenberry asked athletic director Dick Larkins of Ohio State to sit in on the committee evaluating Woody's exams. When Fesler abruptly resigned, Eikenberry immediately offered to recommend Woody to Larkins for the job. Shortly afterwards, Woody went to the NCAA coaches' convention in Dallas and ran into Larkins. They had breakfast together, and Larkins promised Woody he could have an interview with the screening committee.

Many interested coaches were still wary of the Buckeye "graveyard" reputation and decided to play it cool and

cutesy. Nobody was ready to take a deep breath and proclaim to the world, "Yessiree, I'd really like that job and I'm
going to take dead aim at it."

But Woody Hayes, no shrinking violet, no equivocator,
came out strongly. He said he sure did want the job at Ohio
State. "A frontal attack is rarely considered good strategy
in military warfare"—he smiles—"but if well-timed, a frontal attack can lead to victory." Spoken just the way you'd
expect a tank commander or a destroyer commander or a
student of military history would say it.

The "Bring back Paul Brown" movement was in full cry,
led by a Columbus newspaper, when Woody Hayes drove
up to Columbus for his meeting with the screening committee. For Woody, a high spot came when, as he remembers
it, Fritz Mackey, a committee member and a former Buckeye assistant coach, asked how Woody would handle blocking assignments against multiple changing defenses. "It
was something I was glad to talk about," said Hayes "because I knew Ohio State had been having some recent
difficulties on that score. I think I satisfied him."

A little more than three hours later the committee chairman looked at his watch and mentioned to Woody that
another candidate was to be interviewed in a few minutes.
Woody got up, smiled all around and said, "Well, gentlemen, I guess the hay is in the barn."

Summing up with a farmer's homily meaning he'd done
what he had to do and now he could rest was the best
parting shot Woody Hayes could have taken. One of the
committee members was Bland Stradley, the university
vice-president, who'd grown up on a farm. Years later,
Larkins told Woody he thought Woody's comment had
nailed down some vital influence.

But if the hay was in the barn, the vote for Woody Hayes was not in the bag. The last candidate—Gillman—had had his interview on February 10. Speculation was that he was hot. He'd been a captain at Ohio State—first and only Jewish football captain the Buckeyes ever had. Woody knew him from hard experience: Gillman had preceded him at Miami and had departed after the 1948 season for Cincinnati, taking many of the Miami stars with him. And a good section of the press were still confident that Brown would be tapped. The average Ohio State fan wanted a winner. Paul Brown was the most logical man to provide it.

Woody Hayes didn't have a chance, said the self-appointed experts. But the experts had no way of gauging any impact he might have made on the screening committee. They also weren't aware of a lot of little facts the committee had warmed up to. After his first year at Miami Woody had pulled off a recruiting coup. From the 1949 annual North-South Ohio High School All-Star game squad, Woody Hayes lured twelve to Miami. Ohio State got two. Cincinnati got two. No other school got more than one. To a screening committee looking for a Midas touch in mining football ore, this had to mean something special.

On February 10 the Athletic Board reviewed every bit of information its screening committee had submitted. Newsmen, almost holding a twenty-four-hour alert on the best front-page story of their careers, by now had eliminated Faurot, Gillman and five others. They figured it would be the comparatively unknown Hayes from Miami or the popular choice, Brown. Popular with whom? Not with the Athletic Board.

On February 10 the Athletic Board quickly voted unanimously for Woody Hayes.

Since their nomination would not be submitted to the university Board of Trustees until February 12 the Athletic Board bound themselves to secrecy against a news leak to the local press and thereby alienated the rest of the press throughout the state. University officials—particularly the Athletic Department—always dreaded this possibility. The Athletic Department at Ohio State had historically been a target for snipers eager to find fault with expensive big-time sports programs.

People still recalled the energy with which the press had jumped on a comment by Martin L. Davey two decades earlier. Davey, the only tree surgeon in history to become governor of a state, had dourly complained that he had most of the Ohio State football team on the state payroll, an allusion to part-time jobs or alleged jobs the Buckeye gridders held down in an era before athletic scholarships.

Strangely, the Athletic Board then went through the formality of holding an early breakfast meeting on February 12 and again called for a "vote on the candidates," although they'd already decided on the chubby, round-faced, thirty-eight-year-old Woody Hayes of Miami. No one quite knew why they were going through the process again. It was somewhat mysterious, as if someone thought everyone should have a chance to change their mind if they cared to.

Once again Woody was the unanimous choice without a word of dissent.

The nomination was immediately turned over to athletic director Dick Larkins in his office, who just as solemnly handed it over to university president Howard Bevis.

Was Woody Hayes now football coach at Ohio State? Uh . . . well, no. Not quite.

The recommendation from the Athletic Department on

this same day was to go to the Board of Trustees, the seven men in final control of everything that goes on at Ohio State—all seven of whom knew that selecting a football coach at Ohio State just wasn't in the same league with okaying funds for a new chemistry building or maybe even picking a new prexy, right?

Four of the seven convened on February 12. But since only three of them were for Hayes, they decided to call a special meeting for February 18. No use to make a crucial decision without having a full majority in favor.

So President Bevis, in a statement to the press, said, "Because three members of the Board of Trustees found it impossible to be at today's meeting, and feeling that a matter of this importance should have the counsel of larger representation of the board, a special meeting has been called for February 18th."

The university daily paper, the *Lantern,* quipped in a headline: "NO COACH—TUNE IN SUNDAY."

It was at this juncture that the wag alerted fans to be on the look-out for "the puff of white smoke."

The days between the board's first meeting and the special meeting were filled with fever and flak. Pro-Brown students accused Walter Donham, one of the student members of the screening committee, of not representing them properly. Donham argued that he had represented them: "I voted the way I thought the students would have voted if they knew what I knew. After all, ninety percent of all students didn't know a single candidate. But I sat in on every interview with all of them." Score a big one for the student rep, said administrators.

Immediately, there was another ploy by the Paul Browners. Petitions began surfacing, calling for the dismissal of athletic director Larkins on the grounds that he had abandoned objectivity and had personally stumped against Brown. Despite a page-one push by the Columbus *Dispatch,* the campaign fizzled. The Columbus *Journal* reported that only twenty-one student names had appeared during a twenty-one-hour display of the petition in the student union.

It was time, now, to hear it from the state legislature, downtown in the capitol. Representative Harold W. Oyster of Marietta, introduced a resolution to investigate the financial status of the Ohio State Athletic Department. It seemed irrelevant to the issue but typified the sort of troublesome meddling in various official quarters.

Down on the campus Dick Larkins reacted vigorously. "We'd welcome it. We're clean and in good shape."

Spring practice was only six weeks distant. There were fans who thought the Buckeyes wouldn't even have a new head coach by opening game in September, let alone spring practice.

Down in Oxford, Ohio, Woody Hayes was sitting it out tensely.

When the trustees held their special meeting on February 18, the original four were present, plus two others, General Motors Vice-President Charles Kettering and Senator John Bricker. In a preliminary showdown, five of the six trustees present voted for Wayne Woodrow Hayes. Later, Carlton Dargusch, still holding out for Brown, went along with the others. It was now unanimous. Ohio State had a football coach.

Larkins immediately gave Woody Hayes the word and then, somewhat belatedly, asked what kind of salary Woody thought he should have. "Oh, I guess $10,000 will do," said Woody.

"We'll do a bit better," said Larkins. "We'll start you at $12,500."

The agreement would be a contract for one year. For an employee of the State of Ohio, that's the only kind of employment contract anyone can get. But there was a gentleman's agreement that it would be renewed every year for five years. Woody knew that Larkins meant it, too. But he also had to know that of the four coaches who'd preceded him in this pressure cooker in Columbus, not one had been dismissed. All four had decided on their own not to continue.

Woody felt no hesitation in accepting.

A few hours later he got a call from President Bevis, who said, "The football coaching job is yours."

"Thank you, sir," said Woody. "Mr. Larkins has already told me so."

"Yes, I know," said Bevis, "but I wanted you to have my personal assurance of it." Then, as Woody recalls it, Bevis asked, "Is there anything in your past that would cause you to turn down this position?"

Two decades later, a vice-presidential candidate would hedge on this question and cause a scandal. Howard Bevis was years out front in knowing enough to ask it.

"No, sir," was Woody Hayes' quick, firm reply.

In addition to the $12,500 per year, they made Woody a full professor of physical education, in which capacity he would also teach one course a week in football. What that course turned out to be, is something deserving special mention, later . . .

He was also told he would have a free hand in picking his assistants and in running his program. As it turned out, football has never known a freer hand at the helm—so free that it shattered all concepts of college football management.

The next day Woody came to Columbus and held his first press conference attended by thirty-five or so sportswriters from all over the state. It lasted more than an hour, and as one now-retired scribe recalled it, "My God, who could have predicted from that pleasant exchange that some day the guy would turn out to be the toughest coach to cover in football!"

A spokesman for the Board of Trustees had the penultimate word on the marathon seventy-day manhunt. "Mr. Hayes," he said, "was far and away the outstanding man interviewed. He was frank, forthright and full of *savoir-faire.*"

There were a lot of football buffs around Ohio who didn't know what *savoir-faire* was, and hoped, vaguely, that it had something to do with first downs.

The ultimate words, as always, were Woody's. The tough, edgy ones about not looking for security at Ohio State. Opportunity was the thing.

Woody Hayes knew what the hell he was talking about.

# 7
# Background: American Gothic

The immortal Cy Young, retiring to his farm after his fabled pitching career, held beer fests and boxing matches in his barn for the town gentry. He would slip five bucks to local kids to flail away with the enthusiasm that only the tough and untutored could display. One of the toughest and most enthusiastic was a sixteen-year-old middleweight with the best left hook in town. His name was Woody Hayes.

*   *   *

On February 18, 1951, Ohio State found itself, finally, with a new football coach, and if there was still anyone saying, "Where the hell did *he* come from?" it was only a natural question. In the case of Woody Hayes the route was strictly American Gothic . . .

Newcomerstown, Ohio, in the 1920s couldn't have been more typical of its genre if someone had built the place from scratch with Currier & Ives prints for background and a Sears Roebuck catalog for inspiration. It was an eastern Ohio town of about 3,500, nestled alongside the Tuscarawas River, with the Clow Pipe and File works its lone industrial plant. It was ringed by the good earth of solid farming land, and a few miles beyond was a colorful Amish community.

There was the prideful volunteer fire department; a main street appropriately named Main Street; maybe three dozen stores that served most of the mercantile interests of the community; a red-brick high school with a senior class of perhaps forty-five students; a single movie house that showed silent films; and just a few blocks away was the meandering old Ohio Canal, still flowing with water but no longer used commercially.

Saturday was the big day in town and Main Street was a cliché that repeated itself fifty-two times a year, except for holidays.

Just as so many Midwesterners have offered testimony about their own local roots, so did local people praise Newcomerstown as a great place to grow up in and a great place to leave.

It was in Newcomerstown that Woody Hayes did most of his early growing up, although he'd been born in an even smaller place, Clifton, in the western part of the state. If Newcomerstown was typical of so many other small towns in Ohio, the Hayes family was far from typical. It was, on examination, an unusual one.

Woody can never talk about his family without starting with his father, Wayne B. Hayes, one of twelve children raised on a farm, and a man whose involvement with education still fills Woody with awe and respect.

"My father," Woody reveals, "never got past the eighth grade in public school. Neither he nor any of his brothers or sisters could go any further because there wasn't a single high school in Noble County at the time. But in those days there was something called the Boxwell examination for certification to teach public school. My dad took it, passed it and was only fifteen years old or so when he got a job teaching for about twenty-eight dollars a month.

"But it was only the start. My father was determined to go on. Within a few years he was principal of a small high school near Springfield, Ohio, and still he felt the drive for more education. He'd already begun taking courses at colleges around the state. Finally he settled on Wittenberg College in Springfield to finish up. When my father was thirty-eight, I was six years old, my brother Ike was eight, and my sister Mary was fourteen. It isn't often that three kids of our age wind up with the unique and memorable experience of watching their father graduate from college when he's thirty-eight years old. I think Wittenberg must have been the fifth or sixth college he'd studied at, while handling his administrative duties, teaching and raising a family."

A year later, in 1920, Wayne Hayes accepted the job as superintendent at Newcomerstown.

Whatever the special ambience of this village, the three Hayes kids turned out to be somewhat special. Ike went off to Iowa State University, received All-America mention as a 162-pound football guard, and became a prominent veterinarian. Mary Hayes went off to college, and then to a music conservatory at Ithaca, New York; there she decided she wanted to be an actress and took a shot at Broadway, where she made it big. At one time she was George Jessel's leading lady in a production that also featured Shirley Booth and William Gargan. She starred in several road-company shows and then got into radio, where she and her husband were a crack writing team in New York for many years.

It is Mary who recalls so well the Hayes family days in

Newcomerstown. "Because dad was superintendent of schools we had to be a whole lot sharper about what we did," she says. "He told us we'd never get special favors in school, and he had a way of keeping us on our toes, academically.

"He'd notice on a weekend that I hadn't done much studying. On Monday morning he'd make his point. Dad was also the Latin teacher, and Latin class was the first one in the morning. If he knew I hadn't spent much time on it over the weekend he gave me no chance to catch up on Monday morning. I'd be the first student he'd call on to recite from Vergil or whatever we were studying, and there I'd be, unprepared. I'd get the message, all right."

Mary still has sharply etched memories of her little brother, Woodrow (nobody ever called him by his real first name, Wayne):

"Since he was the youngest, Woody was usually very obedient—but once in a while he'd make up his mind to something and then you couldn't budge him. I remember someone gave him a big Mexican straw hat for a present. It had a lot of little bells on it, and Woody wore it wherever he went, day and night. We couldn't get it off his head, and he'd have slept in it if it hadn't been for the bells.

"Woody was an industrious little kid. He mowed lawns and delivered newspapers but he was a terrible business-man at handling his accounts. He was always neglecting to collect from his newspaper customers, and our mother con-stantly had to remind him. I think if she hadn't, weeks would go by before Woody would ask people for the money.

"Our father, incidentally, always encouraged us to culti-vate older people. And I mean *much* older. People in their sixties and seventies. He thought young people should learn to establish a warm bond between them and older folks, that it led to understanding and a sense of compassion. I remember how Woody became attached to elderly 'Uncle' John and 'Aunt' Flora Chapman next door. They weren't really related, but Woody always called them Uncle John and Aunt Flora.

"Woody was a leader, even as a boy. In those days Halloween wasn't the gentle house-to-house trick or treat that today's kids engage in. It was a day of nasty pranks and even vicious things perpetrated on older people or their property. Woody was always the kid who would talk the others out of any nasty plans they had.

"He never lacked for energy. When he and his friends weren't playing ball they'd be building a shack or cabin on the banks of the old Ohio Canal, which ran right past our house. In the summertime I guess they fantasized camping out in it, and in the winter they'd use it to keep warm while skating on the frozen canal.

"The one thing Woody didn't like was fishing. He just never had the patience for it. He couldn't tolerate just *sitting* there, doing nothing until a fish would bite. Woody had to be active."

Quite apparently there were few in Newcomerstown as active as Wayne Woodrow Hayes. A local hero was, in fact, one of the great men of American sports—Denton "Cy" Young, who had long since been retired after pitching the greatest number of victories in the history of baseball: 511. Every schoolboy in Newcomerstown knew every facet of Young's career, including the derivation of his nickname. Hitters swore that Young could throw the ball with the speed of a cyclone, and cyclone soon became "Cy."

Retiring to a farm near Newcomerstown after his fabled career, Young, among other things, liked to hold beer fests for the local gentry, who longed for something a bit zingier than the pale brew sold during Prohibition.

As an added attraction Young would hold boxing matches on a ring pitched in his barn, and would slip five bucks to local kids to flail away with the enthusiasm that only the willing and untutored could display.

One of the most willing and enthusiastic battlers was a tough sixteen-year-old 160-pound middleweight with the best left hook in town. His name was Woody Hayes, and if the Amateur Athletic Union wants to declare that his five-buck stints make him a retroactive pro, let them take their case to Denison University, in Granville, Ohio, where Woody Hayes was to get his first taste of college ball.

At Newcomerstown High School, Woody played football, basketball and baseball. Newcomerstown was a small school and didn't play the kind of schedule that brought college recruiters flocking to the ball park. The young Woody Hayes gave and took his lumps in spirited anonymity, and nobody from Ohio State, Purdue, Michigan or elsewhere sought him out. When he graduated from high school in 1931, he set his sights on Denison, not too far from home. Denison had fine academic stature and played its ball against such as Ohio Wesleyan, Kenyon, Marietta, Wooster and others. Woody was a hard-nosed, 200-pound tackle on a team that struggled through 2–6 and 2–5–1 records in his first two years but had a fine 6–1–1 year in his senior season of 1934. In baseball he was an outfielder with no apparent future.

Woody Hayes' future, as far as he could tell, was to teach and perhaps do some coaching in those Depression years of the mid-thirties. He had majored in English and history at Denison. (Later, one of his professors, Dr. William Utter, was to tell Woody that he was the best nonprofessional history student he ever had.)

When Woody graduated from Denison in June, 1935, he toyed with the notion that law school might be his next stop. But it wasn't too compelling—and besides, there was still a Depression out there in the real world, and law school meant a big expense. So he shunted the notion aside for the time being and accepted a job as English teacher and assistant football coach at an exotically named town called Mingo Junction, about two traffic lights larger than Newcomerstown. His salary was to be a bit more than $1,200 for the year.

To prepare himself a little better he hit the road—literally—the day after graduation. He wanted to save the price of a bus ticket so he hitchhiked 160 miles to Toledo to spend a few days at a coaching clinic, where the two main speakers were Richard Harlow of Harvard and Francis Schmidt, the offensive genius from Ohio State. Law school was still in the back of his mind. But he thought he'd coach and teach for a year before dealing with Blackstone, torts and writs of habeas corpus.

Mingo Junction was one of those tough little Ohio River towns just south of Steubenville and across the river from the West Virginia panhandle. The ambience was coal-mine steel-mill hillbilly and later Woody would recall that it had a tremendous influence on him. A big percentage of his seventh-grade kids turned out to be what his administration called "slow learners."

"But they really weren't," Woody recalls. "They were just *neglected* learners, and there's a heck of a difference. I worked with those kids and they responded, and it taught me a lot about education."

In June 1936, after his first year at Mingo Junction, Woody looked at his bank balance, did some wildly optimistic figuring and estimated he had enough to give him a leg up on his first semester of law school at Ohio State. There was one big hitch. He found out there were no entering classes in the summer session. "But I didn't want to waste the summer," he said, "or the psychological momentum I'd worked up, so I took a shot at graduate school instead."

He thought he'd get his master's degree in educational administration and be all set to follow his father's path to a principalship or a school superintendency. It meant he'd have to take a couple of courses each summer for a few years and could drop the whole idea if he eventually settled on law school. Nothing like touching all the bases.

He didn't know it, then, but it would take many, many more summers of part-time work before the master's would be his. And each summer would take him further and further away from the possibility of law school and closer to a goal that was predestined for him . . .

His year at Mingo Junction, meanwhile, had led to a better assignment at New Philadelphia, Ohio, where he would teach history and be assistant football coach. It meant a few hundred dollars more per year in salary, and the football was a big step above Mingo Junction. With a population at that time of more than 12,000, New Philadelphia was county seat of Tuscarawas County and played in a faster league.

Woody served there as line coach under John Brickels in 1936–37 and again during the summer continued with his work at Ohio State toward his master's degree. He and several other grad students saved on their expenses by living at the Sigma Chi fraternity house, and it was there that Woody got into gab sessions with another grad student, not about educational administration but about football. The other student was head coach at Massillon High School. His name, of course, was Paul Brown.

In 1938, when John Brickels left New Philly to go into college coaching, Woody Hayes became head coach. It was a successful tenure for three years, but his 1940 season was his last. With his natural sense of history he was troubled by the events of the first two years of World War Two. By midsummer of 1941 he was convinced that America was going to be involved and he wanted to be sure of his own personal preparedness. He enlisted in the Navy, was sent to officers' training school and ultimately commanded a destroyer-escort in the Pacific. He was not mustered out until the spring of 1946. But even while his ship, the *Rinehart*, was stationed at Long Beach, California, Lieutenant Commander W. W. Hayes wasn't sure what direction he'd be taking when he took off his uniform. Maybe now would be the time to chuck everything—his master's degree, his incipient desire for school administration, and his high school coaching career—and enter law school full time.

While he was in New Philadelphia he'd met a local girl named Anne Gross, a bright, vivacious graduate of Ohio Wesleyan. It had taken Woody four or five years to convince her she could do a whole lot worse than take up with him, and they were married in 1942.

So in that spring of 1946 while he was waiting for his discharge, Woody had a wife and an infant son, Steve, to consider in making his plans. The easiest thing to do would be to return to his job at New Philadelphia, but a letter from his former coach at Denison, Tom Rogers, settled everything.

Rogers was leaving Denison and the head coaching job for 1946 would be open. Was Woody interested in jumping from high school to the college game?

As Woody recalls it, the most critical thing about the letter was the fact that it had been chasing him around the Pacific and up and down the Pacific Coast for a month. Hayes was not only interested in the job but was lucky. He fired off a telegram to Rogers telling him he sure wished to take a crack at it, but probably couldn't get to Granville, Ohio, for a few weeks. He had to bring the *Rinehart* through the Panama Canal, up to the East Coast and take care of necessary paper work before coming out to Ohio for an interview.

Luckily the job wasn't filled before Woody got there, and after an interview with the Athletic Board and the President he found himself hired. He was now a college coach. Law school was out of his life forever, but he told his new employers that he still intended to continue work toward his master's degree in summer school. He was undoubtedly wise enough to know that although coaching college football was considerably more prestigious than, say, safe-cracking, it was not much more secure.

Enter Woody Hayes, head coach, Denison University, September, 1946, just a couple months removed from command of a DE in the Pacific, where the opponents had been the Japanese. He would have difficulty adjusting to a different sort of combat problem.

William J. Wehr of Cleveland, who played for Woody in Hayes' first year at Denison, recalls how many of his teammates felt.

"We could tell from the start," says Wehr, "that he was going to have a tough time of it. We had a fullback who walked into his office one day and informed Woody that he'd held as much rank in the Marines as Woody had in the Navy and implied that he wasn't going to take the kind of shoving around that Woody seemed to be giving us.

"We never trained, and I think in 1946 we lost at least four games in the fourth quarter as a result of it."

Another player walked in, sat down, propped his feet on the desk of the new young head coach, and informed the coach that he'd been a regular the year before, then asked what plans the coach had for him this year.

The new young coach's plans were for the guy to get his goddam feet off the bleeping desk, and get his bleeping tail out of there and onto the football field, where all of the coach's plans for him would be made.

Whether it was Woody Hayes' evolving personality, or his Navy background, or a combination of the two, Denison football players—youngsters and returning vets alike—were stunned at what was being asked of them in terms of drive, discipline and a coaching philosophy that had as its watchwords: "We're gonna do it again and again and again and again until you do it right—do you understand that, goddammit?"

They understood what he was saying, but couldn't understand *why* he was saying it. Football wasn't supposed to be like that. What they didn't know, perhaps, was that Wayne Woodrow Hayes had made a commitment to a lifestyle. He was going to be a football coach. This was the way he was going to do it. There would be only one way. His way.

Quite obviously Woody's approach to college coaching was that he still had the quarter-deck beneath his feet and that he would apply Navy command philosophy to the football field. It didn't work with returning GI's who were in their mid-twenties and not the nineteen-and-twenty-year-olds of prewar days.

It just might be that the watershed year for Woody Hayes' eventual greatness came in his disastrous 2–6 first season. He could easily have mishandled his troops the following season and had still another failure.

"But at the end of the year," Wehr continued, "Woody, as I recall, publicly declared his approach had been all wrong with the returning veterans. But he convinced us that we had real potential and predicted that we'd go on to be a great team.

"Before he was through with us we'd caught his competitive drive. We were impressed by his thoroughness and follow-through. Now we could see purpose in his attitudes —purpose for the team and not just him."

Woody had realized that the men who'd just come out of military service were actually in poor shape for football, although it might have seemed just the reverse—that life in the service would have better prepared them for the game.

He knew that football had tremendous demands for intense physical energy, and that it was impossible to get those kids into instant shape. As he described it, "If a man isn't in shape he'll hold back because he doesn't want to get too tired. I found that breaking training was more a symptom than a cause, and once they got in shape these symptoms would disappear."

He was absolutely right. In line with what Wehr reveals, Hayes that first winter appointed a committee of five players whom he considered leaders and would inspire others. Hayes met with them frequently over the winter and spring, molding them to his philosophy that nobody could win football games unless they regarded the game positively and would agree to pay the price that success demands of a team.

Just before spring practice in 1947 Woody heard that his star halfback Eddie Rupp was going to pass up spring drills because he was captain of the golf team. "I went over to his fraternity house and talked to him," Hayes recalls. "Eddie had just come out of the Air Force prior to the 1947 season. He'd played football and then basketball, and he said he was tired of all the discipline. Golf would give him the kind of relaxation he needed. So, no spring football.

"I explained to him how much the football team needed him and asked him to come out for the first week of drills and I'd excuse him for the rest of the sessions.

"I saw how upset he was, how drained and emotionally tired."

It was obviously a moment of decision not only for the boy but for the coach. A lot was riding on the moment. His decision could set an emotional and disciplinary pattern for the whole squad. It could provide just the motivation the club needed.

"He hesitated a moment," says Hayes. "Then he said, 'Okay, Coach. I'll be with you.'

"At the end of that first week we had our first scrimmage. Rupp broke three long touchdown runs and after the third one I told him he could go in and get dressed. As he trotted off the field toward the dressing room everyone on the field applauded him. They knew what he'd contributed. It made a successful spring practice for us."

Instead of another disastrous season in 1947, it led to a perfect 9–0 record, the first undefeated season in Denison's history. Woody followed it with an 8–0 perfecto in 1948, and after his two straight unblemished campaigns Miami University at Oxford, Ohio, decided they'd talk to him when Sid Gillman announced he was leaving for the University of Cincinnati.

Talking to Woody Hayes is to invite a one-sided discourse, but Miami liked what they heard and signed him. Hayes got to Oxford, Ohio, just in time to put in a couple of weeks of frenzied recruiting and to plan his spring football drills.

A pudgy, 190-pound offensive tackle named Glenn "Bo" Schembechler who was hoping to crack the starting line-up in his junior year, recalls the startling impact of the gathering tornado that hit the Miami campus shortly before spring practice in 1949.

"I was looking forward to playing a lot of tackle starting with my junior year that fall," Bo recalls. "This guy Woody Hayes had come over from little Denison University and we didn't know anything about him. We knew we'd just lost a brilliant coach and a great guy in Sid Gillman, who'd left to take over at Cincinnati. We all loved Sid and here was this grim-looking guy taking his place.

"Hayes said he wanted to meet all the players so we all lined up his first day on the scene and he came right down the line shaking hands with everybody, looking everybody smack in the eye, with something to say to each one of us. He seemed direct and honest as hell. I had a hunch right then and there he was something special.

"But it wasn't until spring practice began that we realized what he was going to be like on the field. I was playing baseball so I'd get the news from my buddies. This new coach was a shouting, screaming fireball who was physically grabbing guys all over the place, spinning them around while showing them what he wanted, all the while yelling at them.

"The players couldn't believe it and were cussing him behind his back. They were still cussing him when the regular season started that fall and we had a 5–4 year. The more we lost the more he drove us. It wasn't his fault that we lost those four. When Sid Gillman left Miami for Cincinnati he took a lot of our best players with him as transfers. They simply loved the guy and would have followed him anywhere.

"Woody never forgave Sid for that. It put a helluva hole in our prospects his first year. But Woody whipped us into the kind of team he wanted, and the following year, in 1950, we were a pip of a football team. We lost to Xavier, 7–0 in our second game and then we went roaring on to win eight straight, including a biggie over Arizona State in the Salad Bowl in Phoenix.

"Along the way, I never saw a man who got as much pleasure out of revenge as Woody did when he led us to a 28–0 smasher over Cincinnati.

"A lot of people were surprised a few weeks later when Woody Hayes became a candidate for the Ohio State job. I wasn't one of them," said Schembechler. "I wasn't at all surprised . . ."

# 8

# —And Now It Begins

The evidence on film is obvious . . . The tackle's footwork was faulty and he got himself shivvied out of position . . . couldn't shuck the blocker . . . used the wrong shoulder for penetrating leverage . . . The linebacker didn't read the play quickly enough and got blind-sided . . . The defensive back gave up too much depth . . . The average fan has no idea of the number or nuances of sins a player can commit.

\* \* \*

So Woody Hayes came to Ohio State. And now let's say it is any given Saturday in October. The last echoes of the victory bell have wafted over vast and cavernous Ohio Stadium, now empty. The 87,000 have dispersed out of sight across the campus. The huge parking fields on all sides of the stadium and across the Olentangy River have long since disgorged their last car. The Ohio State dressing rooms and the visitors' dressing rooms are empty, and only the lingering scents of adhesive, bandages, shower soap and stale perspiration remain.

The last state trooper is gone, the last patrol car. The

portable first-aid station gone, along with Bell Telephone's huge rolling public-telephone unit. Pieces of newspaper and programs are sucked up from the soaring scarlet and gray seats by a brief updraft of chill autumn air.

High up in the pressbox, the last dispatch has been filed by a couple hundred sportswriters. The pressbox lights are out. The radio and television lines have been unplugged. Over the stadium, in place of airplanes with advertising streamers, flies a flock of Canada geese winging southward in silent splendor. Dusk is settling, a blue-amber haze that is inevitably and suitably the third-act curtain of a hit show.

There is no desolation like Ohio Stadium ninety minutes after the gun has sounded following an Ohio State football game. The 87,000 have dispersed to fancy dinners, cocktail parties or reunions with sons and daughters on campus, or are on the road home to Cleveland, Toledo, Canton or Coshocton.

For Ohio State football, the aura is one of well-deserved repose, a sense of fulfillment, and for the average spectator or fan, the feeling that the week is truly done with.

But the week is never done with for Ohio State football. Two hours after the final gun, Woody Hayes, the hardest-working football coach in America—maybe the hardest working coach the game has ever known—has showered, dressed, hurried home for a quick dinner and then stepped right back onto the turntable that revolves to next week. Without a bit of lost motion.

By 7:00 or 7:30 P.M. at the latest, Woody Hayes is back in his conference rooms at Biggs Athletic Facility across the river from the stadium.

"They may beat us by outplaying us," says Woody Hayes. "They may beat us by outcoaching me. But I resolved a long time ago that nobody would ever beat me by outworking me."

And now it begins. In no corporate board room, in no industrial executive committee, nowhere in the varied American pattern of enterprise will there be a more intense week of evaluating, planning and execution of corporate tactics.

Films of that day's game have been shot by two different camera crews high atop the stadium. One crew shoots nothing but Ohio State on offense. The other shoots nothing but defense. Each crew has two cameras, the second one always loaded for immediate use when number one starts running out of film so that not a single play, not a single second of action can be missed. A play missed by either crew could bring down wrath from Woody Hayes that would be soul-searing.

The work from here on is highly organized and departmentalized. To begin with, Hayes has divided Ohio State football into two camps, both preparing to make war on their own and with little communication between the two camps.

Woody and his offensive coaches do their work in Biggs Facility. Defensive coordinator George Hill and his aides do all the defensive work in their offices in St. John Arena, more than a mile away. They rarely if ever see each other except when they come together on the practice field each afternoon at Biggs. And even then they work at different ends of the field. Their only close working proximity is at an all-out scrimmage early in the season. Visiting coaches and pro scouts who drop by during spring drills sometimes find the system hard to understand and accept.

By early Saturday evening after a game, the system has

slipped into its well-oiled, well-ordered design. Offensive film has been developed and sped to Biggs for Woody and offensive assistants: George Chaump, quarterbacks; Rudy Hubbard (recently appointed head coach at Florida A & M), offensive running backs; Joe Bugel, guards and centers; Ralph Staub, tackles and ends. Defensive film has arrived at St. John Arena for defensive coordinator George Hill and assistants: Esco Sarkkinen, ends; Chuck Clausen, tackles; and Dick Walker, backs. Hill himself is also responsible for linebackers.

Both groups start checking the film and then grading the individual players on every play, each coach checking the players he is responsible for. If the player did the job he was supposed to do he gets a check mark. If he doesn't he gets a zero. On defense, for instance, was something wrong with his footwork? Charge the wrong way? Did he fail to read the ball?

Did a defensive back fail to come up fast enough to keep the play inside? A cornerman is supposed to take the lead blocker with his forearm and shoulder to the inside, "stuffing" the play. Did he execute properly? On a pass pattern the defensive back must get to his zone area and then play the ball, all the while gauging the right angle of his drop-back in playing the ball.

So, after Sarkkinen has graded his defensive ends, Clausen his tackles, Walker his defensive backs, and Hill the linebackers, they tote up the checks and zeros. Suppose there were seventy plays run by the opposition. Of the total, they take the number of check marks and number of zeros and figure out the percentage. To do a job well, a defensive back should grade out to 90 percent. If a tackle does 85 percent he had a super day. A linebacker has to get

75 percent for a superior day. The percentages are a clue to the number of things that can go wrong at any position, with the linebackers obviously having the toughest jobs and being more vulnerable to error.

Meanwhile, of course, the same grading routine is being conducted by the offensive coaches. Woody Hayes plays no part in the grading. As commander-in-chief, he has delegated full authority to his staff. But he will look at the grading reports when they are tabulated and he will have some crisp comments on the number of failures.

By Sunday morning, every assistant coach will have completed his film check. Each coach has a student manager assigned to him who now does the paper work to record the grading sheets. By noon Sunday the paper work must be finished because the varsity squad comes in Sunday afternoon and each player will be handed his individual sheet, notating each play he was involved in (whether it was one play or the entire game) and his checks and zeros. Then the coaches take forty-five minutes off for lunch.

By 3:00 P.M. Sunday, when the players arrive at Biggs and St. John to meet with their individual coaches, the student managers have gone one step further in the film breakdown. They have been taught to edit film, and they prepare for their particular assistant coach all plays dealing with his position. Thus Walker will have a reel of film that shows nothing but plays involving his defensive backs in action. Clausen will have a reel that shows only his defensive tackles; Sarkkinen, only the defensive ends; Hill, just the linebackers.

Now, Walker will sit down with his seven or eight defensive backs; Clausen with all his defensive tackles, and so forth. Each coach will run his particular reel over and over, interminably, until every kid has seen his various errors. Appropriate comments will have been spelled out on each boy's sheet, but each coach embellishes the record with some provocative remarks that leave little doubt what they have in mind.

There's no rebuttal. The evidence is only too obvious on the screen. The tackle's footwork was faulty and he got himself shivvied out of position. He didn't use his hands forcefully enough and couldn't shuck the blocker. He used the wrong shoulder for penetrating leverage.

The linebacker didn't read the play quickly enough and got himself blind-sided by the offensive guard. The defensive back gave up too much depth, provided too much of a cushion between the interference that was forming, and the spot from which he decided to commit himself. The average fan has no idea of the number or nuances of sins a player can commit without being the slightest bit obvious to the spectator.

Offensive coaches Staub, Bugel, Chaump and Hubbard, of course, are doing the same thing for their players. It is the grading-out of his players that enables a coach to judge his kids and drop a boy to a second unit and bring up another whose grades indicate he rates a chance at a starting spot.

"It's as close as we can get to objectivity," Woody Hayes says, "and it's the kind of thing I find difficult to argue against when one of my assistants makes a switch of personnel."

The players go home about 4:30, either to their dorms, fraternity houses or apartments. They will have Sunday night off. Not so Woody and his nine assistants. At 5:00 P.M., they go home for dinner, then return at 7:00 to look at films of their opponent for the next game.

Personal scouting of Big Ten foes is now banned in the league. Prior to 1973 each school was allowed to send two scouts to two games of each opponent. Now the teams merely exchange films—two game films of each team to be played. (Actually, through some "friendly relations" with nonconference teams, a Big Ten club may obtain a copy of this nonconference club's game with a mutual Big Ten foe.)

Woody, meanwhile, has assigned various assistants to be entirely responsible for collecting a complete dossier on every team the Buckeyes will be playing during the season.

From every source possible earlier in the year, Ralph Staub or George Chaump, for example, will have to do a fantastic in-depth investigation of, say, Minnesota or Michigan State, or whomever. Names, height, weight, playing number and class rank of the enemy's starting teams, offensive and defensive. "When Woody says 'in-depth,'" says Clausen, "we take it to mean whether the player prefers chocolate ice cream to vanilla, and whether he has a mole on his left hip. We have to find out how much playing time he logged the previous year; when he first broke into the starting line-up if he came up from second or third string; and, by studying his films, what his best talents are and his weakest.

"Then we have to get all their pictures from the other school's sports information director. On Monday of the week before the game, Woody wants to see those pictures posted on the bulletin board at Biggs, along with position, size, year, and so forth. He wants each of our kids to get a mental image of the guy he's going to have to play against and beat. Just let me say that the assistant coaches come up with all the information . . ."

So there they are on Sunday night, these nine assistants of Woody's, at Biggs and St. John. Up and down the darkened corridors there is no life, no movement. No light comes from open office doors except the eerie flicker of a projection machine; no sound except the whirring of film threading through; the clicking of the automatic buttons as the coaches—each in his own office, each with his own copy of the enemy's film (duplicated, by now in the university photo lab)—runs his film back and forth, freezing it here and there, peering intently at a particular piece of action, straining for a helpful clue from an enemy fullback's mannerism as he lines up or takes (or doesn't take) a hand-off from the quarterback.

The defensive coaches are trying to evaluate the other team's offense. Esco Sarkkinen is trying to read how the enemy's option play is coming toward the defensive ends. Dick Walker is looking for a reading on a bootleg pass. Chuck Clausen is looking for his foe's techniques on trap plays or how they double-team a defensive tackle; George Hill is getting a reading on how the other club might work an isolation play on his linebackers, or how a running back might come in on a linebacker with another running back right behind him.

As a defensive unit, they all contribute to analysis of the enemy's attack. They study the pass patterns and draw them on the board for further analysis. They determine how the enemy comes out of their option plays, how they run the draw and the sweep.

They try to spot tendencies on down-and-distance situations. Every good team has strong tendencies to do certain things in a certain situation. By the time Hill and his staff pore over two or three or more complete game films play by play, often frame by frame, these tendencies will be spotted.

What they have spotted must now be translated to the Buckeye defenders.

At Biggs, the offensive coaches headed by Woody himself are evaluating the other team's defenses, deciding Buckeye blocking assignments which may best be used against them, looking for weaknesses that can best be exploited, determining which of Ohio's plays might work best on particular down-and-distance situations against the foe. It is this complete evaluation that will go into making up the Buckeye offensive game plan.

It is all done in silence, except perhaps for the occasional, muffled exclamation or curse that can either be surprise, respect—or contempt. Over and over. Back and forth. For three or four hours. Scrawling notes in the gloom on long yellow legal pads. At about 10:30 they turn on the lights and elaborate on what they've noted, putting it down in a concise way that can be translated thoroughly and methodically to Woody and the players during the week.

Sometime between 10:30 and 11:00 P.M. Sunday night at St. John and at Biggs, the nine assistants get up groggily, stretch, try to tell themselves that their muscles aren't really cramped and their eyes aren't really burning, realize it's a lie, and go home.

Monday morning at 7:30 A.M. they will assemble again.

# 9
# Woody at Work

A guard pulling wrong or blocking down improperly on a
linebacker would bring forth a sulfurous bellow from
Woody. Then he would snatch off his baseball cap and
tear it asunder, pulling it apart at every seam with three or
four frighteningly quick movements of his hands.

* * *

The Ohio State offensive guard fires out at the snap of the
ball and blocks down on the linebacker to force him away
from the flow of the play. He doesn't execute too well and
in his zeal he hooks an arm too tightly around the defensive
player. Almost with the movement there is a shrill whistle
and a black-and-white-striped-shirted official is tossing a
flag and rushing in toward the action.

"Holding!" he hollers. "Number 68!"

This is not a game—it's a routine practice at Ohio State.
Number 68 bends his head an instant, then looks up guiltily
and fearfully at Woody Hayes standing grimly, arms folded,

just a few yards away. The official is one of three fully uniformed, fully accredited officials hired every day at full fee to attend Ohio State practice sessions and call 'em as they see 'em.

The routine is a sort of live-ammo drill that mentally gears the troops for the real battle ahead. It costs Woody Hayes a couple of thousand dollars extra each autumn for these practice officials, but nobody dares question the expense. Everyone is aware that Ohio State teams over the years have had fewer yards in penalties called against them than any team in the Big Ten.

No practice session at Ohio State is run as a dummy drill, soft-pedaling the action. All the work is called "hit and fit." It means that every time a play is run the offensive man takes his full pop into the defensive lineman, fitting his body fully into the technique and the defender's body. But he not only fits but hits as well, right up to game force and velocity. Few teams do this except in scrimmage. The Buckeyes do it all the time, day after day, week after week in unit group practice. "That's why we have those great blocking lines every year," says Ralph Staub. "And that's why Woody Hayes' teams are still so physical in the third and fourth quarters."

But success comes from more than hard hitting and practice officials. Organization is still the key word, and on Monday morning, the coaches take up where they left off Sunday night. George Hill's defensive coaches sit down as a staff and look at a single game film, approaching it collectively for the first time. For example, discussing the option play that will be coming at them: how will each coach plan to play it and how will their individual players mesh as a unit? Sometimes it doesn't come easy. There can be heated differences of opinion, and a stranger walking down the hall may think he has blundered upon a brawl.

Hill may want to do something with his linebackers on a particular pass pattern, but Walker will claim it won't jibe with what he wants to do with his defensive backs on the same situation. Impasse. Walker may look for support from the defensive tackle coach, but Clausen has his own problems on the same pattern. Walker rushes to the blackboard and furiously erases what Hill has diagramed, and just as furiously chalks in his variation of the theme. Hill grabs up his own piece of chalk. The X's and O's are now proliferating all over the place. Hill hammers on his theory. Walker screams that the cornerback can't hold up that long and re-commit, if Hill's linebackers do such and such. Sarkkinen warns both that his defensive end may not be able to drop off if they read the play differently, so there is now a new consideration. It isn't really bedlam—by Monday afternoon they must get together.

Then Woody and Hill, his defensive coordinator, get together and complete a game plan, based on everything they have learned about their opponents and what they know of the Buckeyes' strengths and weaknesses. Large visual charts of the plays the Buckeyes will now use will be made. By Tuesday night the game plan is firm and no changes may be made.

On Monday afternoon before practice there is a squad meeting. Woody makes some pertinent remarks on the Buckeye performances of the previous Saturday followed by some preliminary comment on the next foe coming up. The preliminary comment simply is that he expects to kick hell outta them but we'll all have to do a little work on it first.

Then comes a ritual which might seem a bit strange if not flakey in a day when college football players are supposed to be very big on sophistication. Woody awards Buckeye leaves—the decals that go on a player's helmet as a badge of accomplishment. The films have revealed who did a good job in last Saturday's game, who executed well and consistently, who made the big plays.

Big deal? Damn right.

"This is recognition," says Woody. "Not everybody can get his name in a headline, so when these kids know that their coaches have singled them out for outstanding performance it means something. They know the fans notice those Buckeye leaves, too."

Even a second-string guard or linebacker, or a member of the specialty team on kickoffs can make a big play and collect a leaf. "And we don't award them lightly," Clausen points out. "We make very serious judgments. There have been times when we only award half a leaf and that kid is going to bust his butt to get another half."

Each day of the practice week is charted by time segments. The day's work is printed up in advance and distributed to all coaches, managers and newsmen attending practice sessions. The sheet is also posted on the bulletin board because it lists offensive and defensive units as of that day: first team and second team, so each kid knows where he stands on any given day. It's the first thing they look at before taking the field.

So precise is Woody's unit breakdown that sessions won't vary for more than a minute or so. A student manager is constantly at Woody's side with a sheet and a stopwatch. Typically, he signals each new session with a loud blast from a portable boat horn which Navy man Hayes has equipped him with.

There is yet another student manager hovering near Woody's shoulder to attend Woody's every need and whim —ready to dash back to Biggs for a rain jacket or a different pair of shoes; to make a phone call; to check for a message; to arrange any of a dozen things that may pop into Woody's mind. And for Woody it has to be instant takeoff.

Student managers are not the only important civilians on the practice field. With his kids' welfare constantly in mind, Hayes insists that one of the team physicians be at every practice session. And a team dentist, too. There is a dental chair installed in the training quarters, "and if something important has to be done to a boy's mouth," says Woody, "we want it done immediately, not fifteen minutes from now."

Most head coaches at big-time schools spend much of their time high on a tower overlooking all work, or wandering around the field checking quietly with their offensive and defensive coordinators. Their general presence on the practice field is less than pervasive.

Woody Hayes is not only in the center of things, he *is* the center of things. "With Woody, there's no question of who is in supreme command," says a former assistant. "Especially on offense. Your direction and coaching technique is under the gun every second. It's hairy at first, but you learn to live with it."

The smooth, orderly procedures of the practice field are sometimes interrupted by Woody's megatons and sometimes a hundred-megaton. A busted play, a missed assignment may be tolerated if practice is going well, but let it happen during a poor practice and Woody erupts, changing the course of things by the sheer drama of his presence.

Veteran sideline observers insist that a half-dozen times or more, Woody has ripped off his wrist watch, flung it to the ground and stomped it viciously over and over until the watch is a shambles. Players stare silently at the display, almost as though they aren't even witnessing it, yet the oaths and anguished screams Woody issues are direct testimony that some cardinal sin has been committed. (The word is that Woody never spends more than ten bucks for a watch . . . )

Only once in anyone's memory did the players' reaction differ. Leon Lindsey, a quietly humorous second-string halfback was witnessing the act for his second time. "Well, there's Woody killing time again," he murmured, and a dozen teammates cracked up convulsively. Luckily Woody was ripping up some charts at the moment and was too enraged to see or hear them. "It could have been the most disastrous moment in Ohio State football history," an assistant coach later reported.

If Woody has destroyed a half-dozen wrist watches he was well on his way to exceeding that number of black baseball caps. A guard pulling wrong or blocking down improperly on a linebacker would bring forth a sulfurous bellow. Followed immediately by Woody snatching off his baseball cap and tearing it asunder in his hands, pulling it apart at every seam with three or four frighteningly quick movements of his hands.

The first time former assistant coach Larry Catuzzi saw that, he had a student manager rescue the remnants for him. "That was one souvenir I was determined to have," said Catuzzi.

One season after he'd destroyed a dozen or so caps by early November, someone goofed, Woody screamed, tore the cap from his head and started to flail away at it. Nothing happened. Again, savagely he ripped and tugged with all his immense strength. Nothing. In a flash he stopped in the middle of his effort, jammed the cap back onto his head and continued with practice as though nothing had happened to excite him.

The consummate strategist and psychologist, he realized instantly what had happened. Phil Bennett, one of the equipment men, had overstitched every seam in the cap with extratough nylon thread normally used to repair heavy leather equipment.

To this day, Woody has never again rent his baseball cap asunder, and nothing has been said about it.

There is one other display of Woody Hayes' temper that has boggled the minds of witnesses. On one occasion he ripped off his glasses, and holding them aloft in scarlet anger, crushed them in his bare hand until the blood flowed from cuts made by the shattered glass shards.

But for the neophyte sideline observer, nothing among Woody Hayes' display of rages comes with such stunning surprise as when Woody lays one on a player. The neophyte will glance at a veteran writer alongside him in disbelief. The veteran has seen it all before and merely chuckles softly, perhaps remarking that Woody's swing is getting rusty.

Like hell it is. The player who fumbles twice in two minutes or goofs up repeatedly on a blocking assignment knows it when Woody pops him a whack in the belly, a hard chop to the short ribs, or a crack on the helmet that rings his bell.

Taking a good belt at one of his players, however, is never a punitive or vindictive thing with Woody. A couple of psychologists, asked to comment, both pleaded a measure of qualification in the distance between themselves and

the subject but offered an observation shot from the hip.
"There's no way the man can mean harm to the boy or
exhibit a hate tendency when he slams him," said one. "He
is obviously too close to the kids for that. But he seems to
be the kind of man who quickly and deeply feels frustration,
and he's such a physical person that this is his release."

The other agreed, generally, and added another note: "I
have a hunch there's such a sense of urgency in the man
that he unconsciously uses the device for dramatic or shock
value—the quickest way to make a point." Then he paused.
"And I'll add this: his desire to win must be infectious, so
overriding that there's an osmosis process at work where
that desire is so keenly felt by his kids that very few, if any,
would seriously resent being socked in that kind of situation."

Well, maybe. And even probably. Woody, himself, adds
still another clue to this behavior. "Let me put it this way.
I've never seen a football player who isn't a better football
player than he thinks he is. And as a coach it's my job to
make a kid realize his potential. One of my basic rules in
dealing with football players is that if I am to expect great
things from them, that's exactly what I'll get. If I talk down
to them or underinspire them and imply that they're not
much of a football player, then that's exactly what I'll get,
too.

"That's one thing that worries me about our life-style
and civilization today. We're too often talking bad about
ourselves. This, as far as I'm concerned, hurts us more than
everything else put together. I know we can't have a winning football team operating that way. Any coach who hints
to his ball club that they're a negative force rather than a
positive force is going to get beat on Saturday—and a lot
of Saturdays.

"I build my kids up—even though I do get a little rough on them out there on the practice field when they're not performing as well as I think they're capable of. And when I explode I'm telling this: 'The only reason I'm mad is because I know you can do better. You can do more.' So the implication is always positive, no matter how I deliver it. No, we don't talk down to a football player. Or let him get away with a mistake without forcefully accenting that mistake."

For accent read a forearm shiver to the chest. Or a six-inch jolt to the midsection. Philosophy at work.

After the brief explosion, it's back to business. Visitors to a Buckeye practice are amazed by Woody and impressed by the careful scheduling, but what they can't get over is the repetition.

A visiting sportswriter watching a Buckeye practice session from the sidelines shook his head. Woody Hayes had just run the same play for seemingly the sixth straight time and still wasn't satisfied with it. "He *does* have another play, doesn't he?" the visitor asked a local writer.

"Sure," was the response, "and when he's satisfied with this one he'll try another."

It would seem that satisfaction isn't enough for Woody. If he carries his preparation to numbing lengths, a clue to his philosophy may be found in things he likes to quote. Pianist Ignace Paderewski, for instance, who said, "If I do not practice one day, I know it. If I do not practice the next, the orchestra knows it. If I do not practice the third day, the whole world knows it."

So Woody simply does it again and again. Perfectionism is part of the reason, but there is also a more personal factor involved.

"All players simply don't learn at the same rate of

speed," he says, "or with the same degree of mastery. If we see a player making a mistake we just don't get him out of there and run the play with somebody else just because the first kid doesn't learn very fast. That would be an indictment of our coaches. We just think we've got to spend extra time on the player."

One of the more interesting factors in an Ohio State practice is the scout team, composed of eager freshmen and sophomores who have good potential but who aren't yet ready for first- or second-string varsity play. They have a special function and they take a lot of pride in it. Upperclassmen with fading varsity hopes make poor scout-team members and are rarely used as such.

Each week they impersonate Saturday's foe, running the enemy plays extracted from the film the opposition has sent. Not only are they meticulously coached in enemy mannerisms for their performance but each week they get a whole new set of jerseys in the same color as Minnesota or Illinois or whoever is coming up on Saturday. They even wear the numbers of the men they're impersonating so the Buckeye varsity can hone in on every possible aid in reacting to the real thing.

At the end of the week the scout team gets to keep the ersatz enemy jerseys and at the end of the year they have quite a collection.

"These kids perform a vital and much appreciated function," says Woody. "Not only is it a learning process for them but we simply couldn't prepare the varsity without them, and everyone knows it, including the starters—some of whom once were scout team players themselves."

In another bit of organizational brilliance, the first two defensive units are called "Bucks" and "Bombers." The scout team first runs a certain sequence of enemy plays against the second-unit Bombers while the first-unit Bucks observe closely. Then the Bucks will defense the same sequence and it's the Bombers' turn to watch. The why and how of defensive adjustments stem as much from observation as from execution.

But what happens on the practice field is not the only important part of the Buckeye workweek. So vital is the quarterback position that Woody insists quarterback coach George Chaump meet four times a week with all four quarterbacks, aside from practice sessions. Chaump, of course, like all assistant coaches, has the kids' classroom schedules in his book. He knows when they're available and Monday through Friday they come to his office for about forty-five minutes, where Chaump reviews every facet of the position.

"First of all," Chaump reveals, "Woody is so thorough that we film not only every game but our three heavy practice sessions on Tuesday, Wednesday and Thursday. Two crews—one for offense, one for defense, and to hell with the expense. Each morning, all the coaches study the previous day's work. Remember, we prepare for a different team each week, which means different things are planned, offensively and defensively. The practice film tells us whether the kids are fully mastering the ever-changing assignments. If they're not, it doesn't mean we have to make changes in the personnel, it just means we should be making changes in execution to accommodate the player.

"With my quarterbacks, I study the film to see what mistakes they made and decide what they must do to correct them—every instant of ball-handling, execution, mechanics, timing."

The average fan will wonder what the devil is so important about meeting every day with the quarterbacks when Woody doesn't let them call the plays. But calling signals has nothing to do with the quarterback's overall function; he is still the most important man in the attack. He is the one man on the team who must know to perfection the proper spot for the other ten when they come out of the huddle and go into a formation and set position.

The linemen rarely make a mistake on this, but there is an occasional lapse on the part of a back because of the immense variety of sets they can take. The quarterback has to check everything before he begins his count. He is the one man who must know where every other back is going to be during every instant a play is unfolding. And although every back has to know the timing of every play, it is the quarterback who has to bail everyone out on a busted play and try to make some yardage out of a bad situation.

"The mental instincts of your quarterback," says Chaump, "must be constantly sharp and in focus on every element of the play. Much of this comes from the nature of the boy, his innate ability to play the position, but most of it comes from constant repetition and drill in every element of the play. There just isn't time enough to do this on the practice field, so we keep reviewing it every day during our meetings."

This has more than just routine significance under Woody Hayes. Former assistant Larry Catuzzi says, "It's hard to realize how much pressure Ohio State quarterbacks operate under. Every day out there on the practice field, there's Ol' Woody taking charge of the offense like no other head coach in the business. Woody has his nose in every huddle. Then he steps back a few feet, crosses his arms over his chest, takes that domineering stance of his, and I swear he's looking for the mistake more than he's looking for the proper execution.

"Ohio State quarterbacks seem to feel this in their bones. It's a form of pressure that not all kids can take. They know that nobody reacts so violently to mistakes as Woody does and they dread that instant when something will lead to a goof-up in a play.

"It takes a remarkable athlete and a well-poised one to stand up to the pressure Woody puts on his quarterbacks," the former coach continues. "Specifically, it takes a Rex Kern. Kern not only had the great physical and mechanical gifts but he had unusual self-reliance and competitive fire. But how many Rex Kerns are there? Damn few."

Incidentally, Kern confused a lot of Woody Hayes' football critics. For years sportswriters had laughed that Woody's teams almost *never* threw a pass. An out-of-town sportswriter once reached into his fund of erudition to describe Woody's passing attack. "I am reminded," he said, "of Dr. Samuel Johnson comparing a woman preacher to a dog walking on its hind legs: 'Sir, it is not done well, but you are surprised to find it done at all.' "

But in 1968, 1969 and 1970, when the slick Rex Kern was at the throttle of the Buckeye offense, the Bucks had one of the finest passing games in the Big Ten, if not the nation, because Kern was not only a sharp, pinpoint passer but also a superb runner on the option. With Kern at quarterback the Buckeyes usually threw between sixteen and twenty times a game, and Woody acquired a new reputation for flexibility.

But most of the perennial strengths of the Buckeye football teams come from Woody's unwavering and inflexible stress on fundamentals. These include not only blocking and tackling but one special area of concern—the kicking game.

Here, now, is a statistic to conjure with. In roughly 225 games during Woody Hayes' twenty-three years at Ohio State, the Buckeyes have punted or kicked off a total of approximately 2,700 times—which means 2,700 times the opposition had a chance to grab the ball and break a long one for a score.

But get this—the other team has scored only six times out of the 2,700. The NCAA doesn't keep records for this particular category, but the Buckeye stat will stand for a record until somebody else comes up with a better one.

The reason is that the last fifteen or twenty minutes of most Ohio State practices are a concentrated drill on the Bucks' kicking game. It's a period when Woody is building an edge over opponents, few of whom spend so much time and planning on this aspect of the game.

"Nothing can turn a game around for you—winning or losing—faster than a blocked kick or one that is returned for a score," says Woody. "It can give you impetus or let you down, depending on which way it goes. A lot of games are won and lost on the kicking game. If we lose a ball game we want to make the other guys win it on their superiority, not on poor planning or a foolish lapse of our own." Only twice in his twenty-three years at Ohio State has Woody lost a game on this kind of lapse on a punt or kickoff.

It is a multifaceted preparation involving punting, field goals and point after touchdown, both Ohio's and the opposition's. Some phase of the kicking game is worked on every day. It all starts with the scouting report extracted from opposition film. The drill for the week is based essentially on tendencies shown by the opposition in their game every day. It all starts with the scouting report extracted from opposition film. The drill for the week is based essentially on tendencies shown by the opposition in their game films. The assistant coach who has made a study in depth of that particular team must translate those tendencies for the Buckeyes to work on. Is it a team that likes to give its punter longer blocking at the line of scrimmage so that he has lots of time to get his punt away? Okay, this means the enemy will be sacrificing yards to the Buckeye punt-return man, and Ohio can peel back its interference accordingly. In 1973 defensive back Neal Colzie racked up 615 yards on thirty-eight punt returns to lead the nation.

When Ohio State is punting, the Bucks like to know where the rush is coming from. This has already been extracted from the films, and Woody sets up his blocking accordingly. Then the men covering the punt must know exactly where the ball is headed. They have no time to look for the ball, so the punter, immediately after his foot explodes against the ball, screams, "Right!" Or "Left!" Or "Middle!" It is the only clue the Buckeye coverage needs.

Meanwhile, the punter, a specialist, has also been meshed with still another specialist, the man who snaps the ball—not always the team's regular center, but a guy who can spiral the ball back fifteen yards in a swift line. Between snap and kick, not more than 2.2 seconds should elapse. Woody likes his punter to hang the ball in the air another 4 seconds, making a minimum of 6 seconds between snap and the safetyman getting the ball.

"Players often tend to deemphasize the need for time spent on your kicking game," says Woody. "They haven't yet realized the true meaning of its tactics, which are both offensive and defensive in nature. They haven't had too

Not at Ohio State. For those who like stats like this, six scoring returns out of 2,700 works out to 22/100 of 1 percent.

On Thursday Woody Hayes begins his countdown toward engagement with the enemy. Before the troops take the practice field for the last heavy work of the week, he gathers them in the conference room at Biggs and sets the tone for Saturday. He rarely lets his emotions get too high.

Typically, he has said, "You will win on Saturday. You will have to do what we have planned to do all week, but essentially you will win because you are Ohio State and they will respect you for that."

And then Woody will get a little warmer. "They know what we do and they respect you, and I'll tell you something else: That respect soon turns to fear, and by the time we've hit them three or four times in that first quarter they know they can't win."

Woody has never shouted or stormed in this Thursday priming session. It is merely a time for the commander in chief to instill that first measure of confidence.

"Woody Hayes is a master at this," says an assistant coach. "It's such a psychic thing it's almost physical. I've been working my tail off all week and I feel the way he does, but when he expresses it, it gets right to me and I know he's right. Maybe that's why whenever Ohio State loses a football game it's a bona-fide upset and that's the way the headlines treat it. But going in, dammit, we figure to win."

Frequently Woody will use a military parallel to make a point, perhaps recounting Lord Nelson's tactics against the French fleet in the Battle of the Nile. He can tell a battle story so masterfully and with such imagery that he can tie it in neatly to his own battle plans for that Saturday.

Sometimes he may sense an opportune moment for an

emotional approach, and he is a master of timing in seizing on it.

A couple of years ago when they were slight underdogs to Michigan in a battle for the Rose Bowl nod, he saw Rick Seifert standing on the fringe of the squad. Seifert had been an All–Big-Ten safetyman the previous season and was touted for All-America in '72. But he tore up his knee and was lost for the season after the fourth game. Now in a cast from hip to toe, he stood on crutches as Woody spoke. Suddenly Woody turned to him. "Rick, is there anything you'd like to say?" Woody, the supreme psychologist, knew damn well that Rick Seifert would indeed want to say something.

Seifert, a handsome blond six-footer, leaned forward on his crutches and stared out at his teammates in the chairs in front of him.

"Let me tell you guys something," he began. "This is Michigan coming up. Well, when I was in high school in Cuyahoga Falls I was a straight A student. I could have gone to college anywhere in this country. Harvard, Yale and Princeton wanted me. My mother wanted me to go Ivy in the worst way."

Rick Seifert's eyes were flashing now and his knuckles were white where he was clenching the handles of his crutches. "But for as long as I could remember," he continued, "I wanted to come to Ohio State and play on a team that would beat Michigan. We lost to them last year, and I was looking forward for revenge this season."

He slapped his cast. "And now I can't play on a team that beats Michigan, goddammit, so you're going to have to do it for me, you understand? You're going to beat those bastards for me!"

Chuck Clausen remembers the moment. "Geez, here I

was a big, tough coach and I'm not supposed to let things like that get to me, but suddenly I had this grapefruit in my throat and I looked at one of the other coaches and damn if he hasn't turned his face away because the tears were in his eyes. Then I looked at Woody and there's the Old Man just standing there with his arms folded, his face pretty much expressionless but you damn well knew he'd pulled off one of his beauts again, just as he'd started off the week with his opening squad meeting on Monday."

At the Monday team meeting, everyone had been seated when Woody said, "John Hicks, stand up."

All-America tackle John Hicks stood up uneasily. "John Hicks," said Woody, "I want you to tell this team what you, personally, are going to do to get ready for Michigan this week."

John Hicks looked at Woody, then glared around him at the team. "I'm gonna get ready like I never got ready before in my life. I'm gonna pop everybody in practice as though he's a Michigan man, and I want him to pop me back the same way . . . I'm thinking about nothing but playing Michigan and beating Michigan every minute we work . . . I'll be telling myself that this is the most important ball game I've ever played in and I'll be putting out every ounce I've got all week long to prove it."

That Saturday Ohio State upset Michigan by stopping the Wolverines for four downs within the 3-yard line—not once but *twice*.

# 10
# Putting It
# All Together

Now comes the epitome of the Hayes' philosophy; the crunching, frontal assault of muscle against muscle, bone upon bone, will against will. Hit the bastards with everything you have. Pound the sonsabitches into the ground and grind meat, grind meat, goddammit! We're better than they are, goddammit! This is where they get to know it, goddammit! This is where they get the fear in their eyes, and this is where Ohio State teams score.

\* \* \*

Suddenly, the workweek is over. All the planning, the give-and-take between coaches, and the fine-tuning adjustments come to an end. All those miles of film have been spun through the projectors. By noon Friday names have gone up on the bulletin board at Biggs. About 65 kids have been picked for the overnight squad to be spirited away to a local motel where they will be held virtually incommunicado. No phone calls in; no calls out. No visitors. No newspapermen. No distractions.

The rest of the squad, although they will dress for the game, will spend the night in their usual dorm rooms.

Following a light workout Friday afternoon the kids pile into two buses for the drive to their motel, along with all the coaches. Everyone is wearing jackets and ties.

They have a bit of time to watch TV before dinner. Some study. Dinner is at 6:00, and right after dinner comes one of Woody Hayes' psychological fixations. At 7:00 the entire team goes to a movie. It has to be pure escapist. A comedy, a musical, a mild Western. Nothing with violence, sex, or a heavy message. Woody wants pure relaxation with no lingering effects on the kids' psyche, which might compete with their last-minute thoughts about the ball game the next day.

After returning from the movie, individual coaches have small group meetings with quarterbacks, linebackers, defensive tackles, or whatever an individual coach desires. Brief, last-minute checks are made against opposition film. By 10:15 all pregame activity is finished. The kids go to their rooms where they are served hot chocolate, cookies and an apple. They can watch TV for another half hour but by 11:00 lights must be out for a bed check by Woody and his assistants.

At virtually every other school, the assistant coaches are now free for an hour or two for a gabfest of their own, more often than not at the bar where they can have a couple of drinks before retiring. Woody Hayes does not allow his coaches to go down to the bar after the kids are put to bed. (Woody doesn't drink or smoke himself, but that is not the reason. He doesn't like the image of his coaches at a bar.)

The assistant coaches go to bed, too. Woody may stay up for another hour, reading a book on history or an historical novel. It is possibly the only hour of the week when his mind is not full of X's and O's.

Breakfast of orange juice, tea and toast is at 8:00 A.M. A few boys have already been up for morning services at nearby churches, and then at about 9:20 everybody meets in the lobby where Woody is waiting. He leads them on a morning walk for about fifteen minutes around the motel grounds. It is nothing strenous nor even seemingly important. Woody just happens to think it's a "togetherness" gambit that allows the kids to loosen up in a freer way.

At 9:40 they sit down to their pregame training meal of steak, baked potato, one vegetable, dry toast and more tea. Then they pile into two buses for a police-escorted trip to the stadium.

In the stadium dressing rooms the kids put away their street clothes, get into their game underwear and athletic supporters, and line up for taping. Eight to ten trainers and assistants tape ankles. For major taping jobs—shoulders, ribs, knees or whatever—where injuries have played a part, two team doctors stand by to supervise the job. The doctors also check special braces that are being used and then examine injury cases to make last-minute decisions as to whether a boy can play. If they rule a boy out, they immediately report it to Woody.

During the taping, a couple of assistant coaches will be out on the field looking for spongy spots if there has been rain, and will notate them for field position during a game. They'll also check the wind.

Taped, the players are now getting into their uniforms. Woody now sits alone in the coaches' room, going over some notes, thinking some special, inner thoughts.

If a boy is starting a game for the first time Woody may take a moment to go over to him casually and put him at ease. He gives no indication that there's any pressure on the kid, that he's expecting anything more than the boy can deliver.

The entire mood is one of quiet but purposeful intensity. Woody wanders through it periodically, highly visible, a combination of the father image and the general seeing to it that his troops are physically and mentally ready for battle. "He infuses a collective calmness," says an assistant, "and the kids take confidence from him. Woody, laying a hand on a kid's shoulder here, patting a butt there, is a psychic influence that simply can't be misread. It's like he's saying, 'Okay, we're ready, we're ready, everything's okay.'"

About this time, a couple of the officials will come in to synchronize their watches with Woody's and the other coaches. The officials will tell Woody exactly when they want his team on the field for the kickoff, and there can't be any excuses for being late.

Then the officials will start checking special braces and pads which players may be wearing to protect injuries. They want to make sure a brace or pad cannot be used as a weapon.

Now, Woody splits his team for final review sessions. Defense, headed by coordinator George Hill, stays on the second floor of the training tower; Woody takes the offense to the third floor. The review will last only ten minutes or so.

Everyone is now in full uniform, including full pads. At 12:20 Woody sends the entire squad out for a thirty-minute pregame warm-up. Most teams hold their pregame drills without shoulder pads. Woody wants his kids to wear full armor, no matter how warm the day. He thinks there should be a full adjustment time to the heavy pads. He doesn't want the kids putting them on two minutes before the game starts.

There's a period of calisthenics, followed by individual skill drills. Woody wanders around to every group. Coaches are clocking the passers and kickers with stopwatches. Passers must set up in 1.6 seconds, release in no more than 3 seconds. Woody prefers 2.5.

He stands with folded arms, narrowly observing all receivers as they run their pass routes: the curls, the square-outs, the post. Once in a while he'll check his own stopwatch on a procedure.

From 1:00 to 1:05 the linemen do some solid bumping again, harder than other teams will do. Then Woody will give a signal and the team goes off to the locker room again. A half-dozen student managers will towel off the mildly perspiring players. Trainers will do some tightening of tape, where players spot looseness.

At 1:10 Woody takes everybody into the main squad room in the tower for a final word. He is low-key, never overemotional as he tells the kids what the game means. Depending on the game he is able to sense how much last-minute psyching and priming the kids need. He is a master at taking a squad pulse and determining how much adrenaline needs to flow.

At 1:20 Woody and his assistant coaches leave the room. Now the team captains take over in privacy for a few words of common-cause inspiration.

The team captains, according to the coaches, often can sense soft spots in attitude that even the coaches don't know exist. Team captains at Ohio State are authoritative and full of leadership or they don't get elected. In this very private, very personal and edgy five minutes a lot of things get said that might not get said in front of coaches.

At 1:25 two game officials knock on the door and tell the captains to come out for the coin tossing. Two minutes later the team forms up at the doors leading to the field. Woody and three assistant coaches join them and at exactly 1:27 they race onto the synthetic turf and across the field to the Ohio sideline. Woody starts out at their head but they soon pass him. By the time he catches up with them at the Ohio sideline they have surged together into a huge, pounding, pummeling wave of scarlet and gray. They bounce up and down, slamming each other. Latecomers— by a second or two—leap up over the fringe to get closer to the core of this sea of insanity. It seems only by a miracle that somebody doesn't get half-killed before Woody Hayes breaks them up. It is the closest thing possible to a public display of holy-war fervor and madness.

Almost in perfect synch, the captains race back to the sidelines from the coin-tossing ceremonies and in an instant the starting elevens—offense and defense—are now gathered around Woody in a final huddle on the field. There is complete silence as Woody Hayes leans forward (sometimes kneels) and offers up a soft-spoken but brief prayer. He never asks for victory. He prays only that no one will get hurt and that each boy will play to the best of his ability. The phrasing may change slightly from Saturday to Saturday, but the essence remains the same.

The huddle breaks, the starting eleven races onto the field, and Woody Hayes slowly retreats . . . no, Woody Hayes does not retreat—returns to the sidelines. An Ohio State football team, under his direction, is about to commit itself to what everyone confidently expects to be a victory. In preparing to knock heads, Woody's kids already know certain predetermined goals he has laid out. Defensively it reads like this, posted on the wall of the training quarters:

- Give up seven points or less.
- Score or set up two scores inside their 40-yard line.
- Get four turnovers on any combination of fumbles recovered and/or interceptions.
- No touchdown passes against us.
- Hold them to less than 250 yards total offense.
- No enemy play—run or pass—more than 20 yards.
- Do not give up more than three consecutive first downs.
- Destroy 25 percent of their passes.
- Hold foe to 40 percent of passes per game.
- No penalties for us.
- We field all punts properly.
- We average 10 yards on punt returns.
- We keep all kickoff returns inside their 30-yard line.

Any kickoff return held inside their 20-yard line brings a Buckeye leaf for everybody on kickoff team.

A look at this list of objectives reveals none which seems unattainable. Putting it all together is another story. Putting it all together—or virtually all of it—just about insures victory, however.

For Woody the list is a battle map, and it's a rare afternoon when a review of the game stats shows more than just a puny few of the objectives unreached. And the kids, say the coaches, get a savage thrill out of accomplishing these things.

Individual recognition, in addition to the Buckeye leaf for the helmet, is also visible each Monday on the huge bulletin boards, with pictures of two kids for Player of the Week and Buck of the Week. It is more Woody Hayes' psychology. The pictures are never seen by fans or strangers. They are seen only by Family: the squad, coaches, trainers and reporters who are on hand daily. Recognition within this close-knit group counts more than anything.

Time was when the sideline at a college football game was a reasonably well-ordered piece of real estate, successfully zoned against confusion, noise pollution and invasion of privacy. Your team was on the field and you had a couple of very long benches where forty or fifty substitutes sat in hunched attentiveness. The head coach and a couple of his assistants—a bit more tense, perhaps, but not much more so—sat there with them. Maybe a couple of student managers hovered nearby to handle routine clerical or housekeeping chores. There would be a modest flurry of activity when a player went into or came out of the game and was slapped on the butt or shoulder. The total effect was one of organized and civilized bustle.

Today you can almost forget the benches, which are there but seldom used; and now there are ninety or a hundred substitutes on the sidelines, and with offensive and defensive platoons the attendant activity on the change of roles resembles, at least faintly, the camera-action call for the cavalry-Indian melee of your average Western.

Virtually everyone is on his feet. This includes the head coach and a flock of his assistants; at least five student managers, a covey of graduate assistant coaches and a platoon of trainers. There'll be more trailing telephone lines than you'll see in the war room of the Pentagon; a mile or two of black spaghetti cable for TV cameras; enough TV cameramen to photograph *Gone with the Wind;* mobile TV vehicles which are a bigger menace than anything on the Santa Monica Freeway; a dozen or so cheerleaders in constant training for a career with the Flying Frabinis; and enough cops and state troopers to quell your average prison riot. And everybody thinks he has Priority. The total effect is organized chaos.

At Ohio State, add to this an important extra ingredient —Wayne Woodrow Hayes—and you've got your show of shows, and everybody better get the hell out of his way because this is HIS PRODUCTION.

A lot of fans—and some newspaper critics—complain that Woody has taken the game from his kids by calling all the plays himself from the sidelines. In the first place, Woody doesn't call all the plays. (We'll see in a moment where they come from.) And the fact that the quarterback doesn't call them on the field is not only defensible but highly desirable, according to Woody.

"Football is so complicated today," says Woody, "that the quarterback has to have a maximum of mental freedom and looseness just to see that the formations are right when the team comes out of the huddle, and to handle the split-second ball-handling and faking that goes on. We relieve him of the extra pressure of play-calling for a lot of reasons."

"To begin with, if we as coaches don't know precisely what play is coming we can't focus properly on the timing and blocking assignments to see exactly what went wrong if the play breaks down. We can make immediate adjustments. Knowing exactly what variation is coming off of a particular formation is a valuable bit of business."

So at Ohio State, the plays are called from high up in the pressbox by offensive line coach Ralph Staub, one of four assistants on duty up there. The other three are Rudy Hubbard, offensive running backs; Dick Walker, defensive backfield; and Chuck Clausen, defensive tackles.

Staub, with large visual game-plan cards in front of him, calls the plays based on down-and-distance and what the Buckeyes figure to do best against the foe's particular defenses on a particular spot on the field.

Staub phones his choice of play down to quarterback coach, George Chaump, who takes a constant position alongside Woody and tells him what play has been sent down. Nine times out of ten, Woody will agree and either sends in the play with a messenger or Chaump will do it by a system of hand signals.

Often enough Ohio State will even break off a good one on first down and come up with second and one. One hundred out of one hundred coaches will agree that this is an obviously swell passing down. If you ask the 101st and it turns out to be Woody Hayes, he'll tell you, "It's an even better running down."

On the occasion when Woody vetoes Staub's play and changes it, Staub simply does what the moment naturally calls for. He blows his stack with the kind of blue-streak cursing that Woody himself would be proud of—except that much of the blistering is directed at the Old Man himself. Depending on the score at the moment Hubbard, Walker and Clausen will either crack up hilariously at Staub or stare grimly down at the field.

Looking for every edge, Woody has also installed an aid which might be unique in college coaching. Directly in front of the four assistants in the pressbox is a photographer with a Polaroid camera. He focuses the instant the Buckeyes come out of their huddle and into their set. But he doesn't take his shot until an instant after the Ohio center snaps the ball, which gives the enemy defense just enough time to take their first step or two to counter the play.

This is the information the coaches upstairs want. What kind of commitment is the defense making? Within ten seconds Staub and the others are poring over the finished print with a ninety-five-cent magnifying glass.

In another five seconds they have what they need to know for future plays. Often it will be Staub's most important clue in his play-calling.

All four coaches upstairs have critical duties. Walker must make instant changes in his defensive backfield alignments. Based on his pregame analysis of the enemy's running and passing games, he must decide what they are liable to do in given circumstances. Clausen must alter his defensive tackle play based on similar background.

The defensive signals are hand-signaled from the sideline by defensive coordinator George Hill. The middle linebacker takes the sign for alignments up front, and the safetyman takes the signal to deploy the secondary. The safetyman may also check off with an audible if the foe shifts out of its original formation and he wants to change things.

The men in the pressbox must also convey information on personnel changes to Hill and Bugel down on the sidelines. Because contrary to what the average fan may think, Woody Hayes does not make the substitutions. It is Walker who decides what defensive-backfield changes must be made; Clausen, the defensive tackles. Rudy Hubbard will spot situations for a change in running backs, and any of the four upstairs can alert Hill, Bugel and Sarkkinen to changes that might be needed for linebackers, defensive ends or offensive linemen.

"We can see so much better from up there," Walker

points out. "Besides, who knows the personnel better than the individual coaches, who are, of course, specialists? If Woody suddenly started to veto our substitutions we'd all feel he'd lost confidence in us. We just wouldn't be able to operate on that basis."

In 1972 Rudy Hubbard, a former backfield coach, was having a tough time convincing Woody about a freshman halfback he thought should be getting more action. Woody wasn't buying it. Hubbard was able to get him into the season opener for a couple of plays but that was all. "Frankly, I didn't like it," Hubbard recalls. "I thought the kid should be playing more. Even starting. The second game came. It was against North Carolina. Woody insisted on starting another tailback. Finally, midway into the first quarter I'd hammered away at Woody so much he finally let me get the kid into the game."

So Archie Griffin got into the game, rushed 239 yards for a new Ohio State record, and a new superstar was born.

Thus it goes, routinely, until a certain critical point is reached in the Buckeyes' field position. The spot is anywhere inside the 10- or 12-yard line. At that point Woody Hayes seems to suck up his gut a few degrees. The thrust of jawline seems to uptilt noticeably. The legs seem to take a firmer hold on the ground; the stance may even widen a few inches.

General Patton has arrived at the critical point of attack in this 100-yard war. There is only one way to go and all the decisions must be his.

Woody Hayes now takes over the Buckeyes' goal-line offense. From here on in, Ralph Staub and the other assistants upstairs agonize and hold their breaths along with every other Ohio State fan in the stadium—and are almost as helpless to do anything about it.

Woody Hayes calls all the plays from here on until the Bucks score. Now comes the epitome of the Hayes' philosophy, the crunching, frontal assault of muscle against muscle, bone upon bone, will against will. Hit the bastards with everything you have, pound the sonsabitches into the ground, grind meat, grind meat, goddammit! We're better than they are, goddammit! This is where they get to know it, goddammit! They've got the fear in their eyes, goddammit! They no longer just *respect* us, goddammit! This is where they fear us and this is where Ohio State teams score, this is where we win our ball games—GODDAMMIT! So pound 'em, pound 'em, let's pound the shit outta them! *Here! Now!*

From inside the 10-yard line, Ohio State football teams score more often than any other team in college football . . .

Nothing too fancy happens here. Woody goes into what he calls his Robust, or his full-house T. It's fullback straight ahead or fullback right or left. Or the tailback the same way (God forbid a pass or even a pitch-out). Occasionally, the quarterback keeper, sliding along the line until a crack appears. The crack is going to appear. When you constantly come up with linemen such as Jim Parker, Bob Vogel, Dave Foley, Rufus Mayes and John Hicks, you're going to get more than a crack, and all that "fitting and hitting" every week is going to pay off. It may take two, three or even four blasts to do it, but few people can remember the last time General Woody has shouted "Forward!" and the attack has failed.

"Let me make one amendment," says Staub. "It's true that Woody takes over on our goal-line offense, but stubborn though he is, he isn't blindly stubborn. He knows that upstairs we can spot the opposition going into a defensive setup especially designed to stop certain sets we use.

"They know what we do best and how we do it, and they've been working all week to stop it. That doesn't mean they will stop us. But upstairs, when we see them start doing things that theoretically will shut us off, we let Woody know immediately and suggest a variation or an alternative to what he has called.

"Often—thank God!—he'll go along with us and switch the play to something we suggest. If he didn't, I think we'd lose our minds up there, or explode. But there's something about Woody taking over completely on the 10-yard line that never fails to remind us how completely he can dominate a situation, how completely he becomes the ultimate military tactician.

"I can just imagine how the opposing coach feels once Ohio State gets down to their 10- or 12-yard line and he knows ol' Woody has him directly in his sights. It has to be a feeling that doesn't come over him on any other Saturday of the season."

Things don't always go as Woody plans, of course. Once, in the early 1960s, Woody was so disgusted with his team's execution of plays that when the first half ended he took them into the dressing room for just two minutes—just long enough to rip them for their shoddy performance. Then he told everybody to follow him. He bustled out the door, his players and coaches following curiously. Then to their utter amazement he led them through the stadium gates and onto the practice field adjacent to the stadium.

"You didn't get it done during the week," he bellowed, "so you're going to have to make up for it now!"

"Making up for it" translated into a ten-minute scrimmage at half time.

Matt Snell, the former All-Pro fullback for the New York

Jets, recalled that moment: "For just an instant we looked at each other in amazement, but we were used to the man and nothing he ever said or did surprised us any more. So we just went out and hit. Then Woody led us back into the stadium for the second half and we got him two or three touchdowns and won the game."

Assistant coach John Mummey, the only one now on the staff who played under Woody, recalls hilariously the time Woody was in a towering black rage because some obvious underdog was leading the Bucks 6–0 at the half.

"He did his thing at the blackboard for a few minutes," says Mummey, "then halted in the middle of some X's and O's and let out a string of curses as though he felt he wasn't getting across to us. 'Goddammit!' he yelled, and suddenly he lets fly with one of his famous left hooks at the black-board, bare-knuckled. His fist smashed right through it. 'All right, let's get out there again!' he roars and out we went and creamed them."

Then Mummey snickered. "I also remember that Mike Ingram, our tough linebacker, looked at the hole in the blackboard just before he went out and said, 'Hell, I'm less than half his age. If he can do it *I* can do it.'

"So Ingram lets fly a punch at the board and barely cracks it. He howls with pain and rage, curses Woody and goes out to make a million tackles in the second half. I think after the game they had to put a cast on Mike's hand and Woody thought he got it honorably in the ball game."

Apparently there's something about Woody Hayes' adrenaline which works in strange ways on the sidelines. Either that or the man is so constituted that his emotions trigger the physical just as they do on the practice field. At least he's consistent.

Once a graduate assistant coach approached Woody—or

maybe just got in his way, nobody really knew—just when something went horrendously wrong on the field. It is doubtful if a dozen people among the 87,000 in the stands saw what happened, because it happened so fast. But Woody's release for that moment of frustration was to cold-cock the young man with a solid right hand. The grad assistant went down as though poleaxed. Woody never gave him a passing glance.

At Iowa one time a Hawkeye had the grave misfortune and the ill-grace to knock an Ohio State player out of bounds and then zing it to him in the neck or kidneys or some indelicate spot. Woody came storming up and in the knot of angry Ohio State players he not only popped the Hawkeye a good one but would have continued with an encore if an Ohio State assistant coach had not leaped on his back to wrestle him into a semblance of submissiveness.

This was one witnessed by a goodly number, however, including Ohio State athletic director Dick Larkins.

On Monday Larkins walked in on Woody's office and told him quite pointedly that there'd been too many occasions on which he'd had to save Woody's scalp and that this time there might be repercussions which would be too tough to handle. The press, as usual, had noted Woody's latest pec-cadillo.

Woody, supreme in his self-confidence, surfeited with the righteousness of his act, immediately went on the attack as befits any disciple of George Patton, and abruptly inter-rupted Larkins. He reminded him in no simple terms of what he'd done for the Ohio State football program in his then seventeen years. The Athletic Board and/or adminis-tration could do what they damn pleased about relieving him, but right now he had a football game to prepare for, so just let him know later what the outcome was. And that, as they say, was that.

Not too many years ago Woody's arabesques on the sidelines included a gambit that would infuriate many officials. A runner stepping out of bounds on the Ohio sidelines, a fumble bouncing astray out of bounds, or a pass receiver bumped out of bounds would find Woody chugging to the spot and marking it with his foot or cap, as if challenging the official to disagree with him. But then the Rules Committee ordered coaches to confine themselves to a marked area between the 35-yard lines or suffer a 15-yard penalty. Truth of the matter is that Woody wasn't the only coach who prowled the sidelines so promiscuously and with such obvious intent, but a lot of critics immediately labeled the new ordinance as the "Woody Hayes rule."

Seconds after any Ohio State victory, Woody is chugging off the field behind his players and disappears into the locker rooms. The instant the last player has entered the doors at ground level, the doors are closed and two state troopers are posted outside, with two more just inside.

Outside these doors there is a strange phenomenon—hundreds of gawkers captivated by the possibility of seeing close up these muscled mesomorphs, these victors of the gladiatorial arena emerging so shiny and showered, so glorified by their conquest. They cannot help being there, these gawkers, because it is part of the mystique of big-time winning football, and quite probably, if they ever cease being attracted it will signal the end of big-time football.

There are only a select few people who get inside that door. Fathers of the players. Newsmen. And anywhere from thirty to fifty Ohio high school stars who have been invited to the game as potential recruits.

The fathers and the high school stars are permitted upstairs to the team dressing quarters. Newsmen are restricted to the lower level and ushered into a first-floor conference room where Woody will hold his postgame interview. But that won't be for almost half an hour. Woody's routine is to first check into all injuries, then talk to his team in private. He'll either compliment them or indicate that the following week there'll be some things that need working on.

Proud fathers are then admitted to see their sons after they've had their showers. Sometimes Woody will recognize some of the dads and go over to say hello. If a kid has had an exceptionally good game Woody won't hesitate saying so to the father, and because it has been in the presence of others, the guy won't feel a single step when he floats back downstairs.

There is one last thing Woody does before going to his press conference room where perhaps twenty-five writers will be sipping free cokes and bitching under their breaths about deadlines they have to make, and why the hell can't Woody get down here sooner, like other head coaches. He bustles up to the team conference room in the stadium tower, where the day's high school prospects have been shepherded. He has been carefully briefed on their identities. And Woody, the consummate host and politician, rarely forgets a name. Woody will talk to them as a group for five minutes or so about the game, reviewing strategy or big plays. The possible recruits listen with rapt attention, and those he happens to greet by name personally wear their delight like a badge.

It is not an elaborate or high-pressure session; in fact, Woody actually doesn't recruit at these moments. He is merely playing host to a special group of kids—some of whom he wants very much to come to Ohio State, but he isn't pressing at this point.

Then a student manager or assistant coach will gently tug him away and Woody finally will hurry down two flights of metal stairs in the cavernous tower and back down to the first floor, where the newsmen are waiting for their post-game interview.

By now it is almost a half-hour since the game has ended. Many writers with deadlines to meet are plainly irritated. Usually, these are writers who may or may not have been here before. The regulars have just lolled around on chairs, sipping cokes, knowing there's no hurrying the Great Man, and when he heaves to he'll be there, and not a moment earlier.

He enters suddenly all by himself, his rubber-soled football cleats not making a sound, and he is pushing rapidly down the aisle even before they know he is there. Now he is up front, settling himself into a chair, reaching for a coke and smiling faintly, complacently.

"Well, how'd we look out there?" he might murmur softly, even before anybody can ask him anything. Not that Woody needs to be told by the press how his club looked out there; he knows only too well. But Woody, when he wins handily, is old soft-shoe, broadly paternal, oozing with cozy comments about his kids and already sounding off about key plays and key situations even before the writers can get cranked up for their own questions.

They do ask, of course, and Woody replies, ticking off generally what they want to know, but most of them would do better to just listen to Woody run on.

You have the feeling that he doesn't think much of their

technical questions anyway, and so he's really steering them onto stuff that will make better copy than what they want to know about. Woody's a pretty good writer himself, and an even better public-relations man (although he hates the phrase); rarely does a writer come away from a postgame conference without some good stuff.

The stuff is even better if the game has been close; if there has been a questionable call by an official; or if Woody feels the opposing coach had come in there with some deep-rooted notion that he was going to knock the Buckeyes off. At a time like that, Woody takes delight in letting the press know where the guy failed.

On the rare occasions when Ohio State loses, a postgame conference produces a Woody Hayes who would like nothing better than to tell the press to get the hell out of there and let him go back to his cave and lick his wounds in private. There will be little if any technical discourse on the loss; he'll blame no one but himself; and any tribute to the opposing coach and his team might just as well be uttered in Urdu. Whatever he says is delivered in less than two minutes. His career record for brevity is fourteen seconds, unless you count the time or two he never showed at all.

# 11
# Road Trip

"On the road, I could tell their writers we have a starter
out with a broken leg or a case of leprosy, for all they'd
care. They don't want to know about our football team. All
they want to know is what Woody's been up to. What he's
said lately, not necessarily about football, and how much
time they can have with him."

—Marv Homan, Ohio State
Sports Information Director

\* \* \*

At least four times a year, Woody Hayes leads the troops
out into a potential ambush. He has never gone into a game
without expecting to win, but out there on the road, in the
booby-trapped precincts of Purdue, Wisconsin or Michigan
State, an opposing coach is harboring delusions of grandeur; he's going to knock Woody's head off. And thereby
make himself a successful season. Never mind a lackluster
or even losing record for the year. Whipping Woody Hayes
and Ohio State is better than a heart transplant. Local
wolves will slink silently back to their lairs. Alumni and
local press will look upon the coach as having pulled off a
minor miracle. Next year he may even walk on water. Even

take us to the Rose Bowl. My God—he beat Woody Hayes and we were there to witness it!

Embarking on an expedition which combines the logistics of a military campaign and a traveling road show, Woody knows what kind of reception awaits him. It has never cost him a moment's sleep. Woody's own road-game countdown, meanwhile, has started climaxing Thursday afternoon in the team conference room for a review of basic offense and defensive plans. It lasts only forty-five minutes and ends up with Woody making his usual Thursday pre-game turn-on. When the meeting breaks, each kid on the traveling squad sets out his own game pads and shoes, leaving them in front of his locker. Equipment managers now collect the gear, adding it to the boy's game pants and jerseys.

Four movie projectors will be taken along. Two will go on the equipment truck. Two others will go on the team plane. Woody Hayes will not tolerate the loss of a moment in projecting film at either staff meetings or at player unit meetings when they reach their motel. He won't even waste time threading new reels; often a manager will be alerted to have two projectors ready for Woody's own screening so that a second one will go on the instant the first runs out.

Every traveling bag and all game equipment for the trip will be stowed aboard a big truck, including foul-weather capes, medical supplies, cheerleader equipment, cameras and camera equipment, and twenty-four footballs. That week, the team has practiced with the type game ball chosen by the home team, whether Wilson, Spalding, or whatever. Woody has left nothing to chance. He doesn't want his kids exposed to an unfamiliar feel of a ball.

By 6:00 P.M. John Bozick, the equipment manager, and

his assistant Phil Bennett take off in the truck for Indiana, Northwestern, Michigan State or wherever. Except for long trips to Iowa and Minnesota, they use the truck and make the journey in anywhere from five to eight hours. Two more equipment managers will follow on the team plane. There will also be a minimum of four student managers with the main party. On Friday morning the equipment managers will hang out the game gear in the rival stadium to be ready for the team's arrival.

By the time the equipment truck has left, however, one very serious and sometimes troublesome problem has already been worked out. Not always with perfect satisfaction.

Big Ten rules limit a traveling squad to forty-eight players. In two-platoon football, this means just a bit more than your first two teams, offense and defense, plus a couple of specialists such as punter and place-kicker. Deciding on forty-eight players is one of the big juggling acts of the week, and can be an agonizing one for the coaches.

At home they can dress ninety or more players and every kid can be part of the act, feel part of the team, with the possibility of sixty or more getting into the game if the Buckeyes get out to a 30- or 40-point lead. (This is the reason coaches are often criticized for running up a score when they get a big lead on the road. They can't help it. The coach can't drop below his second team in getting substitutes into the game. And he can't ask second stringers not to do their best when most of them are trying to convince the coaches they should be starters. But at home a coach can dip to his third and fourth stringers to keep a score down.)

Leaving a boy off a traveling squad can be a bitter disappointment for him. Especially at a big-time school where kids are often recruited with a suggestion (not necessarily a promise) that they'll be good enough as sophomores, or even freshmen, to make the traveling team.

So Woody Hayes makes sure there's a lot of give-and-take among his assistant coaches, who for the most part decide which of their ends, tackles, running backs, linebackers, and so forth, will make the trip. Depending on the opponent's strengths and weaknesses, Ohio State's own position strengths and injury problems, plus a sense of fairness toward the kids, a team roster will be made up Thursday morning.

Maybe this week, Esco Sarkkinen figures he can get by with four defensive ends, but George Hill claims he'll need a minimum of five linebackers. Dick Walker wants six defensive backs this week because they'll be up against a particularly tricky offense, and one of his best backs is slightly subpar because of a leg bruise. There absolutely must be three quarterbacks, and Woody is so fullback-oriented that no one would dare suggest that he get along with just two. Or that he would venture into enemy territory with fewer than five offensive tackles. Maybe four defensive tackles, but never four for offense.

Then there's the consideration of who went on the last road trip; let's do some juggling here and there, with a couple of new faces if we won't be hurt by it . . .

"The prospect of making a road trip is one of the chief incentives for a boy to go all out in practice," says Woody. "If he never lets down, gives us everything he's got and stays sharp, the coaches are going to notice. All other things being equal, this is the boy who will make the trip."

In cases where the other coaches can't work out the give-

Woody Hayes as a seven-year-old on a bridge over the old Ohio canal in New-comerstown; at sixteen as a high school center; at thirty-eight in his first year as coach at Ohio State.

Woody runs off another reel of film and prowls the equipment room at his hideaway in Biggs Training Center. At left, his wife Anne.

Saturdays with Woody: left, protesting a pass interception call against
Buckeyes at Michigan in 1971. Moments later he ripped up a yard marker,
making national news. Above, on another occasion, he steams furiously
down sideline to debate an official's call.

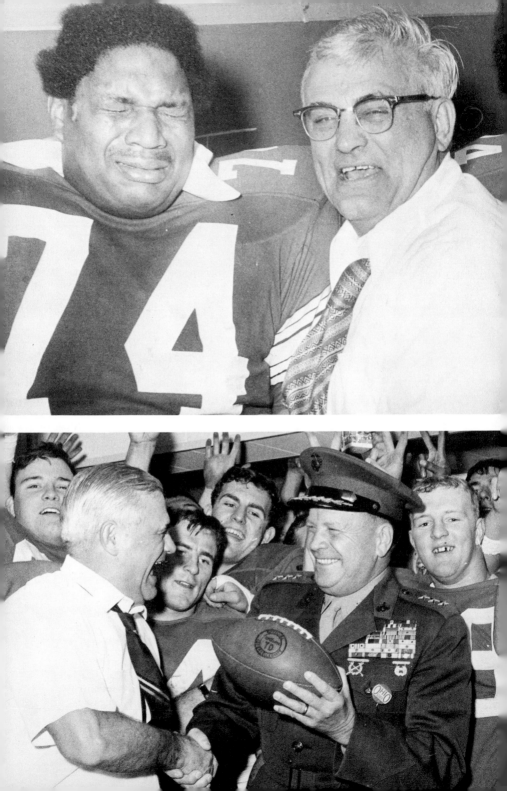

Top left, post-game emotions hang out as Woody and All-America John Hicks tearfully mark a big win over Michigan in 1972. Bottom left, Woody's friend, Marine Major General Lewis Walt, receives a souvenir ball after a victory in Ohio Stadium. Top right, Woody leads pregame cheers in 1973 Rose Bowl, but his Buckeyes lose to Southern Cal. A year later, after beating Southern Cal, Woody astounds the press by bringing Buckeye players to post-game interview (below). Left to right: Archie Griffin, Neal Colzie, Pete Johnson.

Woody, connected by phone to coaches in pressbox, may accept or veto a play they send down, as he surveys action on field.

and-take between them, Woody is the final arbiter. Rarely does he listen to an appeal. Unlike many head coaches, he is so aware of every nuance of his practice week that he's virtually mistake-proof.

Following practice on Thursday, Woody holds his final pregame press conference, a relaxed session in which he sounds a gentle warning about how tough or how upset-minded the home team is going to be, and what he thought of his Bucks' final practice and which of his people looked particularly good that week.

"Most of it," says a writer who has attended many of these sessions, "is strictly yawn-type stuff and I can't remember when Woody ever gave us any really meaty stuff —except for declaring a kid out of the game because his injury hadn't come around. As often as not we'll get some very printable stuff completely disassociated from football, and on days like that we'd be blessed. I can count on my readers quoting Woody's latest comment on some political peccadillo, or his prescription for quicker legal justice in America, but I could rarely relay to them anything that would grab them in a football way."

In one final press conference last fall, according to Kaye Kessler of the Columbus *Citizen-Journal,* "The best item we got, for some fey reason—and you never know where Woody will branch off—was a discourse on how Field Marshal Rommel blew the D-Day invasion because he was hanky-pankying with some *Fräulein* back in Berlin. Probably the best note in my pregame story."

Following his conference Woody and his coaches shower and go home to dinner. For the coaches it is the only night of the practice week they have dinner with their families. It is the only night when they're not holding meetings or viewing another mile of movie film. Except for Woody. Woody will come back to his hideaway at Biggs and the projector will whir away until 10:30 or 11:00, with no one to keep him company.

The traveling squad has been posted by the time the team reports to Thursday practice so that when the kids are dismissed by 5:30 Thursday for training table dinner, they know whether they'll be on the road.

They are expected to be in bed by 10:30 at the latest, with their personal traveling bag packed. The average football fan—and a lot of students on campus—would be stunned to know that almost every bag contains at least one classroom textbook.

The duties of one of the student managers on Thursday night is to arrange for a fleet of taxi cabs which, at 8:00 A.M. Friday, starts making pickups at dormitories, fraternity houses, or apartments where players live. All players will be wearing their Ohio State blazers and ties. Woody, his nine assistant coaches, four or five student managers, the athletic director, the assistant athletic director, the ticket manager and two team physicians are also picked up at their homes. A half-hour later they are brought together at the airport dining room for breakfast. There they will be joined by members of the Columbus press corps, who will also fly out on the Buckeyes' chartered plane.

The flight, if to a Big Ten destination, never takes more than an hour or two. During that time Woody Hayes may choose to take a seat where the one next to him is vacant. It may remain that way throughout the flight. "Nobody," remarks an assistant coach, "will sit down there unless Woody summons him. It just isn't done unless the person has something important to tell him."

Woody may read for an entire hour, although that is rare. He may decide to hold a brief meeting with one of his coaches or with the quarterbacks. Or he may prowl the length of the aircraft glancing at his players. He doesn't make it mandatory for them to study aboard the plane; he knows that some feel it necessary to immerse themselves in silence or tight introspection. But many of the kids have learned to make up necessary study hours on a flight, and will suddenly discover Woody hovering over them, zeroing in on their zoology book, history book, notebook or whatever. It never ceases to impress them when he checks into the material they're studying, or asks the kind of question that lets them know he's right on top of the subject.

The team will arrive at Lafayette, Indiana, or Champaign, Illinois, around 11:00 or 11:30 A.M., and will be met by buses which take the squad directly to the Purdue or Illinois stadium.

There they will get into sweat suits and helmets already set out by the equipment men, who had arrived the night before. The team will limber up for about forty-five minutes, getting rid of stiff leg muscles, run a few plays and review their kicking game; then, accompanied by Woody and all the assistant coaches, they'll slowly walk up and down the field, "taking in the environment," as Woody puts it. They shower, climb back aboard their buses and go to their motel, where student managers have already collected all room keys and now distribute them to the entire party before they go in to lunch. The motel has been carefully chosen for a combination of luxury, service, discreet personnel, fine food and distance from traffic or commercial din.

The room list has been made up by Woody and his

coaches on Thursday morning after deciding who would be making the trip. The room arrangements aren't just any slapdash pattern. A lot of thought goes into them. Woody is big on psychology and interpersonal relationships that can affect his ball club. He prefers to pair the kids off by offense and defense, and often by the same position. Rarely, however, do two kids pair off who are competing bitterly for the same starting job. Otherwise, however, quarterbacks, tailbacks, fullbacks or linebackers may room together.

Woody also likes to have veterans share a room with a young sophomore who may need exposure to pregame poise and confidence. Roommates at the same position often have common problems and goals and can discuss the coming game in that light.

Woody also makes sure there is no natural gravitation of black to black or white to white, and mixes them up all over the place. The room assignments are rotated over the whole season, including home games, so that a lot of sensible juggling can be done over ten or eleven games.

The players immediately deposit their traveling bags in their motel rooms and the entire Ohio State party goes in to lunch which, on Woody's orders, is served promptly at 1:00 P.M.

Sometimes Woody gives his players Friday afternoon off for napping, studying or television-watching. But more often than not he piles them back onto the bus for a tour of the home team's campus, with his personal commentary. Often, too, Woody has arranged in advance to take his entire squad to a class in session on Friday afternoon, usually a lecture class and usually history.

"I think we've drawn some startled stares," Woody

chuckles, describing how his party of fifty-five or so files quietly behind him into a lecture hall, everyone resplendent and shiny in their scarlet and gray blazers and ties. (He also insists that his assistant coaches trot along.)

"I guess the local students aren't used to seeing a visiting football team share their lecture the day before a big game. But it's a way we have of letting our kids know that education is a continuing and diversified thing, and attending a good lecture on somebody else's campus might have a pretty good rub-off effect."

Depending on where they are, Woody may, in fact, deliver lectures of his own back at the motel. "This is Lincoln country," he invariably tells his squad when they go to Illinois, "and what better place to hear about it than in Lincoln's own backyard." And then he'll proceed to unwind two or three Lincoln tales more colorfully and provocatively than most professors or biographers can do. And he does it so dexterously that it can be interpreted as a psychic viewpoint directly in tune with tomorrow's game.

But if a campus tour or classroom visit has been part of Woody's routine for this particular Friday, it is still back to the motel by 3:30 or 4:00 for complete relaxation. "For the next two hours we want them completely off their feet," he says. Dinner is at 6:00, a training table dinner of steak, vegetables, tea and light dessert.

At 7:00 there is Woody Hayes' ritual of a movie. On the road there have been complications. A few years ago Woody was preoccupied with other matters and failed to hear of the choice that had been made. But he happened to be outside the motel when the kids came back a couple of hours later. "What'd you see?" asked a student manager who hadn't gone along. *"Easy Rider,"* replied one of the players. "Wow, what a picture!" he added, with a shake of his head.

Woody was incensed. Within seconds he had grabbed an assistant coach and was screaming, "You've killed us! We're gonna lose the ball game! How could you let them see a scruffy, gruesome thing like that! It's gonna be on their minds for hours!" And on and on and on, while the poor assistant coach summoned up visions of extreme social consciousness whirling around all night inside the minds of linebackers and halfbacks.

The next day Ohio State won, 42–7 or some such, but nobody went up to Woody Hayes and said, "See, Woody, it didn't affect our kids at all."

Otherwise, Woody takes the movie bit seriously. At East Lansing, Michigan, one year, there wasn't a suitable movie in the entire city. Woody finally located one twenty-five miles out of town at a drive-in. But when the student manager phoned for the team buses he found they weren't available for that night.

As former assistant Lou McCullough tells it: "Woody called an Oldsmobile agency," says McCullough, "and had them deliver enough cars to take the whole squad to the movie. Everyone was to be ready, promptly, for a 7:00 P.M. departure. You know what 7:00 P.M., promptly, means to a commander-in-chief?

"Well, at 6:40 he told me to have two separate rooms ready for our offensive and defensive meetings following the movie. All film was to be threaded and ready on four different projectors because Woody, of course, never likes to waste time changing the reels. Two other assistants and I hustled like hell and had everything set up by 7:01. We rushed back to the lobby to meet the team. They had left.

Woody saw us charging toward the door and exploded.

"First he smashed himself with a good right hand. Then he said: 'You sonsabitches have lost the game!'

"But it was just a megaton and not a hundred-megaton because he's left-handed.

"Then he said, 'Don't just stand there, you jackasses! Get to hell out there with your team!'

"I told him there wasn't a cab in sight, there wasn't a rent-a-car available, and after checking, I reported that the only thing we could rent was a thirty-six-passenger bus. He said to rent the goddam bus and get to hell out to the drive-in with the team. I don't know what he expected might happen to our team—get kidnapped, or something —but you don't argue or even reason when Woody gives an order. You mentally salute, fall to and carry out the order.

"Can you imagine this great big bus pulling into a drive-in theater with three coaches? The girl at the ticket booth thought we were loony. She said we couldn't take the bus into the lot. So I bought three tickets, sent the bus back to town and we began looking for a flock of new Oldsmobiles. But by then it was dark and a lot of condensation had formed on all the car windows in the place. I ran up to a brand new Olds and jerked open the door, only to find a young couple making love.

"We finally found our players, but Woody was right. We lost the game the next day."

There's no predicting Woody Hayes' moods (some people say fantasies) on the road. Ohio State officialdom still recalls the time at Michigan when, on Friday afternoon before the game, an assistant coach made an offhand complaint about the food at their motel. "That salad at lunch today," the assistant coach said with a small grimace. "I think something was wrong with it. Like the lettuce was spoiled or something."

Woody reacted in a flash. "Spoiled, hell!" he barked. "I think the bastards are probably trying to poison us or something!" He grabbed the assistant coach impetuously. "Cancel the dinner here tonight," he said excitedly. "We're making other plans."

He had the assistant get in touch with the manager of a fine Detroit restaurant whom Woody knew. "Tell him I want seventy-five of his best filet mignon steaks," he ordered the assistant. "He knows the kind I want. Have them shipped here by special truck or any way he has to. Helicopter, if necessary."

Then he made arrangements to have the dinner prepared and served at a private club a few miles away, and gave the assistant coach a final word of warning. "Make sure nobody touches those steaks except the chef." The assistant coach thought it remarkable that Woody himself didn't guard the steaks when they came, such was his suspicion of anything connected with arch rival Michigan.

Virtually always there is a press cocktail party hosted by the home school for the visiting coaches and athletic department personnel from about 6:00 to 7:30 on Friday, but unless it's a homecoming weekend for the hosts, Woody and his staff never attend. The visiting obligations are handled by the athletic director and his people. Woody Hayes will let nothing intrude upon the close-knit unity of his team and coaches. Nobody or nothing can drive a time wedge between them. On this he is almost fanatical. Hosting schools, their president, athletic director and coaches at first were upset by Woody's policy on this, but over the years they got used to it and now shrug it off with a small smile as just another Woodyism.

No matter where Ohio State goes, the chief attraction as a visiting club is never the team. It's the coach himself. Invariably there will be a dozen or more writers and radio and TV reporters awaiting the arrival of the Buckeyes at the home team's stadium.

Marv Homan, the Ohio State sports information director who goes out as an advance man on the Tuesday before the game, has never been able to sell much information or color to the home media. "They don't want to know much about the club," he sighs. "Hell, I could tell 'em we have a starter out with a broken leg or a case of leprosy, for all they'd care. They don't want to know about our football team. All they want to know is what Woody's been up to. What's he said lately, not necessarily about football, and how much time can they have with him." Homan shrugs. "It's the same wherever we go. The story is Woody, not the football game. Of course, for the most part, the football game is never much in doubt, and I don't say that in arrogance or in a demeaning way. But I know what kind of copy these guys are interested in."

Woody himself is not much for interviews on the road, but he knows something is expected of him and for three or four minutes or so he'll face a television camera or a knot of reporters and be the most charming guy they've seen all year. He simply doesn't want to tell them anything that isn't a god-awful generality or pure pablum. And he knows how it probably registers. Last year at Madison, Wisconsin, after the obligatory interview he confided to the Columbus scribes with a chuckle: "From the looks on their faces I must have sounded like a chapter of the *Bobbsey Twins at the Farm.*"

Saturday morning the normal home-game routine goes into effect. There is one notable difference, however, on a road trip. Unless it is at Michigan there will not be the wildly enthusiastic 87,000 to be found in Ohio Stadium. Now the Bucks will perform before 40,000 or perhaps 50,-000—the great majority being home fans.

Meanwhile, rarely does an Ohio State team go on the road—at least in Big Ten country—without at least 5,000 or more fans from Columbus tagging along. The famed Ohio State marching band—often greeted by the opposition with more grace than is Woody when he plows onto the field at the head of his legions—makes at least one out-of-town trip a year, and the cheerleading corps performs at every game.

For the host crowd, the prospect of an historic upset bursts into sullen and flickering flame at the sight of Woody, and there are boos and the derisive whistles, none of which Woody Hayes hears. They are the kind of hopes that are rarely fulfilled, of course. And the plane ride to Columbus immediately after the game on Saturday night is a model of relaxation and *Weltschmerz* as Woody brings 'em back, the usual mission accomplished.

\* \* \*

There is one road trip, however, that is far out of the ordinary—the trip to Pasadena, California, for the Rose Bowl game on New Year's Day. Woody and his Buckeyes have been invited more often over the last twenty-odd years than any other team. And always the trip is an unmatched extravaganza for everyone concerned. The university stands to make about $125,000 on the Rose Bowl

every year, whether the Buckeyes play or not (Pacific Eight
and Big Ten teams split the take evenly). But the big attraction in playing is the all-expenses-paid journey—one heckuva party. Woody Hayes and the athletic director make sure
nobody is slighted. Want to know who goes along? Okay:

Sixty football players who can dress for the game. At
least forty more squad members who aren't allowed to play
but are rewarded with the trip. Woody and nine assistant
coaches. John Bozick, the equipment manager, and three
assistants. The head trainer and five assistants. Five student
managers. Two team doctors and the team dentist. The
athletic director and four or five assistants. The business
manager, ticket director, two sports information directors
and two secretaries from the football office. And how about
the president of the university, a couple of his cabinet; the
alumni secretary and a few functionaries not here ac-
counted for?

And everybody's wives, including those of a half-dozen
or more players.

And the band.

And ten cheerleaders.

And all that equipment.

And following the official party, several thousand red-hot
alumni, local citizenry and students, many of whom go into
hock for the rest of the year for their spending money. All
that way to California.

A Rose Bowl game is not just a game or a junket. It is a
hunk of mystique; lemmings do not race any more blindly
for the sea than Buckeye fans toward Pasadena.

The first Buckeye foot is barely planted on California soil
before the visitors begin what Woody Hayes clearly figures
is not the real reason they're out there. There'll be an orgy

of official luncheons and dinners, ornamented with people like Bob Hope, John Wayne and Governor Ronald Reagan. The commissioners of the Big Ten and the Pacific Eight will exchange the expected banter; the two teams will mix pleasantries at one or two of these functions; their stars will pose together for pictures and TV, displaying a lot of teeth in the fancied camaraderie of sportsmanship, and everybody trilling about how wonderful it is to be getting to know each other better, and what a great contest this is going to be, and how educational it's going to be to visit the movie studios and Disneyland and Marineland, and Hollywood and the Sunset Strip and . . .

*And bullshit* is no doubt what Woody Hayes is thinking as he delivers his own bons mots, and charms the pants off everyone except the Los Angeles press, which is hovering on the fringes, pencils poised, their own teeth bared, not in camaraderie of sport but in zestful anticipation of zinging it to the Old Man once again. If it were up to Woody, they'd come out there for a week or so to get used to the climate, practice behind locked gates, take a bus to the Rose Bowl and start hitting.

Practice is held at nearby Citrus Junior College, and for Woody the last ten days, in the words of one observer, "seem more like the culmination of a crusade." John McKay of Southern Cal, his ofttime foe, always gives his team three days off for the holiday. "We consider the Rose Bowl a reward, not a punishment," says McKay. "It isn't fair to players who start training in August to beat them to death in December." In fact, he usually practices his Rose Bowl teams only twelve days of the sixteen allotted by the rules. Woody Hayes, until 1974, used all sixteen, plus several double sessions.

With today's more independent-minded players, Woody's former no-nonsense, two-a-day, pregame regimen once got him into trouble with his players for the first and probably only time in his career.

He had taken his great 1968 team of Rex Kern, John Brockington, Jack Tatum, Jan White and others, to the 1969 Rose Bowl and trimmed O. J. Simpson's USC team. Woody had worked his squad with his usual tough sessions, and that was that.

Two years later the same group went out to Pasadena as seniors. This time Woody sensed something and had told his kids that things wouldn't be quite as grim; there'd be time off to take advantage of more of the local goodies.

Dandy. But after a couple of days of continued old-fashioned Hayes' drills, a committee of senior stars came to Woody and suggested that it would be wise to get around to the promises he made. There was no denying that the kids would not be put off—or else. It was the only time in Woody Hayes' long career that anything approaching rebellion by the troops had been witnessed in the Buckeye camp.

With characteristic efficiency, Woody sets up a command post as soon as the Buckeye contingent checks into the Huntington-Sheraton, a stately and elegant hotel which serves as a headquarters for Big Ten teams at the Rose Bowl. The two football secretaries, Lena Biscuso and Linda Fiscus, are established in an office to handle and coordinate the welter of business, social and football matters with which, as Woody points out, a Rose Bowl is "afflicted."

There are also some very important recruiting chores to be filtered through the secretaries. About 125 prep stars on the Buckeyes' master recruiting list are sent a Christmas card with special Rose Bowl greetings from Woody. Copies of the colorful official Rose Bowl programs are also sent to these kids so they can have them in time for the televised game—and to conjure up some dreams, perhaps, of playing here some day. It is always a big recruiting pitch by Woody: Why not play with the team that gets here the most often?

On balance, long-time observers of the Rose Bowl scene marvel that Woody Hayes maintains as much tolerance as he does during these days in never-never land. After all, this is a man who goes buckity-buckity from one mental or physical chore to another when there's a football game to be played and won, and he has a short fuse for the slightest interference.

Up until last year, too, Woody always took his team out of the Huntington-Sheraton the night before the Rose Bowl game and slipped away with them to the Passionist Brothers Monastery in the nearby mountains. There, in spare, ascetic surroundings, each boy to his own cell, the sanctified and spiritual atmosphere was supposed to get the kids all cranked up for the holy war they would wage on the morrow.

In 1974 Woody changed his mind. The Buckeyes had lost their last two Rose Bowl outings and Woody suddenly decided the monastery bit was too eerie and confining. His kids were too gregarious, too family-conscious, and too young for that sort of thing. He opted for the genteel surroundings of the Huntington-Sheraton and went out the next day and flayed the hide off the Trojans.

At a buffet supper for the players and their families after the victory, somebody asked why the Buckeyes hadn't spent the night in the monastery. "Not any more," was the reply.

"Woody doesn't like that hair shirt the monks ask him to sleep in. Y'know, Woody isn't as spartan as he used to be. The mellowing process comes to everyone."

Before the game Woody even allowed his players to stay out later at night on this trip. "But they're coming in fairly early on their own," Woody pointed out, "because they're tired and don't want to abuse the privilege.

"Y'know, I have such great people this year," he continued, "that they've softened me up. I actually have to go out of my way to kick a helmet. Maybe I'm a nicer guy because I'm dealing with such nice people. The psychiatrists call it a reflected image."

Several days later, somebody suggested that maybe it had just been the greatest trap-up-the-middle ever seen in all pre-Rose Bowl action. Because softened-up Woody's Buckeye team went out and simply took Southern Cal apart.

Of approximately a hundred sportswriters polled that week in Pasadena, close to seventy had picked the Trojans to win. "It occurred to us too late," said one writer, "that this time Woody had been all Jekyll and no Hyde."

By Rose Bowl time, however, Woody and his staff have other things on their minds, too. Recruiting season begins December 1, and the coaches' busiest times may be ahead rather than behind them.

# 12
# The Blue-Chippers

Among the fans there is little understanding of the recruiting business. No sales organization ever approached its
goals with the zeal and drive of the Ohio State recruiting
staff. But then no sales organization ever had a Gen'l Sales
Mgr. like Woody Hayes. Yessir, gentlemen—Quotas Will
Be Met.

\* \* \*

The boy was a six-four, 240-pound tackle, and Woody
Hayes was convinced that among high school linemen in
the state of Ohio he was easily the best in the business—
an opinion just slightly south of the prevailing notion
among about 150 coaches elsewhere that the boy might
even be the best prep lineman in the nation. In the parlance
of the trade, he was a "blue-chipper" or even a "super
blue-chipper," and he was the object of a recruiting war
which, as usual, recognized few of the rules laid down by
the NCAA, college sports' Geneva Convention. This kid
was going to be a defensive coach's franchise, and it was

clear from the very start that the boy wasn't going somewhere just because he liked the climate, the coeds or the coach's brand of persuasive snake oil.

At the moment, as Woody Hayes was talking to the father of this superstud, Woody quickly recognized a ploy that was about as cleverly concealed as a go-go dancer's modesty.

"We're awfully pleased that so many people are interested in our boy," the father smiled blandly, "and it looks as though we don't have to worry about not having enough good choices." Then the innocent, boffo laugh: "Heck, the only thing we're worrying about around our house is a leaky roof." Followed by an observation that "one of these days we're gonna have to put a new roof on the place before we have us a trout stream in the living room."

Ho-ho-ho!

While Woody Hayes did not heave the guy out by the seat of his pants he did set a new speed record for terminating a recruiting conversation. The father got his new roof from a school in another part of the country and the kid continued on to stardom in the NFL.

The name of the game is recruiting, and no big-time coach ever suggested he won championships on his sheer football genius. "You've got to have the horses" is the one bromide that will live as long as there's big-time football.

The horses—the highly desirable recruits—are those boys who have the height, the heft, the agility, the great speed for forty yards, and an appetite for the game that translates into "he likes to hit—and doesn't mind being hit in return."

There are about 1,000,000 boys who play football in the nation's high schools, and about 200,000 of these are seniors, the class which produces the mother lode of talent for the hundred and twenty-five or so colleges listed as major football powers by the NCAA. And it's a safe bet that fewer than 2,000 of the 200,000 are the supers being bird-dogged by the major powers.

You'd think there'd be enough to go around. Uh-uh. Not when you see so many of the big-time powers going after the same kids with the fervor of a crusade or the hysteria of a guy double-hustling to keep the sheriff from foreclosing the homestead.

They're not only getting better high school coaching than twenty-five years ago but because of our outdoorsy, better-fed, vitamin-enriched, nutritionally balanced society, they're taller, heavier and faster. Herman Masin, editor of *Scholastic Coach* Magazine, which selects the official high school All-America team, looks at his honor list of twenty years ago, compares it to today's and shakes his head. "We're developing a race of monsters with winged feet."

So, the rush to put pads on these monsters is on . . .

Not only are the super blue-chippers known to every big-time school in the land, but anybody now has a shot at them. The jet plane is the reason. Until about twenty years ago a boy's choices of college were pretty much limited by a reasonable automobile trip, convenient rail travel, or ordinary prop plane—and flying wasn't the universal thing it is today.

Today, the boy from Ohio is only four hours away from Southern Cal; two and a half hours from Nebraska. The hot halfback from Georgia can now be easily wooed by Michigan State, and the good kids from New Jersey are flip-flopping all over the map.

Staying close to home so the family can see him play is still a consideration for a boy, but it is no longer an overriding one. Boy and family are buying the recruiter's pitch that the kid should make the choice "which is best for him and his future." ("Come to our school and that's what you'll find.")

Corraling the horses is supposed to begin with some thou-shalts and thou-shalt-nots graven in the athletic scholarship tablet handed down by the National Collegiate Athletic Association—otherwise, hailed, or hooted, as the NCAA.

On the tablet it reads: "Tuition, books, room and board."

From there on the wording gets a bit blurred.

The legal lure for the hotshot recruit is carefully spelled out by the NCAA, beginning with the requirement that he be academically eligible under the rules. The academic rules state that on the basis of his high school's computation the boy has done the equivalent of C work for his high school career. Anything less than that makes him ineligible for a grant in aid, as the scholarship is called.

His standing can be measured any way his high school wishes: class rank, academic average, College Board scores, and sometimes by a formula so arcane that it's known only by maybe the guidance counselor or principal. It's not uncommon for fervent high school coaches or administrations to do some rather imaginative and artful dodging through the thicket of academe to come up with a formula that opens the scholarship door for their local hero. Nor is it any less common for overzealous college recruiters to suggest to the high school coach that it would indeed be appreciated if A Way Could Be Found.

Thus, while certain kids are signed and admitted on the basis that they can, indeed, spell *cat*, you'd better not try them on *kitten.*

Ask Oklahoma. In 1973 the Sooners lost the services of their great quarterback, Kerry Jackson, and were X-rated off the college TV schedules for 1974–75 for committing hanky-panky on Jackson's Texas high school transcript.

There are some very sensible, explicit rules on how you go about recruiting these hotshots. Without these rules the general recruiting chaos would only be compounded. Still, the breach of ethics runs a full range from obvious to horrendous. Wait. You'll see.

* * *

The Ohio State active recruiting period starts the week after the final game of the season, roughly December 1. By the middle of the month Ralph Staub, offensive line coach and Woody's recruiting coordinator, has huddled with the entire staff to come up with a master list of somewhere between 100 and 125 names of blue-chippers.

"Our aim," says Woody, "is to sign approximately twenty-five of them, depending upon our needs, by position. If we have a bumper crop of good tackles, say, in our present freshman and sophomore classes—maybe six or seven—then our needs aren't too pressing at that position. We're not hurt too badly if we only wind up getting a couple—although in a two-platoon system, and at Ohio State, we can never have too many tackles. But if the majority of our top tackles are going to be seniors the following year we know damn well we're going to have to concentrate on that position, or any other position where we're thin in underclassmen.

"Naturally, we're going after the great ones at any position and in any numbers we can land them, but at Ohio State we don't try to overdo it."

Ohio State signs fewer freshman recruits than any team in the Big Ten and probably fewer than any other major football power. Woody doesn't believe in numbers. He wants his staff to choose carefully, insuring that every recruit will be fairly certain to play.

"For one thing," says Woody, "it helps keep unhappiness off the bench. When you have too many kids not getting into the ball game you've got unhappiness and a morale problem.

"We don't hand out scholarships just to fill our legal limit," Woody adds. "A scholarship at Ohio State costs the athletic department an average of $3,000 per year, and there's no use spending thirty times three, when twenty-four times three will do the job for us."

Besides, Woody would rather spend the money on more productive things. One of them is the recruiting budget. Mention "recruiting budget" to certain Athletic Department officials and they'll either snicker or, more pointedly, send up some outright hollow laughter.

"That'll be the day," somebody observed. "Woody is really a frugal man and will not spend one penny more than he has to, but don't saddle him with a budget. I'll bet you that if it exists on the books he won't give a half-hoot in hell for it."

Knowledgeable unofficial sources report that Woody never spends less than $60,000 a year on the mechanics of recruiting, and routinely probably spends as much as $85,-000. If the Buckeyes sign twenty-four recruits—which has been their average over the last half-dozen years or so—

this works out to a neat $3,100 per player just to get his signature on a scholarship tender.

To those insensitive enough to suggest that this is an exorbitant expenditure of department funds, Woody has snapped, "These kids fill Ohio Stadium six times a year, 87,000 and more each Saturday. When you consider the total take, we're not investing very much in the product, are we?"

\* \* \*

Among the fans there is little understanding of how Woody Hayes and his staff operate the recruiting business. No sales organization ever approached its goals with the zeal and drive of the Buckeye recruiting staff. But then no sales organization ever had a Gen'l Sales Mgr. like Woody Hayes. Yessir, gentlemen—Quotas Will Be Met.

Recall, now, that master list mentioned earlier—the 100 or 125 prospects representing the high-assay ore which the Buckeye staff will now try to mine.

It would be instructive for the average fan to know just how a boy comes to the attention of the Ohio State (or any major college) recruiting system. In a few cases a boy himself will write to Woody and tell him he'd like to play for Ohio State. For this particular kid it is only too obvious that Ohio State has generated some sort of charisma, some sort of attraction. But the real blue-chippers rarely seek out the school. They sit back cagily and wait for the Ohio States, the Notre Dames, the Michigans, the Oklahomas or whoever to come to them.

Most high school coaches know soon enough when they have a real prospect. And they'll start getting the word to a few of the major colleges that have previously taken kids from their school.

Avid alumni (who may not know a gap six from an inside reverse) may see a headline in their paper and fire off a clipping about the local hotshot to Woody. But for years Ohio State football recruiting has been mostly a home-grown product, and many of the 600-odd high school coaches in the state are Buckeye-oriented. Woody Hayes has done his homework and his missionary work thoroughly, throughout Ohio, and the chances of a *Wunder-kind* going unnoticed are rather remote. The Buckeye staff knows by experience which prep coaches really recognize big-time talent.

The all-league and all-state selections not only from Ohio but adjacent states, released in late November or early December, are carefully screened but are often sus-pect. Too much politics. AP may lean toward kids in their client paper areas; UPI will do likewise for their patrons. An all-star may be a sure-fire comet or a celestial fraud. (John Hicks and Randy Gradishar, two of Woody's greatest all-time All Americas, never even made All-Ohio as preppers.)

Woody's assistants who check other states will know high school coaches in every area whose judgment they trust. In fact, an early line has already been established on blue-chip talent. "The great ones will show their real ability as high school juniors," says Woody.

So in the spring of each year, hundreds of questionnaires are sent out by his assistant coaches to every high school in Ohio as well as many in New York, New Jersey, Pennsyl-vania and New England.

The high school coach is asked if any of his upcoming seniors is a Big Ten caliber player. If so, he notates size, speed, academic standing and whether the boy might be interested in Ohio State, at least in a preliminary way. From the hundreds of questionnaires sent out, the Buckeye staff may come up with not more than twenty or thirty of these hot juniors who will be put on a "check-further" list and will be evaluated after the boys finish their senior seasons. (It is against Big Ten rules to actively recruit a junior.) Gradually, a solid list of apparent blue-chippers begins to emerge.

Now the organization gets down to business with typical Woody Hayes military-type planning and execution. First of all, the state of Ohio is divided up among the staff. It's the Buckeye state itself, which will provide the basis, the bedrock of success for any good recruiting year.

Starting in December, recruiting coordinator Ralph Staub takes the Cincinnati area—a critical sector which a strong Michigan alumni group has turned into good pickings for the Wolverines. Dick Walker will get Cleveland and Toledo, plus their suburbs. John Mummey goes into Dayton and west central Ohio. George Hill gets Canton, Massillon and east central Ohio. Esco Sarkkinen takes Columbus. There isn't an area of the state that isn't covered.

Until quite recently Ohio State prided itself on fielding a mostly home-grown football team from a state that is a bottomless cornucopia of talent. That cozy condition no longer exists. Witness the thirty-three Ohio kids on Michigan's varsity squad; the sixteen on Notre Dame's; just as many at Purdue, Northwestern, and Indiana.

"It's getting tougher every year," Woody Hayes admits. "So we're finding it necessary to look eastward. We've got to bring in at least a half-dozen or more boys each year from out of state."

So George Chaump, once a very successful high school coach in Allentown, Pennsylvania, combs eastern Pennsylvania. Joe Bugel, in addition to spot work in Ohio and

Michigan, takes western Pennsylvania. Chuck Clausen covers New York City, Long Island, New England and northern New Jersey. Hill or Walker will make an occasional foray into the Deep South.

Each assistant coach winds up with thirteen or fourteen candidates from the master list. The toughest work begins. And film sessions and phone calls during their travels can broaden the master list.

An enthusiastic high school coach may think his star is the greatest thing since peanut butter, but he's blinded by partisan emotion. Or, as Chuck Clausen puts it, "he just doesn't realize what it takes to play football under Woody Hayes at Ohio State, or in the Big Ten generally. He doesn't know how physically tough our football is, or how much concentration and dedication it takes."

The high school coach may not realize that his great halfback may have had the benefit of a fine blocking line which has blown apart nine straight mediocre or lightweight defenses. So in comparison the halfback looks like an All-America. The same for a big fullback who apparently can blast through a brick wall. Perhaps the bricks had some pretty thin mortar between them.

Tangentially, a high school coach may also overlook the fact that the halfback really is only capable of 4.7 for forty yards; the fullback 4.9 or 5.0. They may have scored 125 points for the season, but they could never play for Ohio State. Too slow.

Too often, a high school coach will deliberately fudge a bit in reporting sprint times. He'll shave a tenth or two in his recommendation. And many high school coaches don't bother to time their boys but offer a guess that isn't within a first down of the facts.

Woody and his staff must first determine who really *is*

good. Their most useful tool in seeking the truth is film. Virtually no boy in the last twenty years has been signed by Ohio State without having his high school game films checked.

How does a lineman fire out and make his blocking contact? How does he control his feet? How does he use his hands on his defensive rush? How strong is he? Can he shuck off blockers? Can he strip interference? Can he handle double-teaming? The Ohio State coach can read the nuances of a boy's game film and know immediately whether this is a kid he really wants to romance.

Here, on film, he can check it all, when the film projector is being run at only half or three-quarter speed to spot small details. But where the unskilled eye can't tell the difference between 4.6 and 4.9, the recruiter's eye knows how to gauge the speed of a back, for instance, against that of a defender angling in on him or in pursuit. The recruiter knows how much of a hole there is, how quickly a normal linebacker can close it, and he's able to judge whether the offensive back handles the situation with speed, agility and balance.

"He's an assassin," a high school coach may say. "He belts them around like tenpins."

Maybe. Because the films show the boy is a 240-pounder making a weekly reputation against 180-pounders and not getting off the mark very fast while doing it.

Or a coach will point out, "His older brother was a whiz at Purdue (or wherever)." But the films indicate that the ferocious genes didn't come on down the familial line.

"Film is our blueprint," says Walker, who has judged miles of it. "It tells us whether this supposedly great defensive end is fast enough to put on a pass rush and agile enough to adjust to a change in the play's direction. The good ones stick right out and you feel a heck of a thrill when you see that real blue-chipper proving it to you. Or when you see a seventeen-year-old defensive back who isn't afraid to come right up there and stick his nose into the play."

George Chaump, who coaches the Buckeye quarterbacks, knows what he's got to see on film to satisfy Woody. Woody loves quarterbacks who can not only throw but who are superb runners, preferably in the Rex Kern and more recently the Cornelius Greene mold. "Naturally, we hope the kid demonstrates the good mechanics of passing," says Chaump. "Such as knowing how to set up, throwing off the right foot, showing us a follow-through and a strong arm. The film shows us that—and one other thing that's a must. The instinct for knowing when to hold onto that ball on the option and cut and run—that great, aggressive instinct so rare in a kid."

The one thing the staff wants to guard against is to mislead Woody Hayes on the talent hunt—to send him off to New Jersey, Long Island or wherever to see a kid who doesn't turn out to be a hot prospect. "It's worth at least fifty megatons," Dick Walker shudders. "Wasting Woody's time just might be the worst sin of all."

So, before Woody hits the road, Rule One proclaims that the Buckeye assistant coaches, who do all the preliminary screening, never take anybody's word as definitive or final in compiling the master list.

Most coaches consider recruiting the toughest, most detestable part of big-time coaching, and they make no bones about hating it. "I think Woody secretly loves it," says a former assistant who has seen him in action. "Woody can be a naturally warm person, but I also think he has a lot of ham in him and he has that mountainous ego. He considers himself one of the world's best salesmen, and probably is. He's at his best in the living room of a recruit, with the boy's parents and maybe a younger brother hanging on every word, and almost struck dumb with awe at the Great Man's presence.''

Coast-to-coast and intersectional recruiting have turned Woody Hayes into football's most indefatigable, most traveled recruiter. Most big-time coaches are content to let their assistants do virtually all the home or school visitations and reserve their own efforts for prize prospects closer to home. Perhaps two or three hotshots will lure Ara Parseghian or Bo Schembechler out of the Midwest, or Bear Bryant or Darrell Royal out of Alabama and Texas. Nobody even comes close to Woody in hours spent and ground covered. Between December 1 and April 1, he goes more than 15,000 miles.

A typical recruiting season will find Woody Hayes visiting at least eight boys in metropolitan New York; four or five in New Jersey; six or seven more in Pennsylvania; two or three in Washington, D.C.; at least two or three in the mid-South, and four or five more in Illinois, West Virginia and Michigan. Add to this the number of times he'll jump into his car and cover the blue-chippers all over the state of Ohio, and you've got the Henry Kissinger of college football, complete with message.

Joe Paterno, the Penn State coach, hurls a good-natured brickbat: "Until about ten years ago I had it made," says Paterno. "My excursions into the New York City and New Jersey areas were leisurely and limited. Suddenly I began to run across Woody Hayes everywhere I went. My God, there were times when I'd be going into a school or a boy's house and there would be Woody Hayes coming out! Now I've got to make those Eastern trips every week or so, or Woody will murder us because you know the kind of impression Woody makes in the home."

Woody has a proud boast that he tries to recruit only the "quality kid," and he isn't talking about the quality of the block the kid can throw or the way he can run Woody's FULLBACK 26. "I've found," says Woody, "that the better the person he is, the better his potential as a player regardless of his skill potential. So I look for that good home background and a good relationship between the boy and his family."

When Woody thinks he's found it he puts on a performance in that living room which, even if the kid doesn't wind up at Ohio State, usually has the parents pulling for Woody.

Many of these he will visit at least twice. On the advice of the assistant coach who has the boy on his list, Woody will visit the kid early in the recruiting season to establish his personal interest in him. Near "closing time," Woody will often make a second visit. More about "closing time" later.

On the first visit, Woody starts talking about education, and it doesn't take long before the Mom and Pop realize they have an evangelistic expert in their midst. The kid may have pro dreams first and foremost in his skull but Woody convinces the parents that a pro contract is not the priority.

Meanwhile, Woody is probing gently but warmly into the whole family situation, and no matter what the Dad does for a living Woody Hayes is able to talk shop with him and make it real, knowledgeable and concerned.

He'll talk cooking with the mother and she'll think Woody spends his weekends in the kitchen. Once he spied an antique watch in a glass case in the family's living room, examined it, recognized its origins and maker and told the family more about the watch than they knew themselves.

What Woody Hayes is doing is selling himself—and Ohio State by extension. When he gets around to football, which he does easily and naturally, Woody tells the boy what he thinks his potential is, and how Woody would use him at Ohio State. No matter how verified-great the kid is, Woody won't tell him he'll start as a freshman. "It's up to you, son," he may say. "We'll be looking at you and if you're better than the holdover who figures to start for us, all you've got to do is prove it."

And then Woody will lean forward, his face a cram course in sincerity, and deliver the ethical clincher, something like: "But remember the key thing, son: You've got to prove it."

An hour and a half with Woody is an evening's entertainment and over-the-back-fence fare for a week for the average middle-class family. A housewife on Long Island actually told a visitor, her voice still tinged with the wonder of it, "He sat right where you're sitting now . . . right there on the couch. Can you *imagine!*" The visitor got the impression that she had come slightly barmy and unstuck over the honor paid their hearth, but it just happens to be the impression Woody Hayes leaves on some people.

In this particular case, the boy passed up Ohio State for Penn State, but Woody knows he can't get 'em all. And his basic pitch is still to sell the entire family rather than concentrating just on the boy.

In the intense, all-out recruiting war, there is no gambit, no ploy, no chore that can stop Woody in looking for an edge. Particularly when it can help sell Ohio State to a recruit's entire family. And especially when it jibes with Woody's honest and sincere life-style.

Lou McCullough, Woody's recruiting coordinator a few years ago (and now athletic director at Iowa State) was roused on Christmas morning by a phone call. "Lou, it's Christmas," Woody began (as if McCullough didn't know), "and I want you to come over here and split this list of recruits with me."

McCullough sensed what was coming next and he was right. "I think we should sit down and call all these kids and wish their families a Merry Christmas," Woody added.

Which is exactly what Hayes and McCullough did. For the next four hours they were on the phone, wishing a Merry Christmas to more than a hundred recruits. "It put a heck of a dent in my own Christmas," said McCullough, "but you just never question Woody's recruiting whims."

Despite his charm, finesse and supersalesmanship, Woody will often get a great football player merely by being bluntly honest in a situation where all the palaver in the world simply won't work.

A few years ago there was a six-four, 228-pound farm boy who lived in Teays Valley, just seventeen miles down the road from Columbus. His tiny high school played in a small-school league which big-time recruiters almost never scouted.

Ohio State never came around to see him. But by mid-February the Buckeye staff began hearing reports that the kid had been a terror and that Notre Dame, Purdue, Michigan and others were after him. "Somebody get out there and check his film," Woody snapped. An assistant went out, checked the film, met the boy and came back gibbering. But it was too late. The boy was miffed that no one had come around earlier and had just about decided to go to Michigan.

Woody went out to see him. "Son," he said, "you know, of course, that Ohio State is a fullback school and you're a great fullback. Okay, we goofed and didn't come after you, and your pride has been hurt. Well, I don't blame you. Pride is a great thing to have. No real football player should be without it."

Then Woody leaned forward and fixed the kid with steely blue eyes. "But if I were you, I wouldn't let pride get in the way of making the right decision. That's one time when pride isn't the priority."

That was all Woody said. Harold "Champ" Henson came to Ohio State. As a sophomore in 1972 he led the nation in scoring with twenty touchdowns. He injured his knee early in 1973, requiring surgery, but was back pawing the ground ready for another great season in 1974.

# 13
# Making the Sale

"A foreign VIP invited to Washington . . . and given the red-carpet treatment by the State Department is not greeted and treated as warmly and obsequiously as a seventeen- or eighteen-year-old blue-chip prospect visiting a big-time football campus."

—Tug Wilson,
Former Commissioner of
the Big Ten

\* \* \*

Eventually, the stage is set for the final prospects to make the all-important visit to the Ohio State campus. In any competition for the truly great ones, there is a limit to the number of weekends a boy has available, especially if he also is playing basketball or wrestling in the winter. Some will collect campuses just to be a big man in their high school corridors and will knock themselves out visiting ten or more colleges. The wiser ones, counseled by their high school coach or a knowing parent, will limit their trips to perhaps five.

When Ohio State, Michigan, Penn State, Notre Dame, Purdue, Nebraska, Colorado and Southern California are vying for the same boy it becomes a battle just to get on his travel list. Rarely does Ohio State fail to get into the finals —and nearly all of the 125 prospects make the visit. It always comes as a small shock when the Buckeyes can't at least get a boy to look them over.

Woody thinks that's demeaning to Ohio State and to Buckeye football. It isn't often he feels insulted. Maybe in 125 prospects contacted, one will say flat out he isn't interested. It's tough for a boy not to at least be impressed by a contact from Ohio State; he's heard of the legendary Woody Hayes; and if he's going big-time, what better basis of comparison is there than a visit to that great, gray concrete horseshoe and a talk with the most famous college coach in the business? That's the way Woody views it.

The boy may not wind up going there, but he and his high school coach know that news of a visit to Ohio State makes him more merchandisable. The mere word that Woody Hayes covets him as a prime prospect confirms for Notre Dame, Penn State, Purdue or whomever that they'll have to go all-out in competing for him.

So, the blue-chipper consents to a legal limit forty-eight-hour visit to Ohio State. It's a visit that will be orchestrated and programed every moment of the route.

The date, first of all, will be anywhere between the first weekend in January and mid-March. The boy's primary host will be one of Woody Hayes' nine assistants. For instance, Clausen. There will be anywhere from eight to a dozen recruits coming in on a single weekend. Each coach will host a couple each. Clausen will make sure of two things: that he'll be able to give maximum attention to them, and that if a kid is a quarterback or a hotshot tailback, that he'll be the only quarterback or hotshot tailback visiting Ohio State that weekend. There's nothing so delicate as having two super-supers at the same position meeting head to head on the same visit. Of course the kids realize they're not the only All-Everything being wooed for their position, but why look for psychological trouble?

So Woody's assistants consult the master list and do a juggling act. Incidentally, they will have to take into consideration that a blue-chipper may be spending several weekends all over the collegiate map and his Ohio State visit will have to be sandwiched into his schedule too.

Okay, let's zero in on a typical visit which Clausen has set up for a kid coming in from New Jersey or Long Island. The date has been cleared and an airline ticket either has been sent to him or will be waiting for him at the ticket counter at Kennedy, LaGuardia or Newark airport.

Often the boy will show up in Columbus wearing a sports jacket and tie, but a surprising number of kids flaunt their cool by arriving in blue jeans and either a windbreaker or their high school letterman's jacket. Some—the poorer boys—just have no choice in the matter. Neither Woody nor the assistant coach acting as primary host shows the slightest flicker of expression. One thing you can't do is embarrass the boy. A casual but well-meant offer to obtain a jacket from an Ohio State footballer for the recruit to wear to dinner can cost you points.

But "a foreign VIP invited to Washington, put up at Blair House and given a red-carpet treatment by the State Department, is not greeted and treated as warmly and obsequiously as is a seventeen- or eighteen-year-old blue-chip prospect visiting a big-time football campus." So says Tug Wilson, former commissioner of the Big Ten.

The NCAA says the boy's forty-eight hours on campus

can be the only expense-paid visit he can make to each school. So during those forty-eight hours, wherever he goes, his hosts are going to do a selling job designed to convince him this is the place for him, and not Notre Dame, Michigan, Southern Cal or wherever. Supposedly the school a boy is visiting on any given weekend is selling itself. It frequently doesn't work that way, however, and on a visit to School A a superstar may face a full campaign against School B—dozens of cogent reasons why he shouldn't go there. This is called "negative recruiting," and some football factories are notorious for it.

Upon his arrival in Columbus, the recruit is met at the airport by the assistant coach who is orchestrating his visit. He takes him out to the campus and immediately introduces him to a varsity player who will serve as the recruit's host. The selection is very carefully made. The varsity host must be a friendly, high-class kid who isn't about to break out a bottle of booze or liberally sprinkle his conversation with profanity. He also has to be understanding of the recruiting mission and its concepts, and most of all he has to be a kid who sincerely likes Ohio State as a university and as a place to play football. At every big-time football school there are a few players who don't measure up to this prototype and who could kill you if they hosted a recruit.

Entertainment will vary from campus to campus, depending on the degree of sophistication of the city or town involved. Sumptuous dining and campus parties are mixed in with elaborate tours of the facilities. On some campuses, sex is an explicit recruiting tool. Some football staffs have been known to cherish a card file of available coeds, who by rights should be entitled to varsity letters for services performed. A date with a downtown go-go dancer has done the job in some places.

At Ohio State, Woody Hayes runs a YMCA operation by comparison. The recruit will spend Friday and Saturday night rooming with the varsity man in his room. The host will get him a date for a Saturday night party, or perhaps just take him to a party where there'll be an informal group, or maybe take him to a rock concert on campus. If the Ohio State basketball team is playing at home Saturday night they'll go to St. John Arena, a spectacle in itself with a 13,000-plus crowd in the beautiful basketball facility.

There'll be sumptuous dinners Friday and Saturday night at two of the best dining spots, accompanied by both the student host and the assistant coach. On Saturday night it might well be at the Top of the Center, a plush spot high atop one of Columbus' modern skyscrapers. As the party enters the room, the four-piece combo on the bandstand will break into the Ohio State fight song, and then the leader will step to the mike and allow as how that little intro was in deference to young Al Rackadovich, a fullback from Cinder Hollow, New York, who just might become a Buckeye.

Cheers from the other assembled diners. A flourish by the captain of the waiters as he spreads a menu the size of a scoreboard before the recruit. An abashed look on the face of the boy. Holy cow! How 'bout this! Geez, they know me already!

He may be one of those kids who showed up in blue jeans and high school letter jacket; ordinarily he wouldn't be allowed in at the tradesman's entrance looking like that, but at the moment he feels as well set up as though he were already an All-America.

If the boy is a can't-miss, super blue-chipper, All-State, All-America, All-World, then Woody Hayes himself may sit in on the dinner, all *gemütlich* charm as he gently offers up cogent reasons why the kid should become a Buckeye.

Between the assistant coach and the varsity host, the recruit gets to see the campus and inspect the athletic facilities. He sees the scarlet-carpeted varsity locker room and the array of impressive training and therapeutic devices. And for once he is treated to a training quarters that smells more like flowers than Eau d' Sweat Sock.

If a boy has already professed an interest in engineering, liberal arts, law, medicine, veterinary medicine, physical education or whatever, Woody has arranged for him to spend an hour with the dean of that particular school. The dean knows that Woody's interest in education is for real, and he's delighted in any case to meet a ham-handed tackle who has an honest interest in his particular field.

"Some of our best recruiting," says Woody, "is done by professors who don't know a lateral pass from a fullback draw, but they sure know how to answer a boy's questions." Then Woody smiles. "I guess they also like to see winners in any university department and if we tell 'em a kid is a heckuva football player as well as a fine student they'll show as much zeal as any of my assistant coaches."

On a football recruiting weekend Woody spreads himself very thin. If ten kids are in town he has to make himself available to all. And part of his guileless selling ability is his utter lack of pretension.

At many big-time football schools, the head coach is ensconced in an office just a smidgen smaller than that of the chairman of the board of U.S. Steel, with carpeting and furnishings to match. A recruit steps into an office like that and he knows—he just knows instantly—that it's the most important inner sanctum he's ever going to enter in all his life. That's the impression he gets when he visits Bear Bryant at Alabama, or John McKay at Southern Cal, or Ara Parseghian at Notre Dame and many others.

Walking into Woody's office on a Saturday afternoon, he's immediately struck by the fact that the Great Man's private precincts are smaller and less ornate than the assistant principal's back home in high school. About nine by twelve feet, with plain metal Venetian blinds on the single window. A plain metal desk, with a single visitor's chair in front of it. Not a leather chair. Just a functional metal chair straight out of an office-furnishings catalog.

Until 1973 the floor was garden-variety nondescript plastic tile. Then somebody covered the tile with some inexpensive red carpeting which Woody immediately felt was a frill. The total look is Parole Officer Functional.

The door to Woody's office is only a stride from the desk of his secretary, Lena Biscuso, and when a recruit shows up for a chat, Woody is right there to greet him as though he's known the kid all his life. The distinction is made by an Eastern blue-chipper who, although he never signed on as a Buckeye, described to a writer his introduction to, for instance, Ara Parseghian, during his visit to Notre Dame.

According to the boy (who ultimately went to a Big Eight school), he had his grand tour and fine meals in South Bend and then was given to feel that the greatest thrill in his life lay in store for him. He was about to be ushered into The Presence. And so he was. He was shown into this spacious, soft-lighted office where Ara Parseghian sat behind a huge desk in regal splendor. Except that Ara was sitting in a rich leather swivel chair—with his back to the boy. As the boy entered, Parseghian swiveled around slowly, imperiously. He eyed the kid coolly and his first words were: "What do you weigh? How tall are you?"

The boy, a Catholic who had gone to a Catholic high school, later recalled he couldn't wait to get out of there.

Woody Hayes' first words are more likely to be: "I hope you remember the things you see here so you can go back home and tell your family about them."

Woody takes a last crack at a boy on Sunday morning when he joins him for breakfast, usually a gargantuan brunch for all the weekend recruits at the university golf course. Everything that needed to be said has already been done so by this time, but Woody uses these final moments to try to get a reading on how much a recruit has enjoyed his visit. If he senses all has gone well he may ask the boy for a commitment. Often a boy will tell Woody on the spot that he is coming to Ohio State. Sometimes he'll tell Woody he still has one or two more visits elsewhere but that he'll make up his mind right after his final visit.

Woody doesn't press at this point. The instinctive salesman, he knows that a boy who has already made three or four visits to big-time schools has been developing some rather sophisticated (and inflated) ideas of his worth as a football player. A lot of big-time coaches have been phoning him weekly at home or have visited him personally. The kid knows he doesn't have to make a final decision until late February or even March or April.

But even when things are going their best, Woody's staff knows he is capable of strange things than can cost them a prospect. A few years ago the Bucks were recruiting the two top quarterbacks in the state. Billy Boyle of Columbus was rated number one by one wire service. Bob Bobrowski of Cleveland was top-rated by the other. Ohio State was after both of them. Two days before Bobrowski made his visit, Boyle committed to Ohio State.

The assistant coach who was wooing Bobrowski was having a fantastically successful visit with him. Everything was falling into place. Everyone felt that Bobrowski, too, would say he was coming before the weekend was over.

At six o'clock Saturday night, just as Bobrowski was getting ready to go out to dinner, Woody Hayes appeared at the dormitory where Bobrowski was staying. "I just want you to know something, Bob," Woody began. "Billy Boyle announced a couple days ago that he was coming to Ohio State."

Bobrowski stared at Hayes strangely, not knowing quite how to react, not quite knowing why Woody had said what he did.

"By the next morning," says an assistant coach, "we knew we had a troubled and confused Bobrowski to deal with. Instead of committing right then and there as we'd expected him to, he put us off. A week later he announced he was going to Purdue."

Nobody ever figured out why Woody did what he had. Was it a typical bit of impetuous, Hayesian honesty? Was he simply warning Bobrowski that the quarterback position was up for grabs? Or was he telling Bobrowski that he already thought Boyle was the better prospect? It baffled everybody.

Boyle never lived up to his promise and dropped off the squad as a junior. Bobrowski went on to stardom at Purdue.

No one knows, either, when Woody's instinct will tell him a recruiting mistake is about to surface. A big, six-six, 250-pounder had been avidly recruited on Long Island as a defensive tackle. Defense all the way. That's where the kid wanted to play. That's where he figured his best chances would be. Defense all the way, said the assistant coach romancing him.

Woody came in to visit the boy. Something didn't click. Something about the kid that didn't impress Woody. But he talked to the recruit with seemingly great enthusiasm. Except that Woody was suddenly telling the boy that he thought he'd make a fine offensive tackle. Offense, all the way. The boy, who'd already committed to Ohio State, changed his mind and went to Penn State.

*    *    *

Unfortunately, in a business where survival at any cost is the bottom-line philosophy, the critical and unvarnished desire to win becomes Priority Number One. The hanky-panky follows. Not in all places, of course, and not by all coaches. But one knowledgeable observer has said, "There isn't a college or university among those listed by the NCAA as major football powers that doesn't bend, break or fracture the spirit or letter of the rules. Not one. From the football factories to the hallowed—and hypocritical—Ivies."

That's what the man said. And he'd been in sports for forty years as player, coach and high-level administrator.

The rationale among coaches and alumni is that everyone does it, right? So we just have to protect ourselves, right? Besides, any sin we commit against the book is just a mere wrinkle compared to some of those others, right?

So, if it's just a matter of degree, it's like a father finding his unwed daughter six weeks pregnant but, shucks, that's not *very* pregnant, is it?

But if anyone thinks a new roof for a recruit's house is

the going price for football talent he's short-changing the system. This is small-time stuff. And Woody conceded that if anything will ever wreck collegiate sports it will be recruiting excesses. Woody names no names, fingers no colleges, blows no whistles on anybody, but his face drops off moodily and vexatiously as he talks about it.

It is a documented fact that poverty-level quarterbacks or fullbacks who have gone through four years of high school with a single pair of pants and a taped-together pair of sneakers suddenly emerge in the late winter of their senior year looking like four pages out of a *Playboy* fashion section. From then on, they are "committed" to someone, as the saying goes.

At certain colleges a boy is promised he'll have a "sponsor." Translated, that means he'll have a local, affluent businessman or alumnus who treasures those 50-yard line tickets and a sycophantic first-name relationship with the coach. Further translation: does the boy need clothes? a car for every weekend? spending money? money for transportation home on holidays? You name it and the sponsor will find a discreet way to provide it.

A prep star from New Jersey comes home from a recruiting visit, puts his hand in his raincoat pocket and pulls out an envelope he didn't know was there. Inside is five hundred dollars in fifty-dollar bills. A simple hand-printed note reads: "This is just for openers, of course."

A Long Island halfback with dazzling rushing stats is told that if he opts for a Southwest school his parents will have a Magic Carpet of unique and impressive style. A Texas oil millionaire's private jet makes weekly business trips to New York and back, and it'd be no problem for the parents to fly out and see the boy play every Saturday. Twice-told tales about high school phenoms receiving $5000 as recruiting inducements are not out of line.

Bubba Smith, the monster defensive star of the Oakland Raiders, has publicly told of the beefy alumnus of one school who breezed into his home in Texas during his senior year in high school. The alumnus confidently tossed a set of keys onto a table, then gestured out the window.

"That's yours, Bubba," he said grandly, "if you come with us."

What was Bubba's, if he wanted to accept, was a flashy new convertible. It so happens that Bubba didn't accept and went to Michigan State.

When former Ohio State and New York Jets' star Matt Snell was being recruited, his mother and father were offered just about every household appliance that could fit into their home, including a refrigerator, a stove, a dishwasher, a washing machine, a dryer, a freezer and a few other gaudy ornaments of our technological age.

The Snells thought they could do without.

"Woody knew the things the recruiters from a lot of other colleges were promising me," Snell recalls. "He leaned over at me across the desk in his office and said: 'You're not going to get a thing under this table. I'm not going to promise you anything I can't deliver and I'm not going to deliver anything I can't promise you.' Then he shook a finger at me. 'You know darn well that if I'm dishonest with you I'm going to be dishonest with a lot of other kids, and you probably don't want to play ball for a guy who's going around being dishonest all over the place.' I knew then that I wanted to play for the man."

It isn't just that Woody Hayes has a moral aversion to that kind of recruiting. One of his more succinct observations comes from his practical nature: "Dirty money leaves tracks!" says Woody.

And Woody also isn't willing to ignore the scholastic requirements. In a glumly frank moment he says, "The academic qualification just may be the biggest problem in the recruiting business today. Undoubtedly, too many boys are being tendered scholarships who just aren't students enough to know or ever care about what the primary purpose of college is all about—which is to get a meaningful education."

In other words, kids who put in four years of college ball merely as their apprenticeship for the pros.

Chuck Clausen, who has had to pass up a few recruiting prospects on academic grounds, has never thought even once—let alone twice—about shortcuts or side-door entrances for a kid. "My God," he shudders, "I'd hate to see one of our coaches try it and have Woody catch him at it. Getting fired would be the pleasantest part of the scene." He pauses and grins reflectively. "A double-hundred megaton. Right off the Richter scale."

*     *     *

If the boy doesn't commit on his visit to Ohio State, it's back to the drawing board. The assistant coach has to make more visits to his home, more drop-in visits to catch the kid during a free period at school, more sessions with the kid's high school coach to try to gain some leverage from him. Then, if the boy has seen all the schools on his list and still hasn't made up his mind, there is one more pilgrimage by Woody.

This is the "closing" visit. If the boy hasn't yet chosen Ohio State, Woody's visit is designed to improve the odds, and the master salesman and psychologist is expert at closing the sale—getting a firm commitment where that's possible.

If the boy finally says yes, he's coming, Woody extends his hand and smiles. "Son," he says, "once you shake my hand I consider it a binding promise. So if you still have any doubts I don't want you to shake my hand."

So sacred does Woody Hayes consider this gesture of acceptance that when a boy reneges any time after The Handshake, Woody is apt to unload a hundred-megaton on the spot. The assistant coach who has to call Woody to tell him of a defection does so with great reluctance. "I can tell from what follows," says one assistant, "that he has flung the phone all the way across the room and up against the wall."

A former assistant recalls Woody in one of his most inflamed moments when a boy phoned Woody personally to tell him he was going to Michigan instead of Ohio State.

"You're going to Michigan?" Woody screamed, his voice beginning to climb into the higher decibel ranges. "Why, you dumb no-good bleep-bleep! You go right ahead! You go there, and when you play against Ohio State we'll just see whether you gain a yard against us all day. We'll break you in two! We'll . . ."

And on and on in the same vein. Woody lost more than just the fullback on that exchange. He'd also been recruiting an end from the same high school. The end had already committed to Ohio State, but somehow got disenchanted when the fullback reported Woody's outburst, and he went to Michigan, too.

In the Big Ten, written tenders (actual contracts) of an offer of athletic scholarship may not be sent out to prospective athletes until February 20. Once a boy receives the tender he has ten days in which to accept and sign it. If he fails to sign within ten days it is considered a pocket veto and he may not attend the school that sent it to him. During this ten-day period, the school is not allowed to contact him.

"Consequently," says Woody, "we rarely send a tender to a boy until he has committed to us verbally that he's coming."

But signing a Big Ten tender only locks up the boy as far as the Big Ten is concerned. He may still sign tenders in several different leagues. But by a date in March designated by the NCAA, he must sign a so-called national tender. In essence, he must then make his final choice among two or more conferences.

So, between the time a boy has signed a Buckeye tender for the Big Ten, and the signing of the national tender, a blue-chipper who has still not made up his mind is subject to plenty of pressure. In fact, this is usually where the most inventive and elaborate hanky-panky comes in. Governors, congressmen, and presidents of TV networks and huge corporations have been known to be among the heavy-caliber hotshots who have pitched in. In Ohio many was the time a big, black limousine would pull up in front of a boy's home, and stepping out would be Jimmy Rhodes, at that time governor of the state. The incumbent, John Gilligan, reportedly uses the telephone or telegram to come to Woody's aid.

Another Buckeye recruiter is John Galbreath of Columbus, one of the nation's biggest builders and real estate developers, and owner of the Pittsburgh Pirates and the Dapper Dan racing stable, which has given him a couple of Kentucky Derby winners. Some of Galbreath's biggest kicks, however, come from his recruiting efforts on behalf of the Buckeyes.

Yet even when a boy tells Woody flat out that he's coming, the Ohio State staff can take no chances. Relying on a heavily recruited boy to mail back his signed national tender can be the worst mistake the salesman ever makes. The NCAA ruling says the boy may not be signed before 8:00 A.M. local time, so somebody from the coaching staff—or a trusted alumnus in the boy's area—takes the tender by hand and is parked outside the kid's house by 7:45 A.M. to make sure that independents such as Penn State, Pitt, Notre Dame or an emissary from another league doesn't sneak by you and con the boy into signing their national tender.

A Long Island alumnus who was asked by the Ohio State staff to get out of bed at 5:00 A.M. so he could be down in New Jersey outside a boy's house by 7:30 mumbled to himself, "My God, what am I doing? This is a seventeen-year-old kid!"

But he got up. And he went.

# 14
# The Off·Season and the Pros

"A pro scout never assumes any privileges with Woody. You wait until you're *invited* to spend intimate moments with him . . . you have to have *permission* to do such and such. That's the general in him . . . his sense of orderly procedure."

—Jim Trimble,
Director, Player Personnel,
New York Giants

\* \* \*

Woody is totally alone now, more so than at any time during the year. He is deep within himself, within the lifestyle that only he can understand—a man completely devoted to the perfection of his art, to the exclusion of all else. Thus goes July . . .

\* \* \*

Like many other big-time coaches, Woody Hayes wants a boy to be thinking football all year round. It's just about the first thing a kid senses once he becomes immersed in the way Woody does things. He will find, for instance, that preparation for any succeeding year will actually start in the winter, just a couple of weeks after the kids return from Christmas vacation.

The NCAA expressly forbids a formal, supervised winter program for football players, but there is enough subtle peer pressure and self-motivation to draw every kid on the squad into Woody's weight-and-running program. And as vigorous as it may be on a voluntary basis, the program falls far short of some of the abuses in college football reported recently.

In *Meat on the Hoof,* a bitter expose of football at the University of Texas, by Gary Shaw, a former Longhorn player, Shaw comments: "What they do to those kids is nothing short of criminal. When a boy doesn't measure up, they put him out there in head-knocking drills until he quits. They've left cripples all over the state of Texas." The process is called "running off the undesirables."

A year ago, players at Florida State complained they were being dehumanized and brutalized because during winter drills they were placed under chicken-wire enclosures, just four feet high, and then told to wrestle to exhaustion without ever being able to stand up.

An Ohio State assistant coach, commenting on drills like that, makes a soundless whistle. "I wouldn't want to be the assistant coach who suggested practices like that to Woody Hayes. Woody wouldn't even give him time to clean out his desk." He reconsidered for an instant. "Well, maybe he would, at that, but the guy wouldn't be able to sit down while doing it."

Woody expects his kids to report at least three afternoons a week for an hour and a half of weight lifting and running. The weight lifting is not designed to produce the rippling muscles of a Mr. America contest, and nobody is going to impress the track coach with his speed or stamina, but the three days will keep the kids very well toned up, thank you.

Woody, incidentally, has some rather pungent views of weight lifters per se. "One of the most important elements in a football player's ability is strength," says Woody, "but even though pure weight lifters are the strongest guys around they'd be lousy football players. Do you know why? Because as big and powerful as they are, they couldn't produce. They're too egocentric. They could never subject themselves to a team principle. They couldn't sacrifice. They like to stand in front of mirrors and admire their muscles, but they couldn't take getting hit."

At any rate, by the time spring drills start the first week in April there are few, if any, kids who aren't ready to knock your head off the first time he hits you. If he isn't, he isn't going to make the ball club.

The coaches at Ohio State will tell you that the time to make the varsity is in spring training. "This is Woody's war within the family," as one of them puts it. "There's no opponent to wage it against. It's a war between the offense and defense right here on our own battleground. There's ol' General Woody over there on his side of the field whipping together the best set of offensive troops he can find, getting them ready for next fall. And the best way he can evaluate them is to put them against the defense, and everybody grinds meat."

Everybody "grinds meat" because George Hill and his staff are doing the exact same thing on defense—looking for the best defenders who must prove themselves against the most ferocious stuff Woody can throw at them.

The kids know this is the way it is. They know—and are told over and over again—that this is when they're going to make it or not. Shortly after spring training ends with the annual intrasquad game of Reds versus Whites, the coaches will sit down and decide what their first two line-ups will be, going into fall practice. After everybody returns the last week in August to prepare for the opener, there is very little reshuffling of personnel unless somebody is injured, somebody goofs up, or a second stringer comes back with a god-awful charge of motivation. But on Day One in the fall, the first team-designate is just that until circumstances dictate otherwise.

Rules laid down by the Big Ten limit spring practice to twenty days over a thirty-day period. This gives Woody a chance to pass up days of bad weather and take advantages of better field conditions. But before the first pads are pulled on, usually the first week in April, another and just as spirited war of sorts has been waged by Woody's two staffs. It's called "Who gets whom" and it takes place in a concentrated two-week period in late March, after the major recruiting drive is over.

The type of football player who comes to Ohio State, or to Notre Dame, Southern Cal, and other big-time football schools, is such a tough, dedicated athlete that he can often fit in at two or three positions, no matter what he was recruited for.

So, going into the spring season, each coach makes an assessment of his needs and then prepares for what often turns into a donnybrook with other coaches—both offense and defense. This is the time for the switcheroos, and the absolute need for the assistant coaches to produce the best results at their assignments. They all want the best material to work with, and they all want to protect, often with ill-concealed frenzy, the riches they have at their position.

A linebacker coach needs help and thinks there's a spare defensive end who'd make a great linebacker. The offensive guard coach wants to shore up his position that seems a bit thin. How about moving so-and-so from defensive tackle? The kid has good agility and would be great at blocking down on linebackers. ("Yeah, maybe so," says the tackle coach, "but I don't think one of those freshmen tackles is going to come on and do the job for me, and I can't spare so-and-so.") An offensive halfback who didn't play too much as a freshman or sophomore seems, nevertheless, to be a hard-nosed kid with quick reactions. "I need a little help at the open-side halfback," says the defensive back-field coach. (Warily: "Well, let's think about it for a while, and we'll see . . .")

All proposed switches are dutifully proposed to Woody. Sometimes he'll deliver a flat-out, cussedly emphatic "Hell, no!" to somebody's idea for a switch. And no amount of argument or practicality will budge him. Other times he'll stay out of it until he sees how the two staffs are working things out, and will then accept whatever decision is made. In any event, no switch is final until Woody okays it.

"Sometimes he'll make up his mind on the basis of best available facts and circumstance," says one coach. "Other times, I swear, he'll just fly his instincts and damn if he doesn't turn out to be right. Meanwhile, it can be pretty hairy waiting to see how things work out because there's just no time to go back and do it all over again."

The spring of 1973 found one of the strangest switches ever made in an Ohio State football camp (or anywhere, for that matter!). Defensive halfback coach Dick Walker counted up his pluses and minuses and decided he wasn't happy. And what he wanted at cornerback was Steve Luke.

Steve Luke? Steve Luke was an offensive center, for Pete's sake!

A switch from offensive center to defensive halfback would normally raise a lot of eyebrows, but Luke, at 193 pounds, had probably been a mite light at center in 1972 as a backup for starter Steve Meyers. But he was quick, tough, and as coaches like to describe certain players, "a helluva athlete." Translated, this means the kid can do anything expected of him; all you have to do is ask.

When Walker saw he wouldn't be getting much flak from the offensive center coach, he marched straight off to Woody. "This kid can play cornerback for us," he said flatly. "Let me get him ready this spring."

"He should be tough against the run," Woody noted, "because we know he likes to hit. But let's see how long it takes him to learn not to get fooled by options and the pass. Let's try it."

With only twenty practice days in which to make a switch, Woody and his coaches have to give a cram course. Not only on the field but in countless film sessions which point up the various situations the kid will find in the new job.

On opening day, September 15 against Minnesota, a team that featured a tricky veer offense that can be rough on cornerbacks, Steve Luke started and starred in the Buckeyes' defensive secondary.

He was just one of two major switches made in the springtime. Bruce Elia had come to Ohio State as a potential star at fullback. He played the position with the Jayvees as a sophomore and looked good—but it didn't look as though he'd ever beat out six-four, 225-pound Champ

Henson, another sophomore who just happened to tear the place apart in his first year to lead the nation in scoring. Behind Henson was a good junior, Randy Keith.

What do you do with a tough kid like Elia when there are two fullbacks ahead of him? If you coach linebackers and need a good backup man you sweet-talk offensive backfield coach Rudy Hubbard into letting him go. Rudy said okay. But Woody was something else. A fullback is to Woody Hayes as a bottle of exotic perfume is to a lovely woman: you can never have enough of it.

Elia wanted very much to go to linebacker. He knew he'd play there. Woody still wasn't sure. There was a lot of strained dialogue between Woody, his coaches and the kid. Elia sort of ducked Woody on the practice field in the spring, making sure he spent most of his time at the defensive end of the drill field. Woody kept lusting for him as a fullback; Elia kept thinking of himself as a nose-for-the-ball linebacker. Somehow he won the little war of nerves and put in his twenty days in the linebacking post. By September he was backup man to Captain Rick Middleton, one of the senior starters, and was logging a lot of playing time, the happiest kid on the block.

In the Buckeyes' second game Champ Henson suffered a torn knee ligament. Randy Keith, who had been projected as his backup, had flunked out of school. On the Sunday after Henson's injury Woody let it be know that it was very nice that Bruce Elia had spent all that spring training time learning the linebacking trade, but from this moment on, Bruce Elia was now the Bucks' number one fullback.

On Monday Elia took over the position and Woody wore one of his happy smiles as Elia continued where Champ Henson left off, tearing up the Big Ten turf for thirteen touchdowns, looking as though FULLBACK 26 and FULLBACK 27 had been his natural habitat.

For 1974, with Henson recovered and sophomore Pete Johnson a talented understudy, Bruce Elia was slated for another springtime refresher course and an eventual move into a regular linebacker spot by opening game.

It is at this critical time that it becomes apparent, according to Woody, why big-time college coaching can be tougher than pro coaching. "The pros not only sign the cream of the cream," says Woody, "but they can keep their stars for six, eight, ten years or more. They're working with proven talent and don't have to be concerned so much with finding and blending in newcomers in key spots. A college coach loses his senior stars every year and a good many of his players are starters for only a single season."

\*  \*  \*

A feature of just about any Buckeye spring practice session is the presence of anywhere up to a dozen pro scouts on the sidelines. This is the time of year when the pros do most of their talent bird-dogging and there isn't a spring when there aren't several of Woody's kids to be checked out. Some may only be sophomores or juniors, but the scouts want to see tham as often as possible.

It happens that Hayes isn't particularly fond of the pro game and has said so publicly. "It can't compare with the college game for diversification of offense," he points out. "And the figures show that college teams run off an average of twenty more plays a game than the pros. About seventy-five to fifty-five per team. At Ohio State, because of our conditioning program and because we don't dally a lot in the huddle, we often run as many as eighty-five or eighty-eight plays a game.

"The colleges outscore the pros by plenty," he continues, "and the growing presence of the running quarterback in college gives the fan a whole new element of excitement."

Still, Woody is courteous and helpful when the scouts flock around. Jim Trimble, director of player personnel for the New York Giants, says that despite Woody's criticism of the game, he is not anti-pro football. "Anyone who says he is," claims Trimble, "is missing the point. It's just that Woody has such a love affair with the college game that it reflects his intense partiality. And I've never known him to be rude or uncooperative with a pro scout."

Alex Bell, roving scout for the BLESTO-V combine (Bears, Lions, Eagles, Steelers Talent Organization, plus Vikings) looks at it from a slightly different perspective. "I think Woody subconsciously favors pro scouts who once had head coaching positions in college.

"In my case," says Bell, "I'm always flattered that Woody allows me to roam around from group to group on the practice field to observe closely. Of course, I'd never dare stand near him or near the huddle when they're on offensive play drill. That's a privilege that Woody grants to nobody. Woody doesn't want strangers near when he's finding fault with things."

"As well as I know Woody," continues Trimble, who has been a good friend for more than twenty years, "I've learned that you never assume any privileges with him. You wait until you're *invited* to spend intimate moments with him and you have to have *permission* to do such and such. That's the general in him, his sense of privacy and orderly procedures. If a pro scout isn't doing too well with Woody it's because he hasn't learned this."

"One thing a pro scout better not do," added Bell, "is to criticize an Ohio State player. The scout can decide the boy isn't a pro prospect but he's got to leave it at that. Woody would hand the guy his head if he ever caught a scout criticizing one of his boys.

"Incidentally," Bell continues, "Woody is one of the more cooperative coaches in allowing us to weigh and measure his kids and talk to them. He has set up a scale and measuring device in a special office and allows us to take the kids there at their convenience. He knows the pros don't like to accept the stats given out by a lot of college publicity offices and allows us to do our own thing. Woody treats us as professional career people who are trying to do our job. In fact, he's proud to see so many of his boys make it in the pros. It's a tribute to their ability and the job he has done on them."

Some colleges designate one full day in the spring, called "Pro Day," in which the scouts have the kids entirely to themselves—measuring, weighing, timing, visiting, and so forth. Woody is cooperative, but he wouldn't turn his squad over for a whole day to the combined resurrections of Walter Camp, Knute Rockne and Vince Lombardi. That'd be stealing a day out of Woody's own coaching life.

Woody has also set up a special screening room and private projector for the bird-doggers and they can get the door key at any time from Woody's secretary. Assistant coaches will set aside special reels for the pros to check out and will answer any questions. The pros have their own questionnaire for vital information on a prospect, but Woody will have nothing to do with it himself. He has his assistants fill them out, and rarely does he even bother to see what has been notated. On page 210, for example, is the Ohio State pro evaluation sheet on John Hicks, the All-America tackle and winner of the 1973 Outland Trophy and Lombardi Trophy as the nation's top college lineman.

Both Bell and Trimble feel Woody is rarely if ever, wrong when he decides to make a personal evaluation of a boy's potential. "A lot of All-Americas flop as pros," says Bell, "but when Woody told us about John Brockington and Jack Tatum he simply stated they couldn't miss, and looking in his face and from the way he said it, you just knew they were going to make it big."

"Once in a while," said Trimble, "I'll make some mild dissent against Woody's opinion. Such as when I was negotiating for the Giants with John Hicks. Woody told me Hicks was the greatest lineman he ever had—even better than Jim Parker, who was a perennial all-pro with the Colts.

" 'You can't mean that, Woody,' I said. 'Nobody is better than Parker. Jim was bigger and stronger.'

" 'Hicks is just as strong,' said Woody, 'and he has better feet.' Woody will always come up with that one fine distinction that ends any argument.

"By the way," said Trimble, "it's absolutely not true that Woody doesn't understand the forward pass. I can jam that down the throat of anyone who says it. I know. When I was starting out in the coaching business many years ago I got hold of—and never mind how I obtained it—a copy of Woody's playbook when he was coaching Miami of Ohio. He never knew this, but I plagarized his pass offense and took it all the way to the pros with me when I was head coach of the Philadelphia Eagles.

"If Woody has grown away from the pass it's not because he doesn't believe in its effectiveness but because of the perfection he has brought to his ground game. Nobody has

BLESTO-VIII SENIOR COLLEGE REPORT — FALL, 1973

Date **10** /**12** / **73**

Player's Name **HICKS**  **JOHN**  School **OHIO STATE UNIVERSITY**
  (last)  (first)

College Pos. **O.T.** Pro. Pos. **O.T./G** Height **6' 2½"** Weight **258** Age **22**

Speed Timed **4.8** 40 yds. _____ 50 yds. _____ 100 yds.

(SELECT ONE OF THE CATEGORIES THAT BEST DESCRIBES
THIS PROSPECT'S FUTURE POTENTIAL IN THE NFL. )

0. STARTER 1ST YEAR. WHY? Hicks is a very positive person and great athlete. He
 has exceptional quickness, balance and body control. An exceptional blocker, either on
 the run or on pass protection. Best blocking lineman we have seen on film.

1. MAKE NFL. WHY? _____

_____

2. PROSPECT. WHY? _____

_____

3. QUESTIONABLE PROSPECT. WHY? _____

_____

4. NOT RECOMMENDED. WHY? _____

_____

| RATING CODE |
|---|
| (0)- Starter 1st year   1 - Make NFL   2 - Prospect |
| 3 - Questionable Prospect   4 - Not Recommended |

(USING THE ABOVE RATING CODE, CIRCLE THE GRADE WHICH BEST
FITS THIS PROSPECT IN EACH OF THE INDIVIDUAL CATEGORIES. )

| Category | Grade | | | | | Category | Grade | | | | |
|---|---|---|---|---|---|---|---|---|---|---|---|
| Type of Athlete | (0) | 1 | 2 | 3 | 4 | Strength | 0 | (1) | 2 | 3 | 4 |
| Attitude | (0) | 1 | 2 | 3 | 4 | Agility | (0) | 1 | 2 | 3 | 4 |
| Character | (0) | 1 | 2 | 3 | 4 | Consistency | (0) | 1 | 2 | 3 | 4 |
| Football Intelligence | (0) | 1 | 2 | 3 | 4 | Balance | (0) | 1 | 2 | 3 | 4 |
| Competiveness | (0) | 1 | 2 | 3 | 4 | Aggressiveness | (0) | 1 | 2 | 3 | 4 |
| Quickness | (0) | 1 | 2 | 3 | 4 | Plays with Pain | (0) | 1 | 2 | 3 | 4 |

RETURN TO: BLESTO-VIII, 316 4th Avenue, Pittsburgh, Penna. 15222

SIGNATURE *Chuck Clausen*

2003235

Woody's pound-hell-outta-them personality and principles, and when you see an attack that so successfully mirrors the man himself, you stop wondering why he doesn't
fool around more with the pass."

* * *

Spring training at Ohio State culminates with the annual
Reds versus Whites intrasquad game the first Saturday in
May. General Woody splits the squad into two even camps
(allowing the kids themselves to help him), tosses out a ball
and invites them to knock hell out of each other—meanwhile displaying what they've learned in the previous
twenty practice sessions.

This is it for the kids. This is where they can nail down
varsity-designate status for that first week of fall practice.
The hitting is awesome. Only Michigan gets hit harder by
Buckeye players.

And there is a crowd of 20,000 on hand in Ohio Stadium
to see it. This for a spring intrasquad game, mind you. It
seems as though a couple thousand of them are pro scouts.

The week after the game is over, Woody and his staff
start evaluating the personnel based on spring performance. The things they expected, plus the surprises and
the disappointments, are put through a staff shake-well.
After a series of meetings Woody knows where he'll be
starting in on the last week of August when his squad returns for the start of another season.

By June the prospectus is finished. The staff takes July
off. But not Woody. He may have gotten away for some
hiking for a couple of weeks in June but the rest of the
summer he retires to his hideout in Biggs. Still going the
film route, studying last year's foes minutely if they are to
appear again on the Bucks' schedule. Again and again he

runs his own Ohio State stuff, including the spring game, focusing on things which need changing or improving.

He is totally alone now, more so than at any time during the year. He is deep within himself, within the life-style that only he can understand—a man completely devoted to the perfection of his art, to the exclusion of all else. Thus goes July . . .

In August his aides return. The interminable meetings commence once again. Plans that have lain cold in the files for a few weeks are heated up again.

College classes have not started yet when the team reports the last week in August for preseason practice. The close to a hundred candidates include the twenty-two to twenty-six freshmen which Ohio State signs each year. Woody has taken over four floors for the players in one of the men's dorms. Even though they are now eligible for varsity, the freshmen are installed on one of the floors.

Woody thinks they can be more easily fitted into the scheme of things by a somewhat special break-in status. A young player's homesickness, natural depression, and often disappointment in his progress is better tolerated when everyone immediately around him is in the same cocoon stage.

Coaches are careful not to embarrass freshmen in early first drills. If a kid doesn't catch on to something right away one of the coaches will suggest casually that he just "step out and watch the next couple of times."

"It takes the tightness out of the kid," says Chuck Clausen. "And tough as Woody is, he's entirely in sympathy with a certain amount of early-season nursing of the younger players."

Reporting to that first week of practice can be a traumatic

experience for a seventeen- or eighteen-year-old freshman. Quite possibly he has come from a small high school in a small town and now *Boom!* Here's the big-time. And that rotund guy over there in the black baseball cap is football's Captain Bligh. Of course, on Day One, Captain Bligh has come down off his quarter-deck and is all avuncular smiles and shoulder-patting. Nobody gets the idea that this is Camp Red Wing and look at all those nice, friendly counselors, but Woody does indulge in at least one bit of subtle hand-holding.

Handsome, personable John Mummey, the freshman-reserve coach, is ordered by Woody to live on the same floor with the frosh and to use the same locker room. He wants Mummey to dress and undress there and do a lot of chatting. He is to be a high-profile buffer between what the young kids have been used to and what they are headed into. And heaven help them . . .

What they—and the entire squad—are immediately introduced to is a test of whether they'd paid much heed to the letter everyone receives in late June, laying out a summer conditioning program.

Up until 1973, Woody Hayes was famed for something called "the six-minute mile." It was a misnomer. It was something Woody pioneered about a decade ago and should more properly have been called Woody's Gut-Buster or maybe Captain Bligh's Revenge.

On the first day of practice, in full pads, everybody had to run a mile in six minutes or less, just like it says, son, and if you don't do it on Monday you have Tuesday to look forward to.

On a late August day in Columbus, under full pads, with no weight allowance or an apprentice bug, you could very easily toss your cookies out there on the track, if not out-right die, which most of them thought they were doing anyway.

The quarterbacks, halfbacks and the split ends always made it the first time; their goal was to impress Woody with how much under six-flat they could do. Show-offs! Ah, but those poor 240-pound linemen. They cursed Woody Hayes with every step beyond the first quarter mile. Happiness was a time of 5:59. A lineman who did 5:50 was Superjock of the Day.

Then in '73, Woody said he was dumping the six-minute mile, but before anyone could start lighting Roman candles, he announced a substitute. Everyone would run a series of eight consecutive 40-yard sprints. Eight of them, one after another, without rest. Tame stuff, hey? Want to try it?

The 40 is football's universal standard measure of quickness as opposed to pure speed. The test at Ohio State under Woody's new system begins during the winter, under perfect conditions in the field house.

Players wear football shoes, shorts and T-shirts, and use starting blocks to assist them. Under these conditions, each player runs the 40-yard dash three times per afternoon on three different days during February or March. Nine sprints in all.

From the nine sprints, a typical time is established. Let's say it's 4.6. To this is arbitrarily added two-tenths of a second to make what is considered a presumed base time of 4.8 outdoors on the football field, without using starting blocks.

Thus "on the morning of the first day," Woody Hayes' practice genesis is set in motion that last week in August with the vital, telltale spring series. Answers Will Now Be Provided: Did You Work over the Summer?

Each kid now has his outdoor base time to work against. He must run his first three 40s within two-tenths of a second of his established base time. The kid with the 4.8 base must now return a 5 flat or better. Then he has to run five straight 40s in which there may be four-tenths tolerance from his base, or 5.2 or better. His only "rest," if it may be called that, between sprints, comes on a clocked 20 seconds from the exact finish of one sprint until he hurries back to the starting line for his next one. Think about it . . .

But the player is not quite through. Now he gets five minutes of real rest. But then he has to run the same sort of series for 30 yards against a prescribed time allowance. If the boy measures up after all this, Woody Hayes now considers him merely a reasonable candidate for what follows.

What follows is General Woody Hayes' three weeks of war games that will make his troops grateful for the battles to come.

The newest NCAA decree is that the first three days must be devoted to conditioning, without pads and without contact work. Then it commences. The two-a-days. The hitting. The driving, relentless, gut-busting drills. The repetitive, again-and-again-and-again offensive patterns measured for perfection in inches and milliseconds.

And don't forget the scrimmaging—the ferocious blood-letting that finally determines who starts in that mid-September opener.

It is a relief, that opener. Finally, all the fire and fury can be turned against a real live foe and not the buddy who rooms across the hall from you.

Maybe that's why—after all this—an opening-game opponent is rarely in the contest when Woody Hayes raises the flag and points his legions toward the field. One statistic says a lot: the last five opening games have been 56–7; 21–0; 52–21; 56–13; and 62–0.

# 15
# The Coaches Remember

"I resolved over and over again that if I ever got my own head coaching job I was going to be my own man . . . I was going to get out from under Woody Hayes' shadow . . .

"It didn't work. A year after I'd had my own team I was going over some things in my den late one night when it hit me. 'My God,' I said to myself, 'I'm on my way to becoming another Woody Hayes!' "

—A former assistant

* * *

The question put to Woody Hayes didn't catch him by surprise or even remotely stump him for an instant. But it was obvious that it was something to which he was bringing some solid thought.

What do you look for, Coach, when you're hiring an assistant?

Choosing a new assistant when a vacancy occurs at Ohio State is news on two accounts: the guy leaving is undoubtedly going on to a bigger job, which reflects credit on Woody; and the new man is going to have to be the kind who'll be making the same move in a few years. Woody's assistants are pretty classy guys.

"First thing I'm interested in," said Woody, "is the man's character and his interests."

(Translation: The guy has to be high on morality and decency and be a good family man, and he'd better like many of the things that Woody likes outside of football. Word has gotten around. It is said that candidates try to find out what Woody has been reading lately before they come for an interview.)

"The second thing," adds Woody, "is his work habits."

(Translation: The guy will have to know he'll be working the longest workweek in college football. Don't try to count the hours. If your wife is competing for time with Woody, she loses. And when you're coaching at Ohio State you'd damn well better be the best-organized guy on the block. No goof-ups; no second-guessing; no *mañanas.*)

"Then there's coaching personality . . ."

(Translation: I want the kids to respect you and like you. You've got to be the kind of coach who can be murderously tough at 4:05, but at 6:05 that kid still thinks you're a helluva guy. And you've got to be honest, friendly, warm and loose as a goose, because one of your most important jobs is going to be recruiting.)

"And, finally, the man must have technical competence."

(Translation: You're an offensive line coach? You'd better know more about guard and tackle play than the guy at Purdue, Minnesota or whoever you play—or at least be on the way to knowing more.)

But it's interesting that technical competence comes last on his specs.

It was not surprising, of course, that Woody was the first coach in the Big Ten to hire a black assistant. He took on Leo Brown, a tigerish 168-pound defensive end and Buckeye co-captain in the late 1950s, and within a couple of years every conference team followed his lead.

"But I didn't hire Leo Brown because he was black," Woody said. "He was simply a tremendous young man with great technical skills who knew how to teach. He went to dental school while coaching and eventually became our team dentist."

In the late 1960s Woody took on another black as assistant coach—Rudy Hubbard, a fine halfback on his 1965, 1966 and 1967 teams, to handle the running backs. This year he became head coach at Florida A & M. "I found out right away," says Hubbard, "that although I knew I had immense respect for Woody as a coach and person, I could fall into a trap and let that respect get in my way. You've got to constantly fight Woody for your ideas and principles when you're out there coaching with him, or you're a goner. Not only do you fail as a coach but you're going to fail as a person with him. And as a black coach I had to hang extra tough.

"Take recruiting, for instance," Hubbard went on. "My friends warned that Woody would use me just to recruit black kids, for obvious reasons. Well, I wasn't going to let anything be that obvious. And I wasn't going to let Woody just assign me to just any old place in the state, small towns and stuff—places with poor potential.

"I asked for, and I got, one of the best areas in the state, the Youngstown, Warren, Niles area where some of the best players are to be found. And that meant I was also going to recruit white kids, not just black, and I'd be going into white homes. I was going to be the Ohio State recruiter in every sense.

"Woody saw it all the way. Not because he had to, but

because I was fighting for something and Woody respects and admires a fighter."

One former assistant coach has formed a different—and less flattering—opinion about Woody's relationships with his coaches. "He adopts a paternal attitude towards them that exceeds that of the toughest, sternest father," he says. "I think he feels they are his to command, and even worse, to put down and even terrorize if the mood suits him. Not viciously or anything like that. I don't think Woody ever toughs-out an assistant without thinking it's for the guy's own good.

"One night he read an article on physical fitness. The next morning at our eight o'clock meeting he was all fired up and opened the meeting by telling us we were in lousy shape and that we should run to the top of the St. John basketball arena each morning.

"He said, 'I'm always standing; now you SOB's stand up, too.' Then he read us the article. After that he said we were going up to the top tier of that seemingly mile-high arena. He lined us up by height and double-timed us up there. A couple of our veteran coaches were in their sixties, and they were dizzy. Some of the younger guys were alarmed.

"Then up there Woody read the article again, and marched us back down to his office and gave us a written test on it. I guess he made his point, because everybody got at least ninety on the test.

"Ever since then you've never seen an Ohio State coach out of shape."

"One of the most astute observations I ever heard Woody Hayes make," says Lou Holtz, now head coach at North Carolina State, "was that 'discipline is 95 percent anticipation.'

"When demonstrations were hitting campuses all over the country a few years ago, Woody would rush to the dorms and get his players aside. He'd say, 'It'll be here on our campus soon, and I want you to know what the full consequences will be before you become a part of it.' He'd appeal to their common sense—in other words, anticipate what they might do if they were uninformed or just plain carried away by false emotion. It had nothing to do with his personal politics.

"Woody also knew how to anticipate overreaction by his players following a big win or after they had lost one in an upset. In the first case the kids might be too high or have delusions of grandeur, and that's bad. Or after a loss they might lose confidence in themselves. His first little speech on Monday after a game would take care of that."

"Let me add this," says John Mummey, one of Woody's current assistants. "Woody expects us to get to know our kids so well that we can almost smell something that's bothering a boy, whether it's a playing problem, a morale problem, or academic or personal.

"Woody feels a boy in a bad mood can infect another kid, and two kids can infect more, until it can affect a whole squad. He's such a bug on anticipation that he'd hand a coach his head if a boy has a problem that hadn't been anticipated by the assistant and passed on to Woody before the matter becomes critical."

"The man is a supreme and natural psychologist," says Holtz. "I'll never forget how he hired me as an assistant in 1968. I was coaching the secondary defense at South Carolina and I'd gone to the annual Coaches' Association meeting in January. Some of the young assistants from around the country were asked to do little chores at the meeting, and I was serving as recording secretary for the Coaches' board of trustees.

"Gee, was I awed by that group. There was Woody, Bear Bryant and I think guys like John McKay or Frank Broyles —a dozen big-name guys—and there I was, nervously scratching down notes of the meeting.

"There was an opening at Ohio State, but what I didn't know was that a couple of the assistants out there had recommended me as a candidate. That's how it works. Woody asks all his guys to post names of anyone they think might fill the bill. They have a big blackboard, and anybody can post a name. I didn't know it, but my name was up there twice. Woody knew it but he didn't let on to me that he knew.

"After the meeting everyone drifted out except Woody. I was still making notes and he sort of started a conversation. I'd heard that Woody was the kind who'd always pick up the 'little guy' at a coaches' meeting and exchange pleasantries. He was like that. He asked me my name and where I was working and, would you believe, we sat there for four hours with him doing most of the talking.

"Once he mentioned casually that he had an offensive line coaching position open, and later he slid very naturally into a question about what ideas I had about handling kids, not necessarily in coaching techniques. Just friendly conversation—you know?

"The next day I was in my room when the phone rang. It was Woody. He wanted to know if he could come up to my room, and I said sure. I thought he wanted to know something about the minutes I'd taken the day before. He walked in and his first question was: 'Would you be interested in a job at Ohio State?' I almost fell through the floor.

It had never occurred to me that he'd been interviewing me the day before."

Despite the earlier marathon four-hour gabfest, Holtz soon found out the truism about Woody Hayes versus conversation: you talk only when Woody wants to talk. "On my fourth day on the job in Columbus we were at a cocktail party and Woody asked me to drive him up to Cleveland, about a hundred and forty miles away. There were a couple of kids he wanted to see. We got in his car. I was to do the driving. I started the motor.

" 'Fasten your seat belt,' said Woody."

"I said it was a nuisance and wasn't comfortable with it.

" 'Goddammit!' Woody said, 'you have a wife and four kids. Fasten that goddam seat belt!'

"I fastened it so fast my hand shook. Then I reached over and snapped on the radio. The music or whatever it was lasted for ten seconds—until Woody abruptly lurched forward and snapped it off.

" 'Goddammit, how can you *think* with that thing on?' he barked.

"Not a word passed between us for the two and a half hours it took to get to Cleveland. He didn't doze or anything. He just wanted to be alone with his thoughts. He is essentially a very private man and nobody intrudes on that privacy."

There is no one more tolerant of race or religion than Woody Hayes. He doesn't have a bigoted bone in his body, but Larry Catuzzi still is unable to suppress a huge grin when he recalls how he was hired as Woody's quarterback coach a few years ago. Catuzzi went on to become head coach at Williams and is now offensive coordinator for Houston in the WFL. Actually, the story is told by Lou

McCullough, now athletic director at Iowa State, who was Woody's defensive coordinator at the time.

"When the vacancy came up," says McCullough, "Woody asked if I had any recommendations. I told him there was a bright young man at Indiana who I thought would be perfect for us. Woody asked what his name was, and I said 'Larry Catuzzi.'

"Woody's reaction was the funniest explosion I ever heard from him, and you mustn't misunderstand. It was just the way it struck him. He screamed, 'Larry *Catuzzi?* Jesus Christ, Lou, I've never had anyone on my staff with a name like Catuzzi!'

" 'Well, then it's time you did,' I told him. 'Besides, he's not exactly some Sicilian bomb-thrower or a member of the Mafia, if that's what you're thinking. He's one helluva fine young man and an extremely capable coach. Why don't you check with Dave Nelson? He played for Nelson at Delaware.'

"Woody glowered at me," said McCullough, "and grumbled once or twice. Then he said, 'Okay, phone Nelson and talk to him.'

"I said, 'Hell no, Woody. If you want Nelson's opinion, phone him yourself.' I think I was the only coach on the staff who every dared talk back to Woody, and I wanted to make it just a bit tough on him.

"He glared at me, then reached for the phone. 'Catuzzi,' he growled and shook his head. 'Jesus Christ!'

"Nelson kept Woody on the phone for a half-hour telling him about the young man."

Catuzzi himself then recalled the subsequent events, chuckling as he did so. "Okay, I got an invitation to come over to Columbus for an interview. Woody wanted to see me at 11:30 A.M.

"You know damn well that I didn't intend to be there at 11:31, nor much before 11:25. I was just twenty-six years old. I was going to be interviewed by one of the Greats, and my knees were made of strawberry jelly. At exactly 11:20, St. John Arena came in sight, where Woody had his office. Perfect. It would take me two minutes to pull up to the building and two minutes to get to his office.

"I drove into the parking lot and approached this huge complex of basketball arena, field house, hockey rink and God knows what. There must have been a hundred and twelve doors spotted around the whole thing. I must have tried every one of them. They were all locked from the inside. My God, I thought, how do you get into this place? One of them *had* to open from the outside. I think it was the hundred and twelfth. It was now also 11:48. Inside St. John Arena I scurried around for another eight minutes until I found the coaching-staff quarters. At exactly 12:00 noon, Woody's secretary admitted me through the open door to Woody Hayes' office.

"He very significantly looked at his watch. My mouth was full of cotton. Finally I stammered, 'I'm sorry, Coach Hayes, but I—I just couldn't find a door that would open downstairs.'

"He looked off dismally for about ten seconds. Then finally he said, 'Jeezus H. Christ—the guy wants to coach my quarterbacks and he can't even find an open door.'

"I was still struck dumb and he grunted a couple of times and said, 'Well, let's see if you can find the damn blackboard and diagram a couple of plays that worked successfully for you at Indiana.'

"After that beginning I wouldn't have given a dime for my chances of landing the job as quarterback coach at Ohio State."

Of the dozens of assistant coaches Woody has had, he has never fired a single one. One long-time Woody-Watcher says this is because Woody would thereby be admitting publicly that he'd made a mistake in taking him on in the first place.

Woody lets go with one of his "bullshit" snorts at this, then follows it with a smile, saying, as a matter of fact, by gosh, once he almost kissed a guy on the forehead when he came in and said he was quitting. "He was a troublemaker," says Woody, "but there was no way I could have predicted that when I hired him."

Some of Woody's present and former assistants crack up, however, at the suggestion that Woody has never fired an assistant. "Hell, there've been some of us who've been fired over and over," one of them grins. "We just never leave, that's all. We understand."

Lou Holtz, describes the terrifying moments when he was "fired" in the lobby of the Huntington-Sheraton Hotel in Pasadena, just a couple of days before the 1969 Rose Bowl game. "Of course, I had no way of knowing." He laughs. "It was my first year with Woody. I was 'Officer of the Day,' which means, in Woody's military philosophy, that I had charge of all security, hotel liaison and communications on that day.

"It also meant I was in charge of bed check that night, at 10:00 P.M. Well, a couple of the other coaches and their wives thought it'd be a good idea if we drove down to the Sunset Strip in Hollywood right after dinner just to see the sights, then drive right back to Pasadena. We figured to be back by 9:00 at the latest. So the Holtzes went along, too. We got caught in the middle of one of the worst traffic jams in Los Angeles history just before we got to Hollywood.

Couldn't move, front or rear. When we finally got off the freeway to a telephone it was almost 10:00 and I was in a panic. I was due back at Pasadena for bed check and it'd take another hour and a half to get back there, even if we were lucky.

"I phoned the hotel and asked for Tiger Ellison, one of our assistant coaches. I had him paged in the lobby. I explained what had happened and asked him to make the bed check without Woody knowing.

"Tiger had a copy of the room list but he never had a chance to use it. Woody was in the lobby and wanted to know why Tiger had been paged, and what was he doing with the room list in his hand. Tiger made some sort of lame excuse about me being trapped in traffic and that he was going to make bed check for me. Woody blew up and said he couldn't trust anybody, and he'd make the goddam bed check himself. He grabbed Tiger's room list and stalked off to the elevators.

"What Tiger and Woody didn't know was that a half-dozen of the players' wives had come in by plane and that day I'd made a new room list so that they could, naturally, stay with their husbands. I hadn't gotten copies of the new list into the coaches' hands. So Woody started up the elevator to make the bed check with the old list . . .

"Next morning he caught me in the middle of the lobby as I was going in to breakfast. If there were any cuss words or variations of them I'd never heard him use before, he sure trotted them out now.

"Man, what a job he did on me. He wound up by telling me I was fired right then and there. Then he stormed off before I could say a word in my own defense, not that he'd have accepted any. I was lower than a whale's belly and I asked a couple of the other coaches whether I should just take a plane back to Columbus or whether I'd be allowed to go back on the team plane.

"They just laughed. They said unless Woody put it in writing I should forget it. So I just showed up at practice that day with my knees knocking, waiting for Woody to set eyes on me. He acted as though nothing had happened."

Woody, asked about it later, raised his eyebrows. "Oh, did he say I fired him? As I recall I just told him to get his butt out of my sight or something like that." He chuckled softly. "Must have scared him a bit."

"I've been away from Woody four years now," said Holtz. "I've had a season as head coach at William and Mary and now three more down here, but I still phone Woody to get his opinion and advice."

Technical stuff? Football stuff?

"No, not so much that," said Holtz. "Usually it'll deal with an organizational problem or a personnel problem with staff, or a disciplinary matter with kids. I'll ask him how he thinks I should proceed and, dammit, the man wastes no time telling me. He tells me, I do it, and I'm full of the feeling that it's right. I guess that'll go on as long as I'm in coaching and as long as Woody's available."

Bo Schembechler, who played under Hayes at Miami and then coached under him at Ohio State, before becoming head man at Miami and then Michigan, was another whom Woody "fired." Schembechler remembers it happened during Woody's worst season, a 3–5–1 catastrophe in 1959. "It was late in the season," says Bo, "and we were arguing over some kids I wanted to get into the line-up, and Woody wasn't agreeing with me. It wasn't exactly a rational discourse, and finally Woody picked up a chair and flung it at me. He missed me by two inches. Make that one inch.

"I did what he probably expected: I picked it up and chucked it back at him as hard as I could. Well, luckily that one missed, too."

" 'Okay, damn you!' Woody yelled at me. 'I'm going to fire you anyway!'

"So I got up and went to the men's room and a minute later he shows up right behind me. 'Get your ass back to the meeting,' he snapped. So I went back to the meeting and that was that—except that I think we played the kids I wanted.

"In the years I worked under him," Bo added, "I fought with the man, argued with him, went home at night and cursed him. But oh how I learned under him. How I learned the values of sheer work. He is a man who is determined never to be outworked, and now I find I'm that way myself. Tell me—where did I get it from?"

One former assistant of Woody's, now a very successful head coach himself, shakes his head in wonderment and asks himself how it happened . . .

"How *what* happened?" he is asked.

"Well, there'd I'd been—subjected to Woody Hayes' moods and attitudes just like a dozen or more assistants before me. Much of it I didn't like at all. I resolved over and over again that if I ever got my own head coaching job I was going to be my own man. I was going to do things my own way—shape my own philosophies, react my own way to certain situations. I was going to get out from under Woody Hayes' shadow and be me, just me."

He paused. "It didn't work. A year after I'd had my own team I was going over some things in my den late one night when it hit me. 'My God!' I said to myself, 'I'm on my way to becoming another Woody Hayes!' It had rubbed off and I didn't realize it. That's the power and the shaping effect of the man."

Still another spelled out his feelings without hesitation. "I just flat out disliked the man," he said simply. "I don't think I could have taken one more year with him."

One of Woody's biggest cheerleaders is Carm Cozza, the head coach at Yale. "I had the good fortune," he said, "to play under Woody at Miami and one of the things that impressed me most—besides his incredible competitive spirit—was his genuine interest in the kids he coached. And I later found, personally, how he enthusiastically maintained that interest when they got out on their own.

"A few years ago he invited me out to Ohio State to speak at their clinic prior to the annual spring game. It wasn't enough for Woody that I just spoke. He insisted that I wear an Ohio State jersey at the chalk sessions and on the field, and he made me get into the huddle when the team was running offensive plays.

"I tell you, it gave me little goose bumps. It made me feel once again like a player under his command. And I think this was exactly what he had in mind. It was a beautiful thing."

John Pont of Northwestern, who also played for Woody at Miami, recalls Hayes' intense desire to win as almost a holy war. "And he was just as aggressive then as he is now. There was no way he was going to change, because few men believe as strongly in their convictions as Woody Hayes does. To change would be to abandon those convictions.

"That's why it's so tough playing against him. His kids make so few mistakes that you just can't go into a game thinking you'll get a break or two. And it's necessary, in turn, for your team not to make mistakes because of the pressure your kids always feel in going against Ohio State."

Opponents aren't the only ones to feel the pressure. Woody puts plenty on his own assistants. "One of the toughest things for me to adjust to, in working for Woody," says an assistant coach, "is his absolute compulsion to dominate a conversation. Once you understand that, you have no problem, but it takes some doing.

"We were having breakfast one morning during preseason practice. One of the other coaches was talking about something he'd just read about the Cincinnati Reds. Woody looked up from his plate and said: 'Goddammit, let's not be talking about any goddam Cincinnati Reds; let's be talking football.'

"So, what happens? Three minutes later Woody glances down at the newspaper lying on the table and notices a headline about some international conference. In a flash he's explaining to us what the significance of it is and what the trends should be, stuff like that, and he rattles on for ten minutes, blithely overlooking the fact that he isn't talking football. And nobody's about to remind him, either!"

Because Ohio State is big time in all sports, Woody has often found himself in conflict with Marty Karow, the varsity baseball coach, and Fred Taylor in basketball. "Often," says Karow, "we go after a high school boy who starred in both football and baseball, and I know he can play for me. The boy asks if he can play both sports, and I say sure, knowing it won't be that simple.

"Woody will go along with it, but he'll tell the kid that he must, however, go out for spring football in his first year to get a full indoctrination to Woody's system. After that, Woody implies, the kid can play baseball in the spring. Yet

Woody's personality is so dominating and he makes the football end of the deal sound so demanding that the kid begins to have doubts and I lose him completely for baseball. It takes a super football player to break away from Woody in the spring to play baseball. Otherwise he won't risk it.

"Hopalong Cassady was a great baseball player. In his sophomore year he passed up spring football and played for me. He'd entered school in midyear as a freshman and starred the following fall as a halfback for Woody while still a freshman because of the Korean War frosh eligibility rule. Anyway, things worked out so that the following spring he passed up spring football to play baseball for me. In the fall he had trouble getting back into Woody's starting line-up. Fans started screaming from the stands, 'We want Hoppy!' Hop still refused to get the 'message' from Woody, and by his junior year, of course, he was an All-America halfback —and still playing baseball every spring."

The same conflict of interests has hit Fred Taylor. "It's almost impossible for a boy to play both basketball and football at Ohio State," he says firmly. "And if Woody and I compete for the same kid and he has to make an agonizing decision . . . well, who do you think wins?"

Then Taylor smiled. "There was one case, though, that was a dandy. There was this big kid who was an All-State quarterback and All-State in basketball. The whole world was after him and nobody knew who'd get him—or for which sport.

"Woody apparently made a great impression on him but finally the kid took a deep breath and said, 'Sorry, Coach Hayes, my choice is going to be basketball.'

"It didn't stop Woody. He simply started in recruiting

the kid to play basketball for Ohio State. Really worked on him. It came out just fine.''

Which is how John Havlicek decided to come to Ohio State where he and Jerry Lucas, another freshman recruit, took the Buckeyes to the heights for three straight years. And for three years Woody watched Havlicek with pleasure and appreciation—but Woody was never really able to overcome the feeling that it was a waste of a great quarterback.

Virtually every assistant coach Woody has had will agree that he doesn't carry his famed rages around in his hip pocket. "He'll cuss you out," says one coach, "and five minutes later you'd never know it happened. But after he cusses you and he himself is subsequently proven wrong about the thing, he'll never show he's sorry. I'm sure Woody thinks an apology is a sign of weakness.

"Sometimes an assistant coach will fight him over a technique. He once made me put in something that didn't work. Then he screamed at me and called me an SOB because it flopped. So I just screamed back at him, 'Yeah, and you're the SOB who made me put it in!'

"We've all found out that if you're right and you back down on it he'll really get on you. He can't respect that kind of attitude from his coaches. We often feel he's 'testing' us that way. He wants to know how strongly we feel about something, and boy, do we ever let him have it!

"Strangely, it doesn't bother us when he yells 'Shut up, I'm talking!' or even 'Shut up, you sonovabitch!' I think we even giggle inwardly, sometimes. We know we have two choices in working with Woody. We know he isn't going to change so we either adapt or leave."

Very few assistant coaches leave Woody Hayes for an

234 Woody Hayes and the 100-Yard War

assistantship elsewhere. Assisting Woody is upward-bound, never sideways. Of his approximately thirty assistant coaches over the years, all but two have gone on to head coaching jobs in college or jobs with the pros.

His assistants know Woody so well, that they're wise enough to keep out of sight during the off-season. "If he sees any two of the nine in a hall," says Ralph Staub, "he'll grab 'em and hold an impromptu staff meeting. He just can't help it. Late June or early July, which is our only slack time, he just can't stand seeing an hour going to waste when there's football to be talked."

Around St. John Arena his assistants are known as the greatest escape artists since Houdini. But they're not always successful. One Sunday afternoon in June an assistant was out jogging and decided to stop in to check his office mail. He got caught at 3:00 P.M. by Woody. He got home at 9:00 P.M., still in his sweat suit.

As he walked in the door, his wife held up her hand and said, "Don't tell me—I know. You bumped into Woody . . ."

# 16
# The Press
# Never Forgets

"I'm able to sustain two views of Woody Hayes. One is of Woody as a football coach, and one as a man whom I as a writer would have to cover on my job. I know how Woody Hayes coaches football, and if I were a young player I'd give my left testicle to play for him. But I also know his general opinion of the press, and as a sportswriter, you couldn't pay me enough to cover him on a regular basis."

—Paul Zimmerman,
The New York *Post*

\*   \*   \*

Woody Hayes was only about two minutes into his postgame press conference when he looked down at a young newsman who wasn't taking notes. He was merely sitting there with a tape recorder on.

Woody skidded to a halt in midsentence, his face darkening. "You there," he barked, "you with the tape recorder! Out!"

There was a stunned silence as Woody heated up, implying that if the young man couldn't do an honest job of reporting, with an old-fashioned pad and pencil like everyone else, he didn't want him in there. The young man, clutching his tape recorder, fled in embarrassment. Woody went on with the conference.

Fifteen minutes later, the interview finished, Woody was bustling back to the dressing room when he spied the young reporter in the corridor. He beckoned to him.

"Now, then," said Woody briskly, "if you'll get out a pencil and paper, we'll see what you need to know . . ."

And then Woody proceeded to give the young man an exclusive ten-minute interview, patiently answering his questions and volunteering material neither the guy nor anybody else inside would have gotten.

It was typical of Woody Hayes' frequent and unpredictable meetings with newsmen. He is forever a creature of impulse, moved by the most mercurial of instincts. Whatever is the priority of the moment governs his actions.

"Woody Hayes," says a veteran sportswriter, "has attracted as much ink with his problems with the press, officialdom and even his colleagues, as he has with his fabulous football teams."

Undoubtedly true. How could it not be? Who else holds forth with such unvarnished directness? Who else has self-starting gut reactions that only a Stanislavsky method actor could match? Who else has the gall and the .45-caliber chutzpah to take on anybody and anything, strictly on his own ground rules?

Here is a man who, first of all, between September 1 and the end of the football season, is unreachable on the telephone. Not just because he doesn't come to his office during this period but because his secretary, Lena Biscuso, knows he is not to be traced down at his hideaway for anything short of the most critical personal crisis. And you can get some pretty spirited comment on what would be critical enough.

Woody is notoriously delinquent in answering mail. Back up. Woody does not answer mail, period, during the season. Lena is an expert at replying to high-level stuff. The merely important can wait a couple of months. Are you wondering about the routine stuff?

To some people this is funny as hell. To others it is downright rude. Woody Hayes means it as neither. Woody just doesn't care—and doesn't care what anybody thinks about his not caring. That, he figures, takes care of that.

"Actually," Miss Biscuso smiles apologetically, "we manage to get a few things over to his hideout. But it's tough. People don't understand Coach Hayes' preoccupation with football."

It's that preoccupation which over the years has triggered his vintage tarantellas that couldn't be believed of other coaches. On Woody, these antic moments have the stamp of the totally expected. So who's surprised or shocked? It's just Ol' Woody again, right?

To be chronological about it, he made his first contentious headlines on his first Rose Bowl venture with his 1954 team led by the irrepressible Hopalong Cassady.

To begin with, it had rained heavily just before the game, and the field was going to be gooey. "And it's not going to get any better," Woody Hayes growled, "with those two marching bands prancing around on it. Let's keep them off it."

Rose Bowl officials did a double take. Howzzat again, Coach? They did not yet know Woody Hayes, and he put it right to 'em. Millions of TV viewers had already seen the bands in the famed Rose Parade that morning, he reasoned, so who cares if they don't do their stuff on the football field? The field was already ankle-deep in mud. Let's save what's left of the decent real estate for the football players.

Bandsmen from both Ohio State and Southern Cal were horrified. They'd worked for three weeks on special material, and now this curmudgeon was trying to close the show before it opened.

It was quite a flap until Woody was overruled.

There was an even greater flap a couple hours later when Woody took on the West Coast writers in the first big skirmish of what would become a continuing war.

He had previously shaken them up during the pregame practice period by not allowing them to interview his players, something unheard of in Rose Bowl history. Then to their consternation Woody refused to let them see his kids after the game in which the Buckeyes smashed the Trojans, 20–7. Now his philosophy was in full view . . . nobody talks to my kids.

Equally odious, as far as the writers were concerned, Woody kept them waiting twenty minutes for the postgame interview. (They were unaware of a Big Ten rule giving coaches privacy for fifteen minutes after a game, and Woody hadn't bothered to explain he was operating on that basis.) When he finally came in to see them he dropped another bomb.

"There are at least four or five teams in the Big Ten," Woody told them coldly, "who could have whipped your Rose Bowl club today."

Howls of rage in the press. The man is insulting. Not even a gracious winner. Downgrading an entire league like that.

Woody Hayes had launched his career as the most un-popular coach ever to visit the Coast. Writers from Seattle down to San Diego began to lay in a supply of needles, pins and voodoo dolls against the day he would return. And he would return again and again. The battle was joined . . .

The fact would soon become plain that headlines of a notorious nature would be Woody Hayes' natural habitat. A year later he found himself being investigated by Big Ten commissioner Tug Wilson for largesse unbecoming a con-ference coach.

The league had not yet embarked on an athletic scholar-ship program and football players paid their own way through part-time jobs found for them on or off the cam-pus. Sometimes the jobs managed to pay enough, some-times they didn't; and sometimes some of the kids collected more pay than their working hours entitled them to.

At any rate, in an innocent interview with a *Sports Illus-trated* writer, Woody, with typical, open-faced honesty, re-vealed there were times when some of his players came up short when term fees were due, or needed transportation home to see an ailing parent, or needed a dinner to im-prove a diet of beans and graham crackers. So Woody sim-ply dug into the fees he was being paid for his TV show and handed out a few bucks here, a few there. Nothing elabo-rate.

"It's only right that I do so," he told the writer. "It's not that I'm paying these kids to play football. I'm just helping out occasionally in private and individual cases on their merits. I see nothing wrong in it."

Maybe he didn't, but Tug Wilson did. The Big Ten com-missioner hot-footed it over to Columbus and took a good look around. "I talked to Woody at great length," said Wilson. "I've been around and I can tell when a guy is holding back or is trying to con me, but this man was being so naïvely honest and open about what he'd been doing that I couldn't be too tough on him. He wasn't trying to defend anything. He was just trying to explain some of his own human and moral instincts. But even though I might have bought it myself, I couldn't buy it for the conference, and told him so. He just looked me in the eye and shrugged. I had the feeling he'd take any penalties handed out to him but that no penalty would ever shake his belief in what he'd done.

"So what with the sloppy job program the athletic department was running, plus Woody's own home-relief program, I put Ohio State on a year's probation. We never had that kind of trouble from him again."

Meanwhile, the headlines blared things like:

WOODY HAYES HANDS OUT CASH;
LEAGUE HANDS HIM PROBATION

* * *

Naturally, relations with the press did not improve. Paul Zimmerman, the football writer for the New York *Post*, vividly recalls his first bumptious postgame briefing with Woody. This was years later, but Woody's attitudes didn't change much over the years. "Woody had just clobbered somebody by a million, and in his postgame conference nobody was asking him why he'd gone for a field goal when he was leading by five TD's or some such.

"So, hell, I had a natural question and I asked it. I piped up, 'Coach, it looked to me like maybe you were trying to run up a score for the polls. Is that why you went for the field goal?'

"There was this big silence in the room, as though some

of the local writers were embarrassed. Woody looked out and bristled.

"'Who asked that?' he snapped.

"I stuck up my hand, told him my name and said I was from the New York *Post.*

"Then he laid it on me. A full blast of sarcasm. 'New *York,*' he said, accenting the second syllable. 'New York *Post* . . . a writer from New *York* . . . I see.'

"He was enjoying it, looking around at the other writers, letting them know he knew whom he was dealing with. One of those New *York* wise guys.

"Well, he finally gave me some sort of flip answer to my question, and that was all.

"Let me add this, though," Zimmerman said. "I'm able to sustain two views of Woody Hayes. One is of Woody as a football coach, and one as a man whom I as a writer would have to cover on my job. I know how Woody Hayes coaches football, and if I were a young player I'd give my left testicle to play for him. But I also know his general opinion of the press, and as a sportswriter you couldn't pay me enough to cover him on a regular basis."

\* \* \*

It was one of those steaming days in early September. Woody Hayes and his Bucks were only a week into preseason drills and things weren't going well this particular morning. A missed block here, an off-side there; a couple of fumbles; a lack of hustle.

Suddenly a group of men—a couple dozen or so—appeared at the far end of the practice field and began filtering toward the sideline. They were the Big Ten Skywriters. The Skywriters are from newspapers in the Big Ten area who each year charter a plane and hop from one conference football camp to another to draw some preseason views of all the clubs.

It's a neat, streamlined operation and the Big Ten commissioner always accompanies the writers. They spend a couple of hours watching practice and then engage each coach in an in-depth interview about his squad, chances for the season, and so forth. Lots of give-and-take. Much accomplished in a brief but intensive time.

There they were, from Chicago, Minneapolis, Detroit, Lafayette, Toledo, Iowa City, Cleveland—all affable and content with their tour and full of *Gemütlichkeit* and goodies from their previous stop at Michigan State or wherever.

Just as they got to the sideline somebody on the Buckeye offensive team pulled a horrendous goof—the second in the last minute or so. It would bring on at least a megaton from Wayne Woodrow Hayes.

But just as he started to flay the kids, he stopped in mid-curse as he spied the Skywriters approaching. His baseball cap had long since been flung to the ground, and now he grimly steamed over toward the assembled writers.

"This practice is closed!" he bellowed. "Everybody out! This session is private!"

They stared in disbelief. "You're kidding, Woody," one of them said. "This is the Skywriters group you're talking to . . ."

"Everybody out!" Woody repeated.

The writers glanced at commissioner Tug Wilson, who was himself busy staring at Hayes. "I've got some very private words for my players," said Woody, "and I don't want anyone around." That was all he would say, but finally added that he'd give them an interview after practice was over.

The writers straggled back through the gate, glaring over

their shoulders. Some demanded that they take off for their next stop and to hell with any later interview offered by Woody Hayes. But the majority said they'd stick it out. An hour later Woody received them in the stadium conference room, his face grim and unrepentent.

"I wasn't happy with the way our practice was going," he began, "and decided to chew out my players. And I never do that in front of outsiders. This was a family affair, and it wouldn't have been fair to my kids."

It was not the end of the affair. In all the years the Skywriters had been operating they'd never been treated like that. Don Wolfe of the Toledo *Blade* echoed, in his story, what seemed to be a consensus:

> Woody's bum's rush on the Ohio State campus of a group of writers and officials was in unbelievably bad taste, particularly when contrasted with our warm receptions at other Big Ten schools . . .
>
> His ill-mannered display was something one would have to see to believe . . . It was like having friends and relatives travel a long distance to see you and having your host throw you out and slamming the door in your face . . .
>
> Merely let it be said that while Ohio State may lead the Big Ten in football success, it is last in hospitality and manners.

Virtually all other newspaper accounts were in the same vein. Some papers called for a public reprimand of Woody. A week later athletic director Dick Larkins wrote a letter to commissioner Wilson in which he said: "I realize the damage has already been done, but I want to apologize for this regrettable incident."

Later, Larkins denied that Woody had been reprimanded by the university. "I talked to Woody and told him I thought it had been regrettable. When he told me he was sorry, that was good enough for me. If you call that a reprimand, I guess it is."

Some of Woody's associates say it was the only time they'd ever felt that Woody brooded over one of his boo-boos, although he never showed it in public. But the following year Woody Hayes demonstrated he had a sense of humor when the Skywriters came calling again.

There on the sidelines were several huge colored beach umbrellas with chairs and tables underneath. On the tables were big pitchers of ice-cold lemonade. With an expansive grin, Woody said, "Welcome, gentlemen."

"How the hell could you stay mad at the guy?" grumped Jack Clowser of the Cleveland *Press.*

* * *

Woody Hayes' neck could have fried eggs as he came off the field after a game, still screaming about the officials. Northwestern had just upset the Bucks and it was all due to those bumbling, inept, myopic whistle-tooters and flag-droppers who had falsely deprived his troops of touchdowns, first downs, strategic field position and maybe their next meal, for all anyone could tell.

Woody didn't say it just once. He spent the next day, too, complaining about the officials, referring to "proof in the game films," and generally deducing that his kids had been flimflammed out of the ball game.

Bill Reed, then the commissioner of the Big Ten, wasn't about to allow league officials to be publicly upbraided like that, especially by a coach who enjoyed coast-to-coast attention in the nation's press.

First, Reed stressed that Woody had run one play from the game three times on his Sunday TV show while point-

ing out how Ohio State had been "cheated" out of two
TD's. Then Reed demanded that Woody apologize on
three counts:

1. It was an action unbecoming to Hayes. (Highly debatable, quipped the fans.)
2. "It was like throwing mud on a painting" to criticize
   a great battle between two fine Big Ten teams.
3. A league agreement forbids coaches from using film
   to criticize handling of games, since the officials have
   to react as they see it immediately on the field, and
   their decision is final.

Then Reed was asked what he'd do if Woody refused to
apologize. The commissioner paused a moment. "He will,"
he said grimly. "He will."

That was the word relayed to Woody by sportswriters
after practice the following Tuesday. They reported that
Woody had no comment except for verifying he'd received
a phone call from Reed, and that he'd sent an apology.

But one reporter had another version of Woody's final
words—by now the expected ending to any cause célèbre
involving the Buckeye coach. According to the writer,
Woody ended it with: "What the commissioner wants, the
commissioner gets. I was wrong—and that makes two of
us."

*    *    *

Losing a football game, as far as Woody Hayes is concerned, is an aberration of nature, and when the uncommon occurs it seems to have the same effect on him as an
eclipse of the moon on the tides. And watch the hell out if
you're a sportswriter on the scene.

In October 1959 the Buckeyes got clobbered, 17–0, by
Southern Cal and took a worse beating on the field, physi-

cally, than they did on the scoreboard. It follows that Woody led his tail-dragging troops back to the dressing room for a chew-out. In an open foyer off the dressing room were Al Bine of the Los Angeles *Examiner* and Dick Shafer, brother of the sports editor of the Pasadena *Star-News*.

Woody spotted them and hurtled out to the foyer. As Shafer reported it, "He stormed out at us yelling, 'Get the hell outta here!'

"We started walking away but apparently not fast enough for Woody. 'Goddammit!' he repeated, 'I said get outta here!'

According to published reports, Woody allegedly then swung and hit Shafer in the back, knocking him off-balance. Next, according to Shafer, Woody hoisted him by the shoulders and pushed him against the wall and out the door.

Next witness, Woody Hayes. Woody denied he swung at anyone. He claimed he asked a group of writers to stand aside to let his players through and when one didn't move he urged him along with a shove. "I didn't hit anyone," he said. "I saw two guys with notebooks who were trying to talk to my squad and I asked them to leave. One did. One stayed with his notebook. Well, I don't even let the president of Ohio State University in when I'm talking to my kids. So I shoved the guy out the door."

Bine came back with: "Actually, Hayes intended that punch for me, and if he says he didn't throw a punch he's a liar."

Woody: "Baloney. If that man got hit I want to know where he got hit. The man who said he saw it happen, didn't. He'd already left."

Whatever happened, Woody had support from some quarters. "For one thing," said Earl Flora of the Columbus *Citizen-Journal,* "any writer with his big ears flapping who invades the early sanctity of a bitter loser's Wailing Wall and whipping post is just begging to get himself cold-cocked."

The Southern California chapter of the Football Writers' Association of America took a more jaundiced view and lodged a formal protest with the Football Coaches' Association, with copies sent to just about everybody they could find a mailing address for, including the Big Ten commissioner, the president of Ohio State, and the Buckeyes' faculty representative to the Big Ten.

Athletic director Dick Larkins once again had to refer to a "regrettable incident," and the Ohio State Athletic Council supported Larkins in reprimanding Coach Hayes—very quietly.

Guess who had the last word. After Woody saw a report on the incident by the committee on ethics of the Football Coaches' Association, he said, "If from this report the implication is taken that I actually struck the man, then the implication is wrong. If the ethics committee said I should not have shoved the man out of the dressing area, then they are entitled to their opinion."

Was it a punch or a shove? As one writer put it quite succinctly: "Woody couldn't possibly have punched him. From what I hear, the guy got up immediately. Nobody does that if Woody busts him."

\*    \*    \*

Kaye Kessler of the Columbus *Citizen-Journal,* one of the more observant Woody-Watchers, has long since made his peace with Hayes' way with the press. "I've established in my own mind," he says, "that the man is a prisoner of his principles and there's no way any writer is going to set him loose. He respects me and I respect him and the mutuality of our interests are founded on that.

"Somebody once asked me whether I thought Woody's cantankerousness and competitive drive came as a result of his success or vice versa. I think the man was just as tough and arbitrary the day he arrived here as he is now. Success didn't shape the man; the man and his moods shaped success. People who claim otherwise simply weren't around twenty-three years ago.

"When Woody first came to Ohio State," continued Kessler, "it was very apparent that he exuded confidence to the point of being defiant. I think he was telling everyone that he knew this was the so-called Graveyard of Coaches and he was determined not to become the latest in a long line of ghosts. You also had the definite idea he was going to pull it off his way and everyone else had better stay to hell out of his way. And I'm talking about day number one."

For several years, Paul Hornung, sports editor of the Columbus *Dispatch,* was moderator of Woody's weekly TV show. "It ranged from dazzling to hectic," Hornung recalls. "On Fridays he'd leave his work at 5:40 to drive to the station for a 6:00 P.M. air time, normally a ten-minute drive. But you could get murdered by rush-hour traffic.

"Many's the time Woody would come rushing down the hall at 5:59 with a technician frantically running alongside him draping the microphone around his neck. But Woody would wheeze into the studio absolutely unflappable even though we hadn't had time to talk over what we'd do on the show.

"Once he said, 'Why don't you just surprise me and I'll take it from there?' I was used to Woody winging it on the air, but that one shook me up.

" 'Like what?' I said.

" 'Like asking me how come we were rated so highly at the beginning of the season and doing so poorly now.'

"So I did," said Hornung, "and darned if he didn't make it a reasoned and fascinating three minutes. Almost had me believing him."

Woody's TV show, incidentally, provides moments of high glee to the aficionados who know Woody's style.

"He'll bring a half-dozen of his studs to the show," says one viewer, "and stand them in a self-conscious semicircle. Then he'll ask a question of one of the kids. The boy gets his mouth halfway open and maybe even utters syllable number one, but Woody has already started answering the question himself. Maybe Woody will wind up saying, 'Right, John?' and all the kid can do by now is nod vaguely, his moment in show business ripped off by the world's greatest nonstop talker and scene stealer. It happens every week and we still bust in two."

\*    \*    \*

The all-out vendetta between Hayes and the West Coast press renews itself virtually every time the Buckeyes go out there, especially on Rose Bowl occasions. Woody knows that the Rose Bowl is a festive thing, a fishbowl sort of thing for the visiting team because everybody with a note pad and pencil wants to invade the Bucks' camp.

Inevitably there is the confrontation between Woody and the writing corps. Can he promise a postgame interview? Yes—he will come around and meet with them. Can they interview Ohio State players in the locker room? And now you can almost see the neck muscles gather behind his ears. The jawline becomes just a mite up-thrust, and there is a flat one-word negative reply, delivered in a tone that couldn't be anything but uncompromising.

One year he grimly mentioned a piece the day before in the Los Angeles *Times*. An anonymous Ohio State player had been quoted at great length about alleged complaints about team mistreatment on the Rose Bowl trip and the way Woody handled his players, generally.

"This boy came to me almost in tears," Woody said. "He was obviously shook up. Someone had approached him on a trip to Disneyland and the boy told me he'd just been chatting and didn't realize the guy was a sportswriter. The boy said he couldn't believe how badly his words had been distorted and twisted, and it had come out a whole lot different from what he'd said."

When the assembled writers at that particular press conference argued that they were all being punished for a breach of ethics by one man, one of them pointedly made a formal request to talk to Buckeye players after the game. He said heatedly that it was the reporters' right.

Hayes stared at him coldly. He paused for an instant and said, "Your rights stop at our dressing-room door. I coach the Ohio State football team and that's the way it's going to be."

They began snapping at him from all sides, and with Woody snapping right back it was apparent to anyone who knew him that there was going to be just one way this press conference would come to an end. On the heels of an unanswered question, Woody wheeled and stalked from the room, trailing clouds of almost visible to-hell-with-you defiance.

* * *

Obviously, when Woody Hayes tilts at the windmills of wayward circumstance he does so in sudden gut honesty. Right or wrong, his impulse is sincere—as was his most choleric of all his public displays of rage, the notorious assault on the yard-line markers at Michigan in 1971.

An Ohio State team severely beset with injuries—at least six starters had been lost for the year—had already dropped three games when they came to Ann Arbor to try to salvage the season against the undefeated and third-ranked Wolverines in the finale.

Woody had done the best patch-up job of his life. He had whipped, goaded and cajoled his kids all week and had them believing they actually had a chance. A crowd of more than 100,000 sat stunned as Ohio State went into the fourth quarter leading, 7–3. A few more minutes and Woody would be pulling off the greatest upset of his career.

Then late in the fourth quarter, Michigan's All-America tailback Billy Taylor got loose on a pitch-out for 22 yards and the go-ahead score.

But the Buckeyes came back and looked as if they might pull it off with one last drive. Don Lamka pegged a long pass to Dick Wakefield on the Michigan 32-yard line. Wakefield went up high for it, but before the ball got to him, Michigan defender Tom Darden came barreling in over his shoulder, smashing Wakefield to the ground.

What's more, Darden somehow got his hands on the ball and held it before tumbling to the turf.

Thousands of fans screamed, "Interference!" Woody and everyone on the Ohio sideline expected an automatic first down with excellent field position. With a minute and a half remaining, they could go on to win or at least tie.

But no flag was tossed by the official nearest the play. No other official was in position to see it, and the ball was given to Michigan as an interception.

On the Ohio sidelines there was incredulity, followed by

black rage. It was infamy in their eyes. And the first man to react was Wayne Woodrow Hayes, charging onto the field bellowing like a wounded water buffalo. What he was screaming to the officials, even loosely translated, would have put any other coach in the stocks, if not purgatory.

He got nowhere with the officials. What he did get was 15 yards for rushing onto the field. A platoon of assistant coaches tried to drag him back to the sidelines.

Water buffaloes, enraged, do not retire gently from the fray. Woody shucked them off and grabbed for the wide colored-cloth sideline marker. He yanked it from its upright position and while an official stared, transfixed, tore it to shreds. Then he flung the remnants on the field. If Woody Hayes was going berserk, 100,000 fans were convinced he was giving an Oscar-winning performance.

In the pressbox, it was said that Wayne Duke, in his first year as Big Ten commissioner, lowered his head as though he couldn't believe it or didn't want to see it.

On the sidelines Woody Hayes was still embattled, still trying to fend off his assistants who were merely trying to keep him alive. Any second, Woody's temperature was going to reach flash-point because the Buckeyes, meanwhile, were being slapped with yet another 15-yard penalty.

Michigan ran out the clock, preserving its 10–7 victory but this was one ball game that would produce headlines that transcended scores. The next day Woody's act was repeated for millions of viewers tuned into the NCAA weekly highlight show.

Newspaper editorialists found it their spiciest topic of the week. The Ohio State student daily, the *Lantern,* pointed out that "Woody Hayes is given to lengthy discourses on the character, leadership and sportsmanship developed by football, but certainly showed a dearth of those qualities himself." The Cleveland *Plain Dealer* urged Woody "to apologize for his immature behavior . . . First it was ludicrous, then revolting. It's one thing to be a fierce competitor—quite another to be a horse's rear end, which he was at Ann Arbor."

There were angry letters from alumni vowing to cut off their contributions to the University Development Fund. Big Ten commissioner Wayne Duke had something to say to Woody the following week, but neither he nor Woody commented on it.

But the betting was that anything the commissioner said bounced off Woody's hide like a spitball off a rhinoceros, because virtually every photo sequence that proliferated in print the next two days—and there were dozens—just about clearly showed that the Michigan defender had committed a palpable act of mayhem on the Ohio receiver long before the ball had reached him. Under those circumstances, nobody, but nobody, was going to rap Woody Hayes for more than uncontrollable conduct—and there wasn't much new about that.

Don Canham, Michigan's athletic director, had a pretty good line on the episode. "I'll buy all the sideline markers Woody Hayes wants to tear up," he said. "Ohio State without Hayes would draw at least 30,000 fewer people."

Still another Michigan precinct was heard from. A few days later a resolution was introduced in the Michigan House of Representatives in Lansing, nominating Woody Hayes as "Sportsman of the Year."

The resolution read, in part: "Despite his disagreement with certain official rulings, Hayes brought the people of

Michigan a few moments of great pleasure, unparalleled delight, and indeed, unrestrained glee."

The resolution went on at great length, gravely tongue in cheek, but died in committee when the legislative body was reminded that Michigan would have to play in Columbus the next year.

And from Woody Hayes? Once again he made good the description pinned on him earlier by Bill Reed, the late Big Ten commissioner, who said: "The man is insufferable in victory, indomitable in defeat."

Woody explained the Michigan incident this way: "I did it for my players. I owed it to them and I would have been derelict in my duty to them if I had done less."

Following Woody's epic display of temper at Ann Arbor, Joe Falls of the Detroit *Free Press* reported that a lot of people around Michigan expected Woody to apologize:

> Well, folks, don't hold your breath. W. W. Hayes is not about to apologize for anything, and if he did it would be the greatest upset intercollegiate football has ever known.
>
> Woody is Woody and at the risk of sounding like a heretic, more power to him.
>
> Not for making a fool of himself . . .
>
> But for being himself . . .
>
> Bless him for that . . .
>
> Woody Hayes is the only coach extant who draws more attention than the cheerleaders. More people follow him through their binoculars than follow all the pompom girls, majorettes and cheerleaders in the land. And this is a fat, dumpy, gray-haired, bespectacled old codger who wears a silly-looking baseball cap as he prowls up and down the sidelines . . .
>
> He is one of a kind. In my opinion the most colorful coach

in the game today. I've hated him for years. We've had a wonderful relationship . . .

My first exposure to Woody was about 16 years ago when I was covering Ohio State against Iowa in Iowa City, coached by Forest Evashevski. These two guys despised each other.

Woody blew his top that day when he saw how high Evy had let the grass grow on the field. Evy wanted to slow down the fast Ohio State backs.

But it doesn't slow down Woody. It was a cold day and Woody sneaked behind the Iowa bench and pilfered a couple of electric heaters for his own players . . .

About 10 years later in a Big Ten meeting, they almost came to blows when the question of sideline conduct came up and Evy said something about Woody being unethical.

"Nobody calls me unethical," Woody screamed. He tore off his coat and lunged for Evy but other coaches broke it up.

So chastise him if you will. Berate him. Even hate him.

But the sad day will be when he's no longer the coach of the Ohio State football team.

But nothing in Woody Hayes' long history of sideline antics drew the attention of his notorious brush with a Los Angeles *Times* photographer named Art Rogers in the 1973 Rose Bowl game.

It happened just a moment before the kickoff. Woody was having a last-minute huddle with his coaches on the field, a few yards from the sideline. Suddenly he looked down and saw a camera poking between two assistants, focusing on him.

The rule is that photographers are not allowed on the field. They must stay beyond the sidelines. "Get the hell out of my huddle," Hayes yelled, gesturing broadly with his arm, lunging toward the man and taking a sidewise swipe at the camera.

Rogers stumbled backward, the eyepiece of the camera still in contact with his face. The region around the eye was bruised and scratched. To play safe, people at the first-aid station suggested he go to a hospital for a further check and treatment.

The next day the story was on page one of much of the nation's press. The photographer had filed battery charges against Woody Hayes. A trial date was set and Woody would be expected to appear. It was, of course, one of the spicier bits of sports news in years.

The West Coast press was feasting on what it hoped would be the last of Woody Hayes' mortal remains. Pasadena detectives had visited Woody for his version. Network TV cameramen had stormed the hotel where the Buckeyes were staying. Reporters had taken up posts outside Woody's room. Woody had been served notice to appear in a Pasadena court on January 15 to answer the charges.

Coast fans were ready for the circus. The Scopes and Dreyfus trials were merely summonses for an illegal left turn. Woody Hayes in the dock. *Wow!*

Press comment was sharper than ever. Wells Twombly of the San Francisco *Examiner* wrote: "Wayne Woodrow Hayes is a temper-tossing boy grown old. His public nonsense isn't even vaguely funny . . . He should retire gracefully, because he has become an embarrassment to the nation."

A dissenting opinion came from Bob Greene of the Chicago *Daily News*, who went to a luncheon Hayes attended a few days after the Rose Bowl:

> He's really not as bad as all of this must sound. Once I was in the Ohio State locker room after a winning game, and an

assistant coach came running. He shouted to Hayes that Richard Nixon, the No. 1 football groupie in the United States, was on the phone. Hayes said that the President would have to be put on hold until Hayes was done talking to his players, and that should count for something.

The legal case never got to court. There were some rather garbled reports of "mutual apologies," and the case was postponed and eventually dropped. "If Woody Hayes apologized," said one wise Woody-Watcher, "then the word, phrase or missive he used should be tenderly wrapped in satin and deposited with the Smithsonian Institution, because it would be an American Original."

Among Woody's most notable words: "I just want people to know that there were eight photographers crowding around us, illegally, on the field, and I asked them to step back. Seven honored my request. The eighth guy even tried to get between my coaches' legs to snap his pictures. As it turned out, he snapped no pictures."

It turned out that for the first time, Woody didn't have the last word on one of his brouhahas. The following spring, John McKay, the Southern Cal coach, successfully recruited a boy named Gary Jeter, a six-five, 250-pound All-Ohio tackle from Cleveland, who had earlier decided on Ohio State. Jeter was so good he started for the Trojans as a freshman. Somebody asked McKay how he'd stolen the kid away from Woody.

"I think Jeter's father is a photographer." McKay smiled.

Well, it wasn't quite the last word. In the 1974 Rose Bowl game, Woody sent most of his classic ground-gainers right over Jeter's position . . .

# 17
# Woody at Large

"In Woody's phys ed course on football, he also lectured a lot on history and the military, but I also remember that he once spoke for two days on prostitution and never once said anything that was crude or off-color. His point was that the easiest thing to do in life is lie down, but he wasn't trying to be funny when he said it."
— Dave Koblentz, a
former student in
Woody's football course.

\* \* \*

Woody Hayes is an American home owner in an upper-middle-class community who has never fixed a leaky faucet, changed a washer, hung the screens, raked a leaf, mowed the grass, watered the lawn, painted a wall, cleaned the garage or, it is suspected, even changed a light bulb.

"No way," Anne Hayes declares emphatically and with a smile. Around the house, Anne Hayes is chief of staff in charge of doing these things or seeing that they get done. She is not only the perfect wife for a football coach, but more importantly, the perfect wife for a coach like Woody Hayes.

"I'd be hard put to recall when Woody has done anything

much around the house"—she laughs—"and I discovered very early in the game that that's the way it was going to be."

She also discovered early that Woody was going to be somewhat polygamous, with two marriages: one to her and one to football. And the way this pixieish fireball handles her part of the affair has made her—at least locally—as much a legend as her famous husband.

Short, vibrant, her salt-and-pepper hair pulled back in a bun and usually caught with a colored ribbon, Anne Hayes is one of the most familiar figures around Columbus. Football coaches at Ohio State have always been major celebrities, but when Woody came to town something new was added. Very quickly, Anne Hayes became a major attraction on her own.

Coaches' wives are supposed to do a good job of pouring at faculty-club teas, serving on minor civic committees, and being loyal to their suffering husbands during losing seasons. But Anne Hayes quickly demonstrated that that would never be enough for her. Not that she intended it that way, but "somehow I just got carried along into the spirit and dazzle of the Ohio State football scene and I guess my natural energies just got a bit unharnessed."

Her first involvement was to be an active spokesman for Ohio State. When it became apparent that she had great extemporaneous speaking ability, she soon became more than just Woody's surrogate in pinch-hitting for him when he couldn't make a luncheon or a meeting. Now she is a star in her own right.

"It used to be," said Frank Tate, managing editor of the Ohio State alumni magazine, "that our alumni groups all over the state wanted Woody for their annual meetings or special functions. It was impossible for him to cover them all, of course. Then Anne got into the act and she was sensational. Now she can't fill all the requests we get for her."

She makes at least fifty varied speeches a year and now finds herself booked six months and even a year in advance. At first, when she'd speak at nonuniversity related events, she did so without a fee. But Woody convinced her that if she was to be the star of the show she'd have to be treated as the star and be paid a fee, which at his suggestion would be given to one of her favorite charities.

When the Hayes arrived in Columbus, Anne and Woody agreed that they wouldn't change their way of life. Among other things, that meant that their telephone number would be listed in the book.

"We were warned," she said, "that it would be vastly different there than it had been at Miami and Denison. This was Crazy Town as far as football was concerned, and all sorts of people had ideas about football—and about the football coach—which they'd just dearly love to tell him in person. Well, we didn't listen to the warnings and although they were right on target we weren't sorry we didn't heed them."

Consequently, over the years, an awful lot of disgruntled alumni, bad losers and armchair quarterbacks have called to speak their piece. Woody, the practical psychologist, says, "If your number isn't listed, the people who want to unload their feelings on you will find the number from some other source. Then they'll bother you to death because they know they have the edge. But if you make yourself available and sort of roll with the punch, the cranks will get tired of it and stop bothering you."

Since Woody is out so much at night during the season, Anne gets most of the calls and has become adept at turning away wrath. "One night a man phoned after we'd lost a game we shouldn't have. 'Your husband is a fathead,' he ranted. All I answered was, 'What husband isn't?' "

Another time she answered the phone at 4:00 A.M. It was another Monday-morning quarterback. "I have to get up at this time every day," he said, "so I'm going to keep calling you and your husband until he gets sick of it or until he talks to me."

"So I suggested to him," said Anne, "that if it was really important I'd put on a pot of coffee and he could wake up his wife and come over right then and there and we'd talk it over. He never called again."

Late-night calls aren't always absurd or from cranks. "Once," said Anne, "the phone rang at 2:30 in the morning. Woody groped for it, listened a moment and then said, 'I'm terribly sorry—I'll take care of it.'

"Next thing I knew, Woody was getting dressed and explaining it to me. 'I've got to drive over to so-and-so's dorm (naming the boy, a football player) and tell him his sister is dying.'

"It had to be handled just right, of course. So, Woody woke up a dormmate of the boy, explaining the situation and told him what had to be done. Then Woody woke the player and broke the sad news to him.

" 'Your friend, here, is going to drive you home. You'll use my car. And just stay home as long as you feel needed.' "

Then, said Anne Hayes, Woody walked the two miles back to his own home at three in the morning. On more than one occasion, Anne reveals, Woody has come home with a player he thinks needs some close supervision for a couple of days. And Anne has helped provide the discouraged or depressed or homesick young man with all the comforts of home.

"One thing that never fails to impress," says Anne, "is Woody's continued relationships with boys who played for him at New Philadelphia High School thirty-five years ago. One of them, not too long ago, was in bad shape, was out of work, was down on himself—the whole bit. Woody found out about it and arranged for a job for him. Woody simply remembered him as a great kid who put out every ounce of effort that Woody ever demanded of him. There was no doubt in Woody's mind that he should help the boy, even after all these years.

"And then there was the former player who was having serious eye trouble and needed an operation. He just didn't know how to handle it. Just couldn't cope with the whole concept of whether he did or didn't need it, and who would do it, and how it would be paid for. Well, Woody arranged the whole thing."

Anne points out that Woody's sense of commitment to people goes beyond those closest to him. One winter he promised to speak at the big winter meeting of the Stark County Athletic Club in Canton. Normally, it's a three-hour drive.

As he left Columbus late in the afternoon it started snowing. The going got tougher with every mile. Stopping once for gas he was told that huge drifts were blocking things up ahead. Woody kept going. He stopped once again at a garage to have his headlights fixed, looked at his watch and mushed on through the darkness.

At 10:15 P.M., more than six hours after he'd left Columbus he walked into the meeting, famished, chilled to the bone and soaked to the thighs from trudging the last mile in the snow.

The alumni chairman shook his hand and said it was marvelous and they appreciated it immensely, but the sensible thing would have been for Woody to find a phone and explain it was just impossible to get there.

A puzzled frown flickered over Woody's face. "But I said I'd *be* here," he told the man, as though nothing else was involved. As usual, without a note he went to the podium and mesmerized 'em for half an hour.

"Let me tell you something else about my husband," Anne Hayes continued. "Sure, you see and hear of Woody boiling over at people, but do you know he's never hated anyone in his life? He'll dislike someone intensely, but he can't bring himself to hate. There's something in him that stops short of that. I think he finds it dehumanizing and demeaning to allow hate to be a human emotion—especially, I think, because he so constantly finds himself in an adversary situation, if you know what I mean. Woody just can't hate people he opposes or who snipe at him.

"Woody, on the contrary, has a lot of compassion for people. When my parents were in their eighties they came to live with us. In fact, we had to bring in hospital beds for them, and they needed a lot of care and attention. Other husbands, I suppose, could have shown some irritation at times, but Woody was completely supportive and sympathetic through all the last years of my parents' lives. He never considered there could be some other arrangement.

"And of course," she adds, "you have to realize that

Woody is never phony. He lets it all hang out. You always know where you stand with him, especially his players."

       \*    \*    \*

Most of his players have no difficulty remembering their football days with Woody and many of them zero in on a common theme: the variety of ways in which he helped.

Matt Snell, the former pro star, recalls the way it was at the windup of his career at Ohio State, when the bidding started for his services with the pros. "We always had the feeling that Woody wasn't the kind who was through with you when you'd played your last game for him," said Snell. "And for the guys with pro potential he wouldn't let an agent come near them. He let it be known that all interviews and negotiations would be conducted right in his office by a representative of the pro team. He'd run an agent off the campus if he found 'em in those days.

"Woody would read all the print on the contracts. And he'd be quick to write in something he thought we should have. At the time I signed with the pros, there was no such thing as an athletic scholarship at Ohio State. We got financial aid based on our need. So if a guy signed a fat pro contract in the early winter of his senior year at Ohio State it was evidence that he no longer needed financial aid, and he'd have to pay his own tuition for the spring quarter. So Woody insisted on a clause in my contract that the Jets would pick up my expenses for the last quarter of my senior year."

Although Woody was a tough taskmaster, players rarely found him unreasoning. The entire squad found poignant proof of that during preseason practice in 1973.

One day Woody found a letter under his door at Stradley Hall (coaches and players all stay at the dorm during these few weeks). It was from a nineteen-year-old sophomore linebacker named Ken Kuhn. Kuhn was a tremendous prospect. As a freshman he'd started two games when All-America Randy Gradishar was injured. He explained that Lou Pietrini, another sophomore, had decided not to come back to Ohio State for the fall term. He was discouraged because he'd been set back by injury and illness. Kuhn and Lou had been good friends, and Kuhn was so upset that he had decided to leave training camp and drive to Pietrini's home in Connecticut to see if he could change Pietrini's mind.

"I'm just trying to do what I think is right," the note concluded. "If I'm wrong in doing this, I'm sorry and I hope the team will forgive me. I'll work extra after practice to make up for what I miss. *Ken Kuhn.*"

Nobody takes liberty with Woody Hayes' rules. Yet, when a boy shows a deep concern for a friend and puts himself in jeopardy . . .

"Here was a boy," said Woody, "who drove six hundred and fifty miles on Sunday to Connecticut where Pietrini lives. He drove his own car at his own expense for the best of impulses. He talked Lou into returning to Columbus, to the team, and they were back before supper on Monday. But he put me on a spot. He left without my permission, and I couldn't condone that."

So Woody, the compassionate, made a deal with Woody the stickler for law and order. He levied a "fine" on both boys, Kuhn for leaving without permission and Pietrini for being "late" to fall practice.

"I made them stay in the dorm every evening for a week," said Woody, "although I let them out to go with the rest of the team to see Sonny and Cher at the State Fair." And then Woody said, "If he'd have asked me, I'd have let him go to Connecticut."

"Strictly a 'family' affair," Woody concluded. "Our kind of families win a few more football games than others."

Lou Fischer, a member of Woody's family in the early 1950s, put a phone call through to Woody one recent spring morning from his office in King of Prussia, a Philadelphia suburb.

"Just thought I'd call to see how things were going," said Fischer. Woody replied that the football team didn't look bad but Fischer detected a grump or two in Woody's tone. With good reason.

Woody was hoping the stadium field could be laid with synthetic turf but funds were a problem. An alumnus was even threatening court action against such a frill.

"How much would the rug cost?" Fischer asked.

"More than $300,000," Woody replied.

"I'll send you the money tomorrow," said Fischer.

And he did.

Lou Fischer had been just another poor kid out of West Virginia when he came to Ohio State and played football for Woody Hayes. Although he never made any all-star teams or saw his name in headlines, he was one of those unsung journeyman guards who got the job done without fuss or flair.

Today he is president and chief executive officer of Gino's, a far-flung fast-food chain along the Eastern Seaboard. After he got out of Ohio State, Fischer joined the business started by two friends, Gino Marchetti, the great Baltimore Colts defensive end, and Joe Campanella, a tackle on the same team with Fischer at Ohio State. Campanella also went on to play for the Colts and eventually became the Colts' general manager.

Fischer had two deeply personal reasons for making a gift of synthetic turf to Ohio State. One was that he wanted it in memory of Campanella, who had died the year before. The other was a debt he was paying to Woody Hayes and Ohio State University.

"Remember, I was just a poor kid," he explains. "Ohio State gave me one heckuva education—and Woody Hayes taught me how to take advantage of it, as well as a lot of other things in life.

"When it gets right down to it, Woody exemplifies conviction and determination more than anyone I've ever met. I've also never met anyone who makes such a lasting impression on you. It's almost physical. Gets right into you.

"Once Woody came storming into the locker room at half time when we were losing. He started screaming about sloppy play and kicked a bench. As it turned out later, he broke his toe and it must have been killing him at the time, but after one quick expression on his face he didn't let on a thing. He couldn't quite conceal the limp, though, when we went back onto the field. A couple of guys almost cracked up but we went out and won the game for him. It was the least we could do for a broken toe, I guess.

"From everything I've observed, I like to think of Woody's character in this way: he tells you where he is— and then he's always there. I've got ten kids, and after I donated the synthetic turf, I took all ten kids out to Columbus for the dedication and introduced them to Woody. They looked at him in awe. I'd told them Woody was something special, and they sensed it."

When Jim Parker, the mammoth, perennial All-Pro guard of the Baltimore Colts, was inducted into the Pro Hall of Fame in 1973, he asked Woody to be his sponsor at the introductory ceremonies at the Hall of Fame in Canton.

Acknowledging Woody's presence, Parker said: "I owe

so much of this honor to Woody Hayes. He was as much a father to me as he was a football coach . . . I even lived with him for the summer before my freshman year, and he prepared me for an adjustment that would have been almost too tough without it . . . For four years he gave me the best bit of advice I ever had. It went like this: 'Play every football game in such a way that you come off the field after a game a better player than when you went on it.'

"I took that right into the pros with me," said Parker.

There may be players who hated Woody Hayes or who found his inspirational oratory and rock-ribbed values unconvincing. If there are, however, they seldom speak out. Despite the flak that Woody got year in and year out from the press, it was almost impossible to find a former starting player who would knock him. Perhaps that is the most significant measure of the man.

*  *  *

Woody's concern with his players, however, often extends beyond football. And although many have been recipients of special kindness from him, a few observers feel his concern goes to odd lengths. Once he was sitting with a half-dozen of his players at a varsity basketball game in St. John Arena. It wasn't one of the Buckeyes' better nights on the court. They seemed flat and listless and were being out-rebounded and outplayed unmercifully. Woody Hayes began to steam. Finally he erupted.

"Everybody out!" he yelled at his footballers, flapping his arms like some huge mother hen guiding her flock. "I don't want you to witness any more of this goddam disgraceful exhibition! I won't let you see Ohio State athletes showing such a lack of hustle! Out! Everybody out!"

And out they went, without a murmur, convoyed by a

furious Woody Hayes still trailing a sulfurous stream of invective over "this disgrace."

It doesn't take Buckeye players very long to adjust to Woody's conservatism and to understand his approach to the personal side of his player contacts. In high school Cornelius Greene, the Bucks' brilliant black quarterback, was a bit flaky. "My nickname was 'Flam'—short for flamboyant," he said. "And I had the name taped to my helmet. It always showed up in photos. I also wore tassels taped to my game pants that twinkled as I ran. No way I could get away with that here. Coach Hayes doesn't even like to have the guys tape their shoes."

Oddly enough, Woody never made an issue of long hair. Everyone thought he'd blow a gasket when the vogue first appeared. Some of his black players started raising Afros the size of a boxwood hedge. "If they can get it inside their helmets, they can wear it," said Woody, stunning everyone. "When they can no longer do that, we'll have to make new decisions."

Consider, now, Woody Hayes' running flap with *Playboy* Magazine. Each year *Playboy*'s request would arrive right on schedule. Each time Woody's answer would be the same: his boys couldn't go . . .

Woody Hayes stands foursquare for Family, the Republican Party and the Fullhouse T, probably in that order, and he has always been offended by *Playboy*'s publishing concept of galloping mammalia. And so each year when the magazine nominated one or more Buckeyes for its preseason All-America team—and not many years go by without a nominee from Ohio State—Woody flatly turned down its request for the players to come to Chicago for an honor-squad photo session.

Woody considered it his coachly duty to quarantine his kids against a two-day exposure to that Bunny Hutch on Michigan Avenue, where God knows what might happen to a clean-living Buckeye tackle or linebacker. So the September issue of *Playboy* would routinely feature a lavish color layout of its preseason All-Americas, conspicuous by the absence of any Ohio State superstar who belonged on it.

Everyone on the Buckeye squad felt it was unfair, and the stars themselves sighed unhappily when they had to forego this Arabian Nights adventure. But Woody was Woody and the kids could only dream and maybe turn to the centerfold.

Anyway, credit *Playboy* with either stubbornness or a sense of humor. They kept the nominations coming. Then in 1973 strange news issued from the Bucks' training quarters. John Hicks and Randy Gradishar, the Buckeyes' all-everything tackle and linebacker, had received invitations to come to Chicago. Woody said they couldn't go—but made a grudging concession. They could appear in the *Playboy* All-America team picture.

Well, first off, Woody sort of admitted that times were changing and so were football players, and what the hell, maybe he was just getting older and mellowing a bit. And here's how it could be done . . .

The photographer who was to make the group picture in Chicago was sent to Columbus with the exact camera equipment, lights and background material that he'd be using for the team portrait in Chicago. He hauled everything over to a spare room in Biggs training quarters and told Hicks and Gradishar to get into their Ohio State uniforms.

He shot color photos of them from the waist up. Then

he returned to Chicago, taking Hicks' and Gradishar's uniforms with him.

A few days later the rest of the preseason All-America squad gathered in the *Playboy* bunny hutch for the team picture. The photographer got hold of a couple of hulking linemen from nearby Northwestern and dressed them in Hicks' and Gradishar's uniforms. He placed them in the group and shot the picture. Then, for the final print, he took the head and shoulders portions of the photos he'd made in Columbus and superimposed them on the stand-ins in Chicago.

It took a lot of doing, but John Hicks and Randy Gradishar were on the *Playboy* All-America team—and in the team picture—without ever setting foot in the Bunny Hutch.

If Woody keeps his players away from the Bunny Hutch, he is equally diligent in keeping them at their studies. His academic relationships with his players begin their first month on campus. He makes a complete survey of their scholastic backgrounds and potential and decides whether they have to attend his famed three-nights-a-week study table. Woody provides tutors for any subject in which a player may be weak. And heaven help the kid if Woody finds he's been giving the study table a short count.

"I hated the sonovabitch!" said one former player years later. "I resented him running my life by confining me to that damned study table for a whole year." He paused. "I was too dumb to realize Woody was doing me the greatest favor of my life. And I think there must be dozens of guys who now feel the same way."

One of the things Woody is most proud of is that more than 90 percent of his football players have completed work for their degrees—a percentage considerably higher than for the general student body. Some of his players weren't able to complete their work in the normal four years because they carried a lighter course load during the football season. That meant they were short some credits after four years.

If the player had gone into pro ball and his time was limited, Woody would immediately get on his back to complete his work for a degree in a portion of a fifth year, or even a sixth year.

"He was like a bulldog," a former player recalled. "I'll never forget how that man pounded at me by phone and mail until I agreed to return."

Woody even tracked down Jack Tatum while the Oakland Raiders' star defensive back was visiting his parents in North Carolina, and all but threw a halter over the former Buckeye All-America to get him back to Columbus to finish his classwork.

Perhaps Woody Hayes values education because he himself holds the rank of full professor and teaches a football course to physical-education majors in the winter time. For football players, even if they're not in phys ed, Woody will take a look at their schedules, and if they have an open spot he makes them all take his course.

"The trouble is, it's hard not to have an open spot," says Matt Snell, "because Woody schedules his class for 8:00 A.M. and he insists you be on time. Nobody is late and nobody cuts that class. He used to shout at us, 'Every man should be up and thinking by seven o'clock in the morning. And dammit, if I can be here at eight, so can you!'

"Woody didn't want the football players there to learn football. That was for the phys-ed majors who weren't on the varsity but would need it for their careers. He wanted us there to do some 'extra thinking,' as he put it."

David Koblentz, who was not a player for Woody but is now a football coach at West High School in Columbus, confirms this. "I had few if any profs at Ohio State who could speak and hold the interest of the class as well as Woody. He could sure make your mind work, especially when he got onto subjects removed from football—which was frequently.

"He did a lot of lecturing on history and the military, but I also remember that he once spoke for two days on prostitution and never once said anything that was crude or off-color. His point was that the easiest thing to do in life is to lie down, but he wasn't trying to be funny when he said it.

"Or he'd talk about religion or prejudice, and you'd hear it in a way that not even your own minister could open up the subject for you. Then at the end he'd look at his watch and very abruptly say, 'Okay, now let's get back to those blocking angles on the pitch-out,' and we'd just wish he'd have kept going on the other stuff he'd be talking about."

And Woody carried his teaching skills right back to the football field. Dave Foley, former Ohio State All-America and now an offensive tackle for the Buffalo Bills in the NFL, recalls the time Woody was having trouble explaining a certain trap play to his troops. "So he paralleled it to history," says Foley. "He showed us on the blackboard how Hannibal used the same play to cross the Alps, achieving victory, and how General George Patton used it to flank the Germans. The guys all laughed about it afterwards, but I've never forgotten it.

"Woody would constantly find military parallels for football," Foley went on. "There was a time when the November weather got way down almost to zero, and some of the school administration people wanted him to hold practice indoors for a couple of days. Woody got us together and told us about the war.

" 'We were getting the hell knocked out of us in the North Atlantic,' he said, 'because all our naval training had been done down in the sunny Caribbean. We couldn't fight in cold weather. Then the Navy got a new chief of staff and he switched all the maneuvers to the North Atlantic. We got tougher and started winning.

" 'So from now on,' Woody said, 'this football team is practicing in the North Atlantic, no matter how cold it gets. No Caribbean for us.' "

"We almost died," said Foley, "but Woody was doing it for *us,* not for him, and we were better players for it."

There is never any doubt on what terms the show is mounted at Ohio State. "People complain," Woody says, "that we are victims of a permissive society. Well, I'll tell you this—we don't have one player on my team who 'does his own thing.' We aren't permissive here. At Ohio State they do *our* thing. Winning is the epitome of group effort.

"It used to be we could expect more conservative attitudes from football players and count on a more consistent status quo attitude toward society. But I think today's players are more reflective of the full range of society's attitudes —much of which is to decry or tear down authority.

"I used to be dead against athletic dormitories. I didn't think athletes should be segregated—that they should be exposed instead to the full cross-section living range with all students. But now I wonder if the athletic dorm isn't the right answer. It gives a coach a better shot at discipline, unity of purpose and at least a small refuge against what goes on in the free-style life the colleges have come to.

"*Loco parentis*—Latin for 'in place of parents'—has virtually ceased to exist as a university procedure all over the land. Kids live where they want and how they want. Sex, dope, marijuana, voluntary class attendance, the whole bit. How can you expect football players not to be part of a whole society when that society puts pressures on all peers to react the same?

"A year or so ago," Woody continued, "it was discovered that a male student here had had a girl living with him for several weeks in his dormitory room. University officials were upset. In fact, they were *very* upset. And do you know why?" Woody paused and shook his head in amazement. "Because she'd been living there without paying room rent.

"Some of our football players heard of it and I'm sure they understood the administration's point of view. Twenty years ago they would have taken a more moral viewpoint. So far, however, I haven't seen these new attitudes affecting the caliber of their play."

Nobody knows better than Woody Hayes that he is a leading symbol of big-time college football, so often criticized for hypocrisy, brutalization and commercialism. He has heard it all and maintains his stoutest goal-line defense against it.

"There is a segment of society," he argues, "which is not only against football but against anything that's well organized.

"There's the old story about the two guys meeting on the street, and one says to the other, 'How's your wife?'

"And the other guy replies: 'Compared to what?'

"Well, as I see it, compared to other activities of young

people these days football is so far out in front in whole-someness that there's no comparison. Our whole show is based on wanting to win, and if you do it cleanly, how can you top it?

"It saddens me," he goes on, "to see that the football player is an antihero so often today. He's just like the student who is sneered at if he works like hell—the overachiever. He's looked down on.

"But what the hell's wrong with dedication? Sure, it's the first demand I make on my kids, but when it comes to the basic aspects of football I'm too old to change. And our players are more dedicated than they've ever been. They work like hell and they hit like hell.

"No, it has nothing to do with brutality. Our kids are never brutal." He pauses, then adds, "Of course, that opposing quarterback better be careful about running a whole lot.

"Because football is such a tough, physical game," says Woody, "I like our coaches to lean over backwards to prevent kids from gaining the false impression that we'd like them to try anything to beat their man . . . that a coach's insistence on "get that man" means stopping him with any possible means.

"That's a feeling I like to erase from a kid's mind. We use a bit of psychology at Ohio State when it appears that some bad feelings are developing between one of our kids and one of the other team. We send in word to our player to pick up his man after the next block or tackle. It's hard to play dirty against a man who picks you up."

Woody has often applied the principle to himself. When John Karas, the Illinois All-America of several seasons ago, got racked up near the Ohio bench, Woody himself helped him to his feet and gave him a pat on the butt. Karas turned in surprise and said, "Thanks, Coach."

It's not violence that Woody sees as the keynote of football—it's coordination and order. "Just consider," he says, "that in football there are eleven men moving at the same time. Of course, other sports have the same element—to a certain degree. But look at baseball, for instance: the emphasis is on nine people stopping just one batter, right? In basketball, there's a lot of one on one, and often there are scoring plays where not all five men are involved.

"I'm not saying the football player has to be more talented than players in other sports. But he is certainly a part of the most highly coordinated group. If the play is to succeed, all eleven men have to do their job."

The same concern for order carries over into his views about society. In 1973, while Ohio State was whipping Wisconsin on the Badgers' home field, some of the home fans started chucking stones, bottles and other debris at the Buckeye bench. After the game, someone asked Woody if he had any comment. Yes, Woody blazed, he certainly did. "The problem comes from people believing they have too many rights, and the word 'rights' to them means acting like an idiot."

In 1972 when President Nixon revealed that U.S. troops had invaded Cambodia and many campuses erupted in violent demonstrations, Woody took personal action to help restore order at Ohio State. University officials, faculty and student leaders seemed helpless as students confronted police and National Guardsmen in a volatile situation that produced rioting, serious injury and closing of the university. Only Woody seemed to know what to do.

He went to the students themselves. Although he was

concerned about his players, he was even more concerned to avoid a tragedy like the one at nearby Kent State, where four students were killed. He brought a voice of sanity to rioters at the dorms, the student lounges, and wherever hotheads were gathering, and appealed for moderation and reason.

He was one of the few voices listened to in those first bitter hours. A day later the Law School held a forum on ethics, legality and other issues raised by the riot. Invited as main speaker was a man the Law School thought would make a lot of sense: Wayne Woodrow Hayes.

* * *

Woody Hayes has an immense respect for his coaching profession. Aside from the fact that he doggedly considers football a medium by which kids learn discipline and lessons in living, he argues that every good football coach does as good a job, if not better, than the average classroom professor.

"Look at it this way," he says. "The classroom professor gives a final examination once each semester, right? In essence, he has been preparing his class for that final exam, right? Well, you can also claim that the way that class is going to perform in that examination is a reflection of his success in preparing those kids for it. I don't care whether it's history, economics or Russian literature. If a number of his students do poorly, by gosh, I say that professor has done poorly!"

Then Woody's blue eyes glint as he moves in for the kill. "Now take the football coach. What he's doing is giving a final examination not just once a semester but every week for at least ten weeks. His expertise as a teacher is on the line every Saturday. How well has he prepared his team for that final exam every game day? That scoreboard is going to tell you.

"And how often do they fire professors because a number of his students have flunked or gotten very low grades? But you know damn well what happens to the football 'teacher' when his students fail. Yes sir, we're just as much a teacher as that chemistry prof or zoology prof, but our failures make the headlines and his do not."

Woody's comparative evaluation of teaching jobs may well be arguable, but it was action by his own Ohio State teaching colleagues that brought on one of the most dramatic confrontations of his career.

The 1961 season had been a great one for Woody and his Bucks. After a 14–14 opening game tie with Texas Christian, which shouldn't have happened, the Buckeyes rolled over nine straight foes, capping things with a 55–20 clobbering of Michigan. Rose Bowl, here we come . . .

The Bowl pact between the Big Ten and the Pacific Eight had run out and everyone expected a new contract would be signed to continue the series, but for 1961 there was no formal agreement binding the Big Ten champ to an appearance. But the champ would, of course, be invited on an individual basis.

And Ohio State, number one in one of the polls, was indeed invited to pack up and come on out. It was a great team led by a couple of guys named Matt Snell and Paul Warfield.

The invite had come on Sunday after the game. On Tuesday night Woody was in Cleveland at an annual alumni bash where Woody was to be the main speaker. What a night. Euphoria.

Woody was getting in some good recruiting licks, too,

with a couple of dozen prospects invited from the Cleveland area, and he was right in there among them, shaking hands, beaming, racking up points all over the place.

Suddenly a man hurried over to Woody, his face grave. He whispered something in Woody's ear. Woody straightened up, a stunned look on his face. "You're kidding," he told the man, his voice incredulous.

The man had told him that the Ohio State faculty council had just voted 28–25 to refuse permission for the team to accept the Rose Bowl invitation. The reason was that it was "overemphasis" and the boys' best interests could not be served by it. Academe had felled Woody Hayes with a blow in the night.

Woody was shaken. He could barely conceal his white-hot rage. A couple of assistant coaches tried to restore him to a semblance of sanity. They wondered what would happen when Woody got up to speak after dinner.

The first thing Woody did was to leave the hotel and start walking, trying to understand what had happened and how to cope with it. He walked for an hour and got back just in time for the banquet. When he got up to speak, two assistant coaches all but held their breath.

It was described later as epic. Woody Hayes made one of the great speeches of his career.

He announced what had happened to a stunned assemblage, then went on to explain why a great bunch of kids were being deprived of a valued experience they had earned and deserved. He was bitter, he was deeply disturbed and dismayed. But never once did he rage against the faculty. The main point of his thrust against them was that he could not question the faculty's sincerity or their right to act, but he did seriously question their judgment.

Then he sat down to the greatest ovation of his career.

Later, he heard what had happened in Columbus. Ohio State students, enraged at word of the faculty veto, marched downtown by the thousands to try to get to the governor. He was out. They came back to the campus, and their mood was ugly. It was a bad scene and things could have gotten out of hand, but one student saved the night. He was football co-captain Mike Ingram, who got up in front of the crowd, held up his hand for quiet and told the rioters that no one was more disappointed in the faculty vote than the players—all of whom were back in their dorms. "They're going to live with that decision," he shouted, "and if they can, then you can!"

The crowd broke up. "How proud I was," said Woody, "that a football player was able to show them the way."

\* \* \*

In the final analysis, nobody understands Woody Hayes' total commitment to his career and life-style the way Anne Hayes does. And she proves it with wit and wisdom. Once, at a luncheon, she told of cashing a check at a supermarket, where the manager asked if she were related to Coach Woody Hayes. "I identified myself," said Anne, "as Woody Hayes' full-time housekeeper and part-time mistress." Her audience cracked up, and she described still more of her hectic life. "I've been on the go so much, a lot of times I show up late. In fact, Woody often introduces me as 'the late Mrs. Hayes.' "

Asked what she does or says to Woody when Ohio State loses, she said sagely, "Nothing. I just stay to hell out of the way."

At another lunch, following the Michigan game in which Woody chewed up the sideline markers, somebody asked her if it was possible Woody might be getting too old for the coaching life. "Too old!" she scoffed. "Did you notice it took three of his younger assistants to drag him off the field when the ref was threatening us with another penalty?"

She understands how much Woody needs a release from his year-round coaching tensions and has never begrudged him the solitude he seeks when he goes off on his June hiking in Colorado, New Mexico or the Alps.

When Woody bought several acres of woodland in rural Noble County, Ohio, where he banged together a small, rustic cabin, Anne understood. "It's not exactly my idea of a vacation spot," she said with a smile, "but it's a marvelous place for Woody to get away on his own, tramping a dozen miles through the forests while sorting out his thoughts."

To get to his cabin, Anne reveals, Woody uses an honest, nonplushy pickup truck which is his personal transportation. Its lone embellishment is a couple square yards of AstroTurf to cover the flat-bed of the truck. It was a scrap left over when the stadium field was covered a couple of years ago. Typically, Woody refused to accept the scrap gratis. He wrote a check for fifty dollars for it and sent it to the university development fund.

If covering his truck bed with stadium AstroTurf was a bit of offbeat whimsy for Woody, Anne was not surprised. Just as she was not surprised by the phone call she received from him the Sunday afternoon in 1973 following the Buckeyes' 10–10 tie with Michigan in the season finale. It was up to the Big Ten athletic directors to decide which of the two teams would receive the Rose Bowl assignment.

Waiting in his office, Woody got the signal that the Bucks had been chosen but was sworn to secrecy until official word had been given to the press.

Finding it impossible to cooperate all the way, Woody telephoned Anne at home. When she answered, Woody said nothing. He merely hummed a few bars of the familiar "California, Here I Come."

"I didn't say a single word." Woody grinned as he told about it later. "I hummed and hung up."

# 18
# Woody's Greatest Games

Woody Hayes, uptight and suspicious over every shadow lurking within a mile of his practice field, was leery of Michigan spies in his own encampment. He handed out scarlet Ohio State jerseys to every nonplayer in the area, including sportswriters, trainers, team physicians and student managers. No one without an Ohio jersey was to be admitted to practice, saving Woody from worrying about unknown civilians on the sidelines.

* * *

All the organization, all the energy and painstaking work in the Ohio State football program is aimed at the few hours each year that the team is on the field. The controlling purpose is winning, and through the years Woody's ways have shown themselves to bring the desired result.

Yet some games have been more important than others. And perhaps the most important of all for Woody was the one played against Michigan on November 20, 1954, in Ohio Stadium.

It was undoubtedly the watershed game of his life. It came when he desperately needed not only a victory but an undefeated season as amunition against the "Goodbye, Woody!" signs which proliferated over the stadium, and the sniping by fans and alumni over three straight lackluster seasons.

Ohio State football coaches who post three straight lackluster years historically do not post a fourth—or else.

Woody's first three seasons were 4–3–2, 6–3, 6–3, and the feeling around Columbus centered on two main themes: (1) if he didn't make a good run at the Big Ten flag in 1954 he might be run out of town, and (2) although he seemed to have more talent this year there wasn't much faith in Woody's ability to capitalize on it.

The talent up front in those single-platoon days included two fine ends, Dick Brubaker and Dean Dugger, and a huge, raw sophomore named Jim Parker at guard. Dave Leggett and Captain John Borton were the quarterbacks; Bobby Watkins was at right half; a rousing sophomore named Hubert Bobo at fullback, and at left halfback a redheaded junior who was about to burst upon the college football world as the most exciting player of the decade— Howard "Hopalong" Cassady.

Woody had fitted them out with the split-T, geared as usual toward running, with a dozen passes a game thrown in. Buckeye fandom mentally crossed their arms and fixed their faces in an okay-now-show-us expression.

The Bucks opened against Indiana and Hop Cassady scored two TD's, one of them coming when he picked off a Hoosier fumble in midair and streaked 68 yards. Okay . . . 28–0 for the opener.

Next, California. Cassady tallied two more, on runs of 26 and 29 yards. Okay . . . 21–13. Okay? The polls now had the Bucks in the Top Ten . . . better than okay.

Next, how about a 40–7 creaming of Illinois at Champaign? By now, Hop Cassady was in the national spotlight and the Buckeyes in number four. Were they for real?

They were. Leading a tough Iowa team 20–14, the Bucks stopped an Iowa drive on the Ohio 5-yard line with a minute to play to win their fourth straight.

Undefeated Wisconsin, second in the polls and led by All-America fullback Alan "The Horse" Ameche, seemed to be the team to end the Buckeye dream. The Badgers were leading, 7–3, and obviously headed for another score on the Ohio 20. A Wisconsin pass on the next play was right on target, but Hop Cassady leaped high, snagged it with one hand and was off toward the Wisconsin goal, 88 yards distant. He picked his way through and around three Badger defenders, was obviously going to be nailed by Badger Pat Levenhagen on the Ohio 30, but fooled 83,000 people, and especially Levenhagen, with a dazzling pivot out of reach, and went on to score on what must have been at least a 110-yard run.

The Badgers fell apart as the slashing Cassady led the Bucks to a 31–14 victory. Suddenly Woody Hayes had the number one team in the polls. The Buckeyes knocked off Northwestern, Pitt and Purdue in a row, and then there it was, the confrontation with Michigan in the finale, a powerful Michigan team that had lost only once in a 13–9 upset by Indiana.

Columbus for three weeks now had had a serious case of Rose Bowl fever. Could this belligerent, still-new, still-suspect Woody Hayes pull it off? After all, there had been only three victories in sixteen years over Michigan. It was a kismet sort of thing now . . .

Woody Hayes, suspicious of every unfamiliar shadow

lurking within a mile of Ohio Stadium and his practice field, worried about Wolverine spies even in his own encampment. He handed out scarlet Ohio State jerseys to every nonplayer in the practice area, including sportswriters, trainers, team physicians and student managers. No one without a jersey would be admitted to practice, so Woody knew just who was—and wasn't—there.

It rained for hours before the game. Woody Hayes, realizing that his future at Ohio State was on the line, was at his edgiest. And one edge he wanted was the best field conditions. He tried to talk athletic director Dick Larkins into keeping the two bands off the field. Larkins put it up to the presidents of the two universities and the kindest word they had on the subject was that Mr. Hayes' request "was unthinkable."

It didn't help things when Michigan won the toss and drove almost 70 yards for a TD. Then the Wolverines began another drive, but Jack Gibbs intercepted a Michigan pass and carried it all the way to the Michigan 11. A delay-of-game penalty cost Ohio 5, but from the 16, quarterback Dave Leggett faked a hand-off and zipped a scoring toss to end Fred Kriss in the end zone to tie the game 7–7. A year later Woody Hayes would repay Kriss by refusing to let him drop out of Harvard Medical School when he was discouraged.

Early in the final quarter Michigan put on a long drive and, with a first down on the Buckeye 4, smelled victory and roses. The fullback got two. The left halfback got one. The fullback got two feet. It was fourth and a foot. Ohio Stadium was bedlam. The ball was snapped. The Michigan fullback blasted straight ahead and was engulfed by a wave of scarlet tacklers. The referee dug for the ball. He found it six inches from the goal line. What had been bedlam now became sheer berserkery as Ohio State took over.

Dave Leggett sneaked for a yard. On the next play he handed off to Cassady. Hoppy bolted over tackle, shifted into high gear and raced 62 yards to the Michigan 37. Two minutes later Leggett pegged a TD strike to Dick Brubaker.

With a 14–7 lead, the Buckeyes, heady with the sweet smell of success, savagely blunted two more Michigan drives. On the second one it was Cassady again, intercepting a Wolverine pass on the Ohio 26 and returning it to the 39. Then the rampaging redhead led another Buckeye drive, capping it with a one-yard smash for a final TD with less than a minute to play. Ohio State had a 21–7 victory.

Moments later, Woody Hayes, for the first time in his career at Ohio State, was being hoisted to the shoulders of his players and carried from the field. Then, for the first time in his life, he was being thrown into the shower with all his clothes on.

And in a more sane moment, after he'd changed clothes and appeared before the press, Woody Hayes was telling about the longest drive in football history, the 99 2/3 yards to a touchdown after stopping Michigan on the six-inch line, a drive that actually carried 2,500 miles to the Rose Bowl in Pasadena.

Beating Southern Cal at Pasadena, 20–7, was almost an anticlimax for this 1954 season. So many other goodies had already been wrapped up: the national championship in the polls; the first undefeated Big Ten title; and first undefeated Ohio State team in ten years; and for Woody Hayes, the feeling that the ghosts in the coaches' graveyard would not have another to join them in their next spectral gavotte along the Olentangy River.

Woody Hayes would not be among them. Woody Hayes
—body, soul and splenetic tyranny, would be around for,
well, forever . . .

*   *   *

When Woody Hayes gathered his legions around the
colors in the first week of September 1968, there was great
expectancy and unfettered excitement in Buckeyeland.
Was it true what Woody was hinting about his crop of
sophomores? That they were the greatest in Ohio State
history? The names didn't mean anything then, but they
included Rex Kern, John Brockington, Jack Tatum, Jan
White, Larry Zelina, Leo Hayden, Tim Anderson, Mike
Sensibaugh, Jim Stillwagon and others. As it turned out, it
was probably the greatest single class ever recruited in
college football, but the real verdict would have to be with-
held until they took a crack at a real live enemy.

It turned out, too, that when the Bucks opened their
season against Southern Methodist, an even dozen sophs
started and looked pretty good, winning 35–14. A 21–6
victory over Oregon followed. Okay, but then on October
12 came Purdue, led by the brilliant Mike Phipps. And the
Boilermakers, touted as a possible national champion, had
taken a great Notre Dame team apart the previous week.

This would be it for Woody and his prodigies. If they
were for real they'd have to prove it against the best. Neu-
tral observers could find a lot of reasons for Purdue to whip
the Bucks. Two of them were Phipps, the All-America quarterback, and a brilliant All-America tailback, Leroy Keyes.
They operated behind a line that averaged 250 pounds,
including two mastodonic tackles of more than 275 each.
The young Bucks seemed to be in for a very physical afternoon.

They were obviously very tight the night before the game. Woody spent a lot of time going from room to room, easing the pressure with some calm chatter here, a pat on the shoulder there. There is something about a martinet who shows his human side before a battle that has a comforting effect on young troops; they absorb his strength and sense of purpose. It has always been part of the Hayes mystique.

His kiddie corps went out the next day, took the opening kickoff and marched 74 yards—including a 38-yard gallop by John Brockington—and didn't score. Penalties for holding and clipping set them back—proof of their tightness—and they gave up the ball after missing a field goal on the Purdue 4-yard line.

For the rest of the first half it looked as though the two brilliant teams might produce nothing more than a scoreless tie. On the sidelines Woody Hayes stared tight-lipped as Purdue took the second half kickoff and were stopped on their own 18. Somebody was going to have to break one soon . . .

Phipps passed to Leroy Keyes on the 27. Then a blast into the line got the Boilermakers a first down. Now Phipps was air-minded, but Buckeye Jack Tatum came up fast and broke up his pass to Keyes. Phipps went to the air again, tossing into the flat. Ohio State's lanky Ted Provost, raced over, plucked the ball out of the air and dashed 34 yards untouched for the TD. Ohio State had a 7–0 lead with only 90 seconds gone in the half.

Then came drama of a high order. The Buckeyes' senior quarterback, Bill Long, had been beaten out of the starting position by brilliant sophomore Rex Kern. But late in the third quarter Kern got racked up and had to leave the game. In came Long. With the ball on the Purdue 14, Long went back to pass on a delay pattern. Jan White, the right end, was his primary receiver. White was covered. So was everyone else. Long shot a glance at the yawning hole up front ahead of him, completely void of Purdue linemen. He set sail straight up the middle.

Before the startled Purdue secondary could converge on him he swerved around a linebacker, tucked the ball tightly into his belly and practically dove into the end zone for the touchdown.

Long had thrown a couple of interceptions the week before against Oregon, and Buckeye fans had expected Ron Macicjowski, another talented soph, to replace the injured Kern. They had voiced loud disapproval when Long went in for Kern, but now they were giving him a thunderous ovation. As Long came off the field Woody Hayes put an arm around his shoulder, smiling widely, no doubt telling himself that when it came to putting in the right guy at the right time, he didn't need any help from anyone.

Ohio State led 13–0, and that was the ball game. There was no more scoring. Woody's fired-up, sophomore-studded club had held Purdue's great rushing game to 69 yards. Phipps, the super passer-runner, had −4 yards for the day. Keyes, the most dangerous runner-receiver in America, had rushed for 19 yards and averaged only 11 yards for the four aerials he caught.

A few days later when a jubilant alumnus flung an arm around Woody and complimented him on a great upset, Woody took issue. "It's never an upset if the so-called underdog has all along considered itself the better team," he said.

There no longer was doubt in anyone's mind that this young team would go on to an undefeated season—which they did—and wind up national champions—which they were. But could they handle number two Southern Cal in the Rose Bowl . . . a Southern Cal team led by the remarkable O. J. Simpson?

*   *   *

O. J. Simpson, two-time All-America . . . blazing speed . . . shifty as Jello on a flat plate . . . the nation's most exciting running back . . . with a great Southern Cal team to back him up.

Number one in the polls, Ohio State would have to prove its claim against him in the Rose Bowl, January 1, 1969. For the first time in bowl-game history the nation's number one and number two teams were meeting head-on. The doubters—of whom there were many—said Woody Hayes couldn't put the frosting on his 1968 cake. Especially with Rex Kern coming off a practice injury that would leave him less than 100 percent. C'mon, they said, this is where General Woody Hayes sees the wrong end of Waterloo, Gallipoli, Caporetto, Thermopylae, the Valentine's Day Massacre, all those losing campaigns. Woody, the historian, knew them well.

Early in the second quarter, 102,000 in the Rose Bowl and the biggest TV audience ever to see a football game were apparently watching the beginning of a Trojan runaway as Southern Cal led 10–0 in the first quarter on a field goal and an 80-yard run by O.J.

In the first huddle after the ensuing kickoff, Rex Kern crouched, looked around at his teammates with just a bit of irritation and then snapped, "Okay, why don't we quit messing around and get to work?"

They got to work. Ten plays later, the Buckeyes had a first down on the Trojan 31. Kern faded back to pass, and the Trojan secondary receded. But Kern, meanwhile, was handing off to Leo Hayden on the draw. Hayden boomed for 13. Two plays later, it was third and 13. Then Ray Gillian made a great diving catch of Kern's pass on the 3. Seconds later, Jim Otis blasted over from the one. With 1:45 left in the half, it was 10–7.

Then came a Trojan mistake. After the kickoff, Sogge was sacked for a 13-yard loss and the Trojans took time out —which they shouldn't have. When they punted, the Buckeyes had a full minute left.

Did someone say Woody Hayes doesn't pass? Give him the passing tools and he knows what to do. Kern hit Jan White for 17. Then he found Gillian for 19. The Bucks had a first down on the USC 16.

Jim Otis ran for 6 and the Bucks used a time out to stop the clock with nine seconds left. There was time for a pass. It was incomplete, but now there were still three seconds left. Jim Roman kicked a field goal to tie it up at the half. If the Trojans hadn't taken the time-out, they would still have had the lead.

Sogge and Simpson spent much of the third quarter dropping the football when they were hit by fierce Buckeye tacklers. In the dressing room between halves, Woody Hayes had told his young Buckeye troops they were now masters of the campaign, and if they made no mistakes there was no way they could lose. When Sogge got smacked yet again behind the line of scrimmage and coughed up the ball, Ohio recovered on the Trojan 21. Rex Kern wasted no time. On first down, with no receiver quite in the clear, he ran for 14 yards. On the next play he lofted a 4-yard pass to Leo Hayden in the end zone, and the Buckeyes led 17–10.

A few minutes later it was O. J. Simpson's turn to take a clobbering behind the line of scrimmage, and his turn to forget what he did with the football. Ohio recovered on the Trojan 16. Kern again went right to work. On first down he pegged brilliantly to Gillian right over the middle and Gillian zipped into the end zone. 24–10.

Southern Cal hopes were soon lost. The Buckeyes kicked another field goal to go ahead by 17 points. With forty-five seconds remaining in the game the Trojans did score again. But the Buckeyes had their spectacular 27–16 victory over O. J. Simpson and a clear claim to the national championship.

A couple of years later, in an AP poll, Woody's 1968 club would be voted the Team of the Decade—not bad for sophomores, even though they had some heartbreak ahead . . .

*  *  *

Revenge is a tarnished word, and nice people don't go around getting actively involved with what it means. But who the hell wants to be nice to people when you're the number one team in the land—maybe the best college club of all time—and a vastly inferior team catches you on the only day of your reign when you've got a collective case of the flats, the blahs and the Bulgarian thrip. And they rip you off as an hysterical TV announcer screams, "It's the upset of the century!"

Well, that happened, of course, on the final day of the 1969 season to Woody, Rex Kern, Jim Otis, Jack Tatum, Jim Stillwagon and all the rest of the greatest collection of All-Americas ever assembled on one team. They were undefeated and favored to stay that way by 20 points or more over twice-beaten Michigan in Ann Arbor. Well, the Bucks didn't do a lot of things right; Michigan did nothing wrong and never mind the details. Michigan 24; Ohio State 12.

There would be Revenge. Write it big, like this: *RE-VENGE*. Preparing for the 1970 Michigan game would be a twelve-month affair. First of all, a Columbus carpet manufacturer sent Woody a rug into which had been woven:

> 1969: MICHIGAN 24; OHIO STATE 12
> 1970 . . . ?

Woody laid that rug down at the door leading to the practice field every day during spring training and throughout the following fall. Every player tromped on it on the way to practice and on the way out every day.

Finally came November 21, 1970. Number two Michigan came into Ohio Stadium undefeated. The Buckeyes had their accustomed number one spot in the polls, but they were in no mood to be playing it cool. They were preparing to go gloriously bananas at the first sight of a blue and gold winged-stripe helmet.

It would be the game of the year. For the first time in history, Michigan and Ohio State were meeting in a season finale undefeated. For the Bucks—for everyone who had been humiliated the year before, which meant most of the starters—it would be the game of their lives.

Woody Hayes wanted it that way. Later he would say it was the most emotional game his kids had ever played. In squad meetings that week he was at his superb, barely controlled, psychological best. He put the pressure on them, driving them to an almost unrestrainable fury in the last week of savage preparation. The coaches could see it and feel it, and smiled thinly and grimly to themselves.

Nobody else saw it. Woody closed the practice field for two reasons; to keep the family frenzy to themselves, and to keep anyone from seeing a new tailback draw play. It was designed to pick apart an intricate Michigan defense, and if it worked . . . *if* it worked . . .

Much of the new blocking adjustment depended on a big sophomore tackle who would have to sort of improvise every time the play was used. His name: John Hicks.

The last thing Woody did before he sent his team onto the field was to read an anonymous telegram to them. Normally, Woody would have nothing to do with an anonymous telegram, but not this time. It said:

THIS ONE LITERALLY IS FOR A LIFETIME.

The Bucks roared onto the field for the kickoff as though they'd taken leave of their senses. As they grouped on the sidelines they clawed and pummeled at each other, and the sounds that came from the huge, frenzied scarlet mass was charitably described as Neanderthal. In the pressbox Paul Zimmerman of the New York *Post* said, "Those guys just aren't sane. I wouldn't want to be a Michigan football player today."

As if on cue, Michigan's Lance Scheffler took the kickoff on the Michigan 25, was hit from at least three directions, including homicidal, and fumbled. Nothing was routine from then on.

Ohio recovered the fumble, got a first down on a Kern pass to Bruce Jankowski, then was held on three running plays and settled for a field goal. Michigan tied it up late in the first quarter.

The rocking and socking for the next ten minutes was

epic. Then Harry Howard of the Bucks returned a punt to the Michigan 47. Ten plays later Kern fired a picture pass 26 yards to Jankowski, who broke over the middle between two Wolverines, plucked the ball out of the air and raced into the end zone.

Michigan came back again and scored. But Harry Howard hurtled in and deflected the attempt for the point-after, so the Bucks still led, 10–9.

It went into the fourth period, a very debatable issue. Michigan hung tough on an Ohio drive and the Bucks settled for another field goal of 27 yards, from Fred Schram. But 13–9 wasn't Comfortsville. A Wolverine TD could still win. But then Buckeye linebacker Stan White picked off a Michigan pass on the Wolverine 23 and raced it back to the 9. If the Bucks could score, they could put the game away, and Woody Hayes was at the controls.

John Brockington got one. Kern kept for four. Then Kern swept to the right on another keeper, faked a run inside the defensive end and pitched out to Leo Hayden, trailing. Hayden flew all the way home and it was 20–9, Ohio State. With two minutes to go, the Buckeyes got the ball back again and were on another TD drive in Wolverine territory when the gun sounded. When the films were graded, John Hicks got the highest marks ever turned in by a Buckeye lineman.

Revenge may be a tarnished word, but an hysterical Buckeye team were making the most of it in the postgame dressing room. Woody Hayes was hugging everybody in sight, sometimes three or four at once, and proclaiming it the greatest victory of his career. Up until that day, it certainly was. But the label would last only three years.

\*    \*    \*

On Sunday, November 25, 1973, Woody Hayes got a reprieve. The previous day his Buckeyes had finished a spectacular season on a sour note—a 10–10 tie with Michigan, also undefeated in the conference. The question was: Who would go to the Rose Bowl?

On Sunday the Big Ten athletic directors decided—despite the tie and despite the fact that Ohio State had gone to the Rose Bowl the year before—that the Bucks were the best team to represent the Big Ten against Southern Cal in Pasadena.

Michigan coach Bo Schembechler howled at the moon, came within an inch of committing hara-kiri, and bellowed some unkind things about the Big Ten commissioner and the conference athletic directors. Something about a grievous error they'd made. There was even an abortive lawsuit by a Michigan student to prevent the Buckeyes from going.

Woody Hayes said very little, smiled a saintly smile and said, "Thanks, fellers, we appreciate the honor; now let's get to work." Woody had a score to settle. Make that two scores. One for himself, the other for the Big Ten. The previous year, USC had absolutely humiliated the Bucks, 42–17. Fullback Sam Cunningham had blasted for a record four TD's. No one had ever done that against one of Woody's Ohio State teams. A return trip to Pasadena for a rematch had been boiling on Woody's back burner all season long.

There was something else. The Big Ten had lost four straight bowl games to the Pacific Eight, two by Ohio State, two by Michigan. Woody wasn't weeping for Michigan, but he was grimly aware of a growing suspicion that the Big Ten had lost some of its luster and could no longer handle the Pac Eight.

"Sez who?" would not exactly serve as W. W. Hayes' answer to charges like that.

Yet out there in California waiting for him were Anthony Davis, Pat Haden, Lynn Swann, Richard Wood, Booker Brown and others on a team which had lost only to Notre Dame in a close one. Although the odds-makers said it would shape up pretty much an even game, seventy-odd sportswriters out of about a hundred polled in Pasadena before the game picked the Trojans.

Woody has seldom agreed with sportswriters, but had he been asked, this is what he knew: he knew that Ohio State's Archie Griffin was better than Anthony Davis. He knew he had the best set of linebackers in the country in Randy Gradishar, Rick Middleton and Vic Koegel. He knew John Hicks was the nation's greatest lineman. He knew that Corny Greene, his slick little quarterback, had recovered from the injured thumb that had incapacitated him against Michigan. He knew that a bull-like frosh fullback named Pete Johnson, who had needed a couple of months to really learn the Ohio State system, was now ready.

He also knew (but who would have believed it?) that Ohio State was going to put the football in the air.

But pregame predictions and gut reactions aside, things still had to be decided on the field. And a 5-foot 5-inch, 130-pound Indonesian kicker named Chris Limahelu sounded the first dramatic note. USC drove past midfield and Limahelu came in for a successful 47-yard field goal, a USC record. Trojans 3, Buckeyes 0.

Late in the first period Blair Conway missed a 36-yard field-goal attempt for the Buckeyes but USC was offside on the play, giving the Bucks a fourth and one. Woody decided to heck with another try for three points. Archie Griffin streaked all the way to the USC 13 for a first down, and a moment later, on second down, Pete Johnson smashed over, capping a drive of 80 yards in 18 plays. But USC regained the lead when Limahelu added another field goal in the second period, and a tricky halfback pass from Davis to Jake McKay got the Trojans another touchdown. After a two-point pass play conversion, they were ahead 14–7.

How was Woody going to settle his scores at this rate? Passing, that's how. Corny Greene hit tight end Fred Pugac for 11 and then to split end Dave Hazel for 15. It was Griffin again, dazzling for 17, and then the big frosh, Johnson, banging in for his second TD. It was 14–14.

Davis got the lead back again for USC, wriggling over from the one, after an 84-yard drive. On the sidelines Woody Hayes gathered the defense around him and the air turned blue above them, and it wasn't from smog. The offense told Woody not to worry; they'd get the TD back.

They did—in only four plays. The big one—believe it!—was a 39-yard pass from Greene to Pugac. From the four, John Hicks and a couple other scarlet shirts blasted a hole the width of a mine tunnel and Johnson came through it like a ton of rock on the fly, for his third TD. Now it was 21–21.

A few moments later, after a 56-yard punt return by Neil Colzie, Corny Greene had a fourth and one, on the Trojans' one-yard line. He slipped Johnson a wizard fake so convincingly that the Trojans, 105,000 fans in the bowl and millions on TV watched Johnson plunge into the end zone. But Greene still had the ball. He wheeled, spun off tackle and scored.

A couple of minutes later Griffin sped 25 yards to the Trojan 2. On the second play after that, Bruce Elia ripped across untouched, giving the Bucks a 35–21 lead.

It was really over then, but with less than five minutes to play Griffin broke over tackle, faked out a linebacker, cut back and headed for the goal. Two defensive backs converged near the goal line and hit him, but Archie slammed over with both of them clutching at him for a 47-yard touchdown.

It was a smashing victory for Ohio State and a day of vindication for Woody and the Big Ten. The Buckeyes had pounded for 320 yards rushing, and Greene had hit on six of eight passes for 129 yards. The total—449 yards—was the most gained against USC all year.

After the game, John McKay said, "Ohio State was the best team we played all year."

But no one had to tell Woody Hayes. Three times they'd come from behind. Their blocking had been devastating; their timing and execution wore the sheen which coaches plead for in repetitive practice sessions and dream of for game time.

The Bucks' poise was superb. They had been forced to punt only twice, had had only one penalty and had fumbled only once—a bobble by Archie Griffin that halted an apparent touchdown drive deep in USC territory. Late in the fourth quarter, on the same play, Corny Greene said calmly in the huddle, "All right, this is the spot. Let's get this one timed up right." And Archie Griffin was off on his 47-yarder.

Woody Hayes said it flat out. "This was my topper," he beamed. "The greatest victory I've ever had—maybe the greatest we've ever had as a team. It's difficult to say this is the greatest team I've ever had, but we've never been as good in six trips to the Rose Bowl, and four of them were victories."

A few minutes later, USC president John Hubbard added

his congratulations and invited Woody to lecture at Southern Cal on World War One.

Woody smiled. "Thank you, sir, but I'd rather lecture on World War Two. That war was not a stalemate."

To Woody Hayes, the coach and military historian, "stalemate" obviously is an ugly word.

# 19
# Goodbye, Woody?

There has been talk of Woody retiring. Woody Hayes retiring? Say it again, slowly, and give it the litmus test for
verity, logic and a few laws of probability . . . It doesn't add
up. Not yet. Inevitably, of course, he must. The heart attack he suffered last spring may hasten the process, especially if he finds it impossible to follow his doctors' orders
to tone down his tempestuous and arduous life-style. The
nay-sayers have their doubts, doctors' orders to the contrary. He'll put retirement off, they say, beyond all parameters of logic and reason.

\*    \*    \*

Ohio State's smashing 42–21 Rose Bowl victory over
Southern Cal in 1974 was barely history when a footnote
to it was being readied. Historians would mark it as an
important date. It had something to do with the—uh—the
new Woody Hayes. Let Wells Twombly of the San Francisco *Examiner* and the *Sporting News* tell you about it:

> Down in a sub-basement of the Rose Bowl, in a chamber
> where the stadium gardeners used to store their rakes and
> hoes, they had hollowed out a genuine interview room. The
> more courageous journalists were huddling together, wait-
> ing for the impending storm. Any moment, one of America's

best-known monsters would come snorting out of his cave. The mere fact that the Ohio State varsity just had pried open a close game and gone on to mutilate an otherwise excellent University of Southern California 42–21, didn't necessarily mean that Wayne Woodrow Hayes even would show up. By proven reputation, Hayes is insufferable in victory, homicidal in defeat.

Everyone sat there, trying not to cringe. The two California sports columnists that Woody is said to loathe most decided to sit together for much the same reason that the settlers used to draw the wagons into a circle when they feared an Indian attack. The danger dissolved so unexpectedly that it was a few minutes before anyone realized what was happening.

Into the room, as warm and cheerful as an old uncle bringing gifts for your birthday, strode this kindly looking man. His face was incandescent with the glow of the recently beatified. His eyes mirrored the serenity of his soul, his love for humanity. With him were five of his players. These young men were encouraged to speak to the representatives of the press with all candor and Woody wouldn't interfere. It had always been suspected that Ohio State players were mute from birth because nobody ever had heard one talk.

"It's a trick! It's a trick!" shouted Jim Murray of the Los Angeles *Times*. "Fall back!"

This was really Woody, although a couple of newsmen wanted to check his lip tattoo and send a specimen to the racing commission. But apparently the head coach of the Ohio State Buckeyes had undergone a personality transplant.

There were indications of such a change even before the 69th Rose Bowl game began. Instead of locking his team up the day before the game, he permitted them to remain in the Huntington Hotel. Instead of refusing to let them take part in the social events that surrounded the bowl, he gave them his blessings and told them to enjoy themselves.

"This was my greatest victory and the greatest victory for

this team," he said, with great feeling. "I promised to tell you members of the press after the game which of my teams was the greatest. Well, this team is the greatest. They came to Pasadena and defeated an outstanding football team by three touchdowns and scored 42 points. That's greatness!"

For the next few minutes, Uncle Woody, who has been known in the past to peel the pelts off fallen foes, described the beaten Trojans as being young gentlemen of impeccable character, perfect manners and lofty purpose.

One writer quietly suggested to another that maybe Uncle Woody had discovered funny cigarettes.

"I'm in such good humor that I'll let you ask me if I plan to retire after this, my greatest victory. My answer is that I enjoy the uplifting values of coaching college football and associating with young men of this caliber too much to leave. I love this game. I'll be back."

A wistful little smile passed across his suddenly benign lips. There was something he wanted to ask the press. This, of course, would have been the proper moment for all the writers to snarl, get up and walk out. But nobody wanted to hurt Uncle Woody now that he had discovered religion.

"Let me ask you fellows who you think the No. 1 football team in the country is. What's that you say, Whitey? You think Ohio State is? Let's have a show of hands to see how many others agree with Whitey. C'mon. Be honest."

It was a true mind-blower. Here was the ogre, the beast, the Piltdown man who scampers on all fours when nobody is looking, making a benign statement. Only about 10 hands went up, an affront that ordinarily would have driven Woody into a screaming tizzy. Instead, Uncle Woody shook his head. Naughty children!

"We didn't come to Pasadena in a spirit of hatred because of last year's loss to USC. You couldn't make my boys hate anybody. We worked hard and beat a great team soundly. And we were No. 1 for eight weeks this season.

"I'm biased. You fellows have your opinions and I respect them."

Then Uncle Woody did the most amazing thing of all. Instead of trying to strangle some writer, he said something sweet: "You fellows have treated me better this year than I've ever been treated before and I think I've treated you better. Gotta go now. Talk to my boys here. I love you all."

He departed into the darkness, leaving behind a phalanx of stunned expressions.

What is the press going to do now that it doesn't have Woody to kick around anymore?

The *new* Woody Hayes? That possibility (Mr. Twombly to the contrary) is as suspect as your friendly neighborhood alchemist's latest formula for turning vinegar into gasoline. The more popular view of a fork-tailed, fire-belching, troglodytic monster would seem to hang in there for as long as Woody stalks the sidelines.

Anyway, your average overview of the old, new or emerging Woody Hayes still has to leave him standing for what he is: a monument to contradiction. Follow with the usual comments: One of a Kind. They Threw away the Mold.

The truth is, as witnessed by many of the faithful, that it just doesn't suffice to proclaim Woody Hayes as merely the Janus of football coaches. Has anyone in sports ever presented the sheer variety of faces which Wayne Woodrow Hayes has turned to players, coaches, fans, writers and a diversiform establishment?

But perhaps, suggests a long-time Woody-Watcher—just *perhaps* the whole thing has been a gloriously effective put-on. The biggest and best put-on football has ever known.

Players he has coached have described him as an unparalled dramatizer, and believe that many of the colorful or controversial things he has done have been consummately self-serving. No one can deny that he has a boldly artistic streak in him, that he is a masterful writer, a licensed ham actor, a pretty good amateur psychologist. Has Woody Hayes, then, been getting away with something? In fact, everything?

Someone once asked him if he pounded all those cheap watches of his into the dirt just to dramatize his points. With a sly grin, Woody simply replied that "only one man knew the answer to that, and he isn't talking."

A new Woody? Is Woody changing? Is it true, for instance, that from now on he'll let his players see any Friday night movie they want to before a game? Even a dirty movie? Yeah, says an assistant coach, but if it's going to be a dirty movie it'll be a *dirty football* movie, and that takes care of that.

Frequently of late there has been talk of Woody retiring. Woody Hayes retiring? Say it again, slowly, and give it the litmus test for verity, logic and a few laws of probability. For those who know him, it doesn't add up. Not yet. Inevitably, of course, he must. The heart attack he suffered last spring may hasten the process, especially if he finds it impossible to follow his doctors' orders to tone down his tempestuous and arduous life-style. The nay-sayers have their doubts, doctors' orders to the contrary. He'll put retirement off, they say, beyond all parameters of logic and reason.

Look at it this way, they say. There's Ol' Woody retiring next year, the year after, whenever. Out to pasture as an assistant athletic director, professor of physical education, or university vice-president. And there's Ol' Woody taking a few minutes off and sneaking over to the practice field, and the kids are belting each other around but looking as though they're enjoying it, and no one has seen or heard of something called a megaton or even a miniton, and coaches are holding up diagram after diagram which show dotted lines of footballs in aerial flight, and the stern-faced guards are gone from the practice-field gates, and . . . and . . . and Woody Hayes is taking it all in and going bonkers.

Or yet again, there's Ol' Woody sitting in the pressbox, high in Ohio Stadium, watching the Buckeye line firing out at Michigan, with the Bucks inside the Wolverine 10-yard line, and the 87,000 loonies in full roar, and the Ohio State quarterback *(calling his own plays!)* isn't going with FULLBACK 26. Instead, there's a pass or an end-around or some other bit of heresy, and maybe the Bucks don't score, and . . . and . . . and, well, does anyone think Woody Hayes could live through it without blubbering to himself or maybe even flinging himself off the 110-foot-high edge of the stadium, so temptingly close to the pressbox?

Woody Hayes *retire?*

A few years ago it was being bruited about that Woody might be invited to Washington to take over as head of Selective Service, or step into some other federal manpower commission or some such, but it was only talk. Woody Hayes had a commitment to football as long as he was physically able, and as long as Ohio State wanted him.

There's a consensus around Columbus that Woody is, after all, a realist, and the retirement situation is one he must eventually face up to. But most agree that Woody won't retire until he has produced one more undefeated national championship team, or until he completes twenty-five years as Ohio State football coach, whichever comes first.

And Woody Hayes' successor? An intriguing thought. A university such as Ohio State does not routinely witness the departure of a living legend, and all sorts of vibes will attend the naming of his successor. Especially in the milieu that is Ohio State and Columbus, Ohio.

The question was put to athletic director J. Edward Weaver: "Would Woody have some say in naming the man who'd replace him?"

"Woody," said Ed Weaver, "naturally will have some feelings about this, and just as naturally, we will be listening to him."

Which doesn't tell Buckeye fans too much, but knowing Woody, his recommendation will be received with something more than studied politeness. Woody is going to try to tell 'em who and *why,* goddammit, and if they don't buy it, it won't be because they haven't heard.

Who? Well, those close to Ohio State football have flatly said he will not be a stranger to Ohio State football, a big name from another school, or someone from the pro ranks. It will be, so it is said, "someone from within the family." Which means someone who either once played for or coached under Woody Hayes.

And if that happens, don't look for too many basic changes in that huge gray stadium along the Olentangy River. The ghost of Woody Hayes wouldn't permit it.

## About the Author

JERRY BRONDFIELD is an Ohio State alumnus ('36). Since the early 1950s he has been an unpaid recruiter for Ohio State football in metropolitan New York, helping to attract such Buckeye stars as Matt Snell, John Brockington and Pete Johnson. He is a frequent contributor to national magazines and is an editor for Scholastic Magazines. He lives in Roslyn Heights, New York.